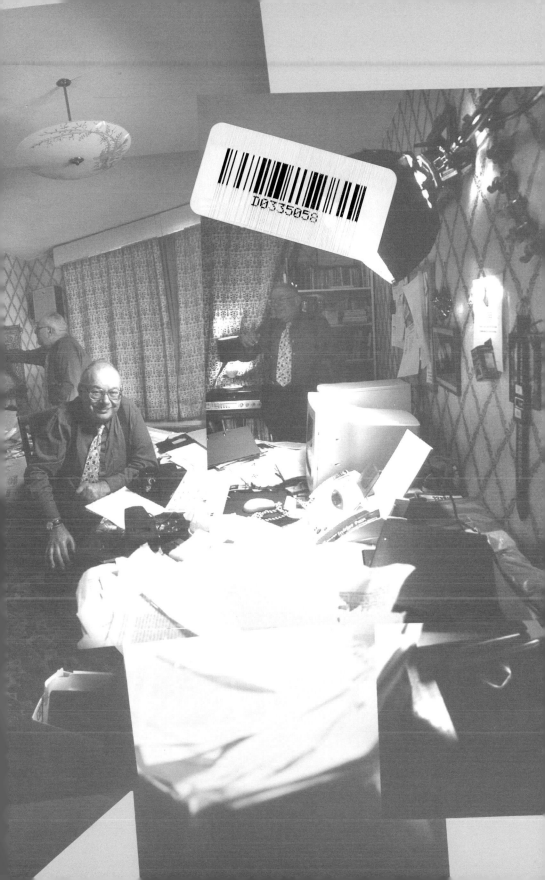

Hitchhiking to Heaven

Hitchhiking to Heaven

AN AUTOBIOGRAPHY

LIONEL BLUE

Hodder & Stoughton

LONDON SYDNEY AUCKLAND

First published in Great Britain in 2004

The right of Lionel Blue to be identified as the Author of
the Work has been asserted by him in accordance with
the Copyright, Designs and Patents Act 1988.

10 9 8 7 6 5 4 3 2 1

British Library Cataloguing in Publication Data
A record for this book is available from the British Library

ISBN 0 340 78660 4

Typeset in Baskerville by Avon DataSet Ltd,
Bidford-on-Avon, Warwickshire

Printed and bound in Great Britain by
Clays Ltd, St Ives plc

The paper used in this book is a natural recyclable product
made from wood grown in sustainable forests.
The hard coverboard is recycled.

Hodder & Stoughton
A Division of Hodder Headline Ltd
338 Euston Road
London NW1 3BH
www.madaboutbooks.com

To Hilary Kates, to James Cummings,
to 'Juno' (Wendy Greengross) and to Vivien Green.

Contents

Contents

To the Reader

The great traditional Scriptures (with their capital 'S') are mixtures of what happened, what people would like to have happened, and what was the meaning of what happened. It is the same with personal scriptures, such as mine, with their small 's'. Just as it is not possible to separate the strands with certainty in the public Scriptures, so it is not possible to separate them in limited personal ones either. Who can hold his hand against his heart and swear his own story is an objective, unbiased account of the passions and quarrels of his youth and salad days? I do not fool myself.

I do know that I have occasionally altered a name, a detail, a time, a place or a gender to avoid needless hurt to living people, though I have kept to the point and purpose of what happened. The prophets could get away with paying off old scores. But I am no prophet nor son of a prophet. Paying off old scores under the mask of pseudo detachment – Ugh!

If you are a close friend and therefore alive, do not feel left out if your name does not appear in this story. My greatest responsibility is to dead friends and teachers. Oral memory is fragile but a printed memory brings the dead to life, like a little resurrection. Also, being alive, our relationship is not complete and your turn is not yet. This is material for another book. God willing!

I have given more space to Eros and carnal love than is usual in a story so concerned with divine love. Agape and Eros are intertwined in most lives and loves. They certainly are in mine. What use is truth on the higher slopes if it can't cope with honesty on the lower ones? Nakedness is honest, and compassion can be the fruit of passion – as appears in the following pages.

I was never good at dates in academic history or in my personal history. My mother made an archive of the latter for me, but where she squirrelled it I do not know. So many strands of my life are intertwined and happened together – my private life, my public life, my professional life, my inner life, my love life, all reacting on each other – that I have found it more enlightening to separate the strands rather than to reconstruct a doubtful diary. The only diary I have ever attempted was a spiritual one, and it was so 'pi' that it was unreadable. I gave it to my poor father, whom it moved to tears. He was a sentimental man.

'The Tao that can be named is not the true, eternal name,' said Lao Tse in the sixth century BC. I used many names for the Divine in this book. I have used, among others: heaven, my soul, Inner Voice, WW (Whomsoever Whatsoever), JC, Fred, God, another dimension, Old Smokey, Holy Spirit, He, She, It and possibly more. I have used so many because my beliefs have not stood still in the last half century, nor have my needs. They are all pointers in the same direction. I have not always used capitals when referring to the divine. The context makes it clear and too many of them are too heavy for a love story.

My thanks to my agent Vivien Green, my publisher Judith Longman, to genial supportive BBC *Today*, to my colleagues and friends Rabbi Professor Jonathan Magonet, Rabbi Danny Smith, Rabbi Guy Hall, Father Bill Kirkpatrick, Sister Mary, and Father (brother) Gordian. You pray for me, I'll pray for you!

Enjoy, enjoy! To my surprise, my life got more joyous with age. And I hope it's the same with you.

1

Lionel, Lion of Judah, Bluestein (Levite)

That's me – the name my parents decided for me in the Salvation Army hospital in Hackney where I first emerged on the 6th of February 1930, resentful and cross. My mother was one of the few married women in the ward so she got special treatment. The others got no compliments for any bastards they were bringing into the world. My mother was amoral but warm-hearted and got my embarrassed father, who had an even bigger heart and a sentimental one, to go around and congratulate them and hand on her own big bunches of flowers. She herself preferred celluloid blossoms with stronger colours that only needed wiping not nurturing. She was never a 'nature girl' though she identified with Jane in Tarzan films, cavorting through the jungle slap up against Johnny Weissmuller's great chest.

She was strangely innocent about sex, more interested in the accompaniments than the main course, whose oddity always surprised her. She thought of it as some form of PT, like the keep fit lessons on the wireless which she exercised to. Which is why she never understood her own pregnancy and was jolly lucky to get to the hospital in time and get me born at all.

To keep her job, she never told her boss she was pregnant. But it all came out when she was pretty far gone and her body being unbalanced fell off a tram. I emerged in a hurry just after she was taken into the ward, which may explain my pique on arrival.

She wasn't really the maternal type. She was more at home with dolls and boyfriends than babies and I wasn't the doll she wanted. The following is of course anecdotal but it sounds true because it was so characteristic of all of my family. I emerged cocooned in black hair, looking malevolent because I'd been pulled around a lot. My mother took one look at me and said, 'My God, it's the devil!' Whereupon her mother, whose only grandchild I was, slapped her and snatched her from me, telling her that she was no true Yiddishe Momma and was not worthy to be entrusted with an angel like me. A ding-dong argument then went on around the bed, unlike any the startled Salvationists had yet heard. My mother said she was a Yiddishe Momma. Her mother said she wasn't. She said she was and this continued until my father and the nurse commandeered the baby both were trying to snatch and shouted at them to keep quiet.

It was one of the rare times he took charge and I only wish he had taken charge more often. But Jewish matriarchy had weakened his masculine will and reduced him to a provider figure. (He hid sexy magazines in his bedside cabinet like many modern males. They had pictures of virgins stashed away in cages by Nazi beasts.) Sometimes in church many years later when I was having another shot at piety, I couldn't help wondering about the domestic life of St Joseph, another good provider type like Dad, and what he relied on for relief. Christians are reticent on the facts of this life, though over-certain about the facts of the next.

Actually Granny was quite right. My mother wasn't a Yiddishe Momma, though she would have given her life for me and did work far into the night for me, denying herself every penny to save it up for me so that I could escape the ghetto and the poverty trap. My mother, who was no fool, knew in her heart she was not the normal Yiddishe Momma and felt guilty all her life because of it, continually trying to make up to me for what she wasn't. Since emotional blackmail was a characteristic of our family, it was a weapon I used against her when the going got rough. We blackmailed each other, and when I was old and she was ancient we used to laugh about the tricks we once resorted to. Time had taken away any animosity. As my mother said, 'What we'd done, we'd done,' and I hope God will be equally relaxed on me when he judges.

At the beginning I didn't like her much. She was a pain in the neck and I far preferred my grandmother and my father who loved me for what I was, not for what I might become. They didn't want me to do anything, just be their idol, which I found restful and rewarding.

But back to my name. Like everything else in my early life, confusion reigned. They all had their own agendas and myths. My mother told me privately that she called me Lionel because she had seen Lionel Barrymore at the pictures and it was the only nice thing that happened to her during the economic slump of 1929. My father, who was a manly athletic boxing type, told me (when my mother wasn't around) that Lionel meant I was a real 'Lion of Judah' who would always stand up for our people. Whether our people were Brits or Jews or both together I never found out. I don't think he worked it out either because he was no intellectual, just a natural British Israelite. My grandmother insisted that I was a continuation of a ghostly ancestor called Levy the Levite, lost in the murk of the marshes of White Russia. Lionel, Levy and Levite all began with L, she said, and this proved it. I would have preferred to have been called Bill but nobody asked me.

My mother's maiden name was Goldstein and her married name was Bluestein. In Eastern Europe Jews had to take surnames in a hurry when they were reluctantly emancipated by the authorities in the nineteenth century and ordered to be like everybody else. They didn't have nice lives but at least they could have nice names. Now roses were nice, so lots of them called themselves Rose. But better than a single rose was a mountain of them – a Rosenberg, or a valley of them – a Rosenthal, or at least a whole tree of them – a Rosenbaum. And the same thing of course with silver and gold, so there were lots of Goldbergs, Goldsteins, Silversteins and Goldfingers. There were also Katzenelenbolgens, cats' elbows, but they must have been Romanian Jews who Granny said had a warped sense of humour.

Later on when I was at county school, my parents (i.e. my mother) decided I must move in the high circles that inhabited the heights of Golders Green and Hampstead where Cohens were Cahouns and Levines, Le Vines. Bluestein was no longer suitable. Now Ma had noticed that English people liked using colours as names – black, brown, green, white – and she acted. What about making me acceptable among the elite by dropping off the last syllable of my surname and calling us all Blue? So I endured the indignity of listening to my form master address the class as follows: 'I have received a letter from Mrs Bluestein now legally Blue by Deed Poll,' he said tersely. 'You are no

3

longer to address her son as Lionel Bluestein but as Lionel Blue.' He went on to another matter quickly and I wanted a black hole to open and swallow me up. I also wanted to drop into it my parents who had perpetrated this indignity on me, which took me years to live down.

The change of name never did any good. My parents, as I was beginning to realise, would never make it to riches. They were too incompetent. The lower suburban middle class was their limit, though late in life Ma was quite a success among intellectuals and in classless bohemia. They also appreciated Dad's kindness. Of all the colours suitable for surnames, Blue sounded a bit odd and later on in slang it sounded smutty. So my last condition was worse than my first. Never mind! My parents had to put up with me as well as dote on me and me likewise and vice versa.

The problem was that I don't think I was ever a real baby at all but a wizened old man in a baby's body. It's only now that I'm becoming a wizened old man that I feel like a child though not a baby. Life hasn't gone the way that I expected – as I've become older, I've felt younger. Mortality permitting. I shall be the *jeune premier* of the Jewish old age homes, if they let me in.

If you're a Jew or Gentile not conversant with the patchy quality of Jewish tradition, I wouldn't worry about the 'Levite' part. There's a bit of honorary status still given to the descendants of the Cohens (priests) and the Levis (the levites, their attendants) who served in the Jerusalem Temple two thousand years ago, but as no one's ever kept reliable family records of who did what in the old Temple, the honours are only anecdotal hearsay. The truth is that my mother's family were probably tailors, pedlars and tinkers climbing out of the Pripet marshes, the Yiddish equivalent of bog Irish. 'Gentlefolk but poor,' said my granny and she was certainly a lady.

2

Home Sweet Haym

In the years after I was born, my mother had to go back into hospital again. She had some strange blood illness. I never knew what it was and it baffled the doctors too. But my father kept her alive by giving her pints and pints of his own blood. (He was a good man.) He couldn't look after me because he was walking and cycling through London looking for a job like everybody else. (It was 'Brother, can you spare a dime?' time.) There was no demand for bespoke tailors in 1930. Later on I remember helping him trying to sell ice-creams in winter and felt both angry and sorry for him, but I loved him. Dr Johnson must have felt the same about his father because years later, when he was the literary lion of London, he returned to stand for hours in the pouring rain of Lichfield market at the exact place where his father once had a bookstall but could sell no books. I was moved by his story, so centuries later I stood too in the rain of Petticoat Lane market remembering my father and his luckless ice-cream barrow.

In the morning he deposited me with my granny, my mother's mother. When he returned home at night, worn out and miserable, she comforted him with his hot meal. Then carrying me in his arms he took me to our furnished room several streets away. My other granny, Granny Bluestein, loved me just as much but she had many children and grandchildren, so at her home I was one among many. At Granny Goldstein's, however, I was a unique, chosen and never-to-be-repeated marvel. With her I led a paradisal life.

As a young kid doted on by my father and grandmother who loved me as I was, I led a paradisal life. After my mother came out of hospital the pace of life abruptly changed, because she loved me as the success she planned for me. Painfully I had to emerge from the womb again. But she couldn't look after me and prove herself the Yiddishe Momma she wanted to be, because she had to go out to work too and for a few years was the only reliable breadwinner of our family. So home for me remained my granny's house. I stayed there till I went to school and after I went to school I got my tea there and waited in my grandfather's cobbler shop (the front room of their house) or in my granny's kitchen at the back of the house until late in the evenings, when my parents came home tired from work or looking for work and took me back to their home.

That little house for me was more than English 'home'. It was *haym*, the Yiddish word, because though at that age I thought in English, I felt in Yiddish and this has remained with me a little till now. *Haym* was for me a little house in an East End side street somewhere between the grander Sydney Street where my father's family lived and wider spacious Jubilee Street where we went to live after my father got a job again. Granny's little house had no hot water – just a cold tap in the kitchen – and only an outdoor loo in the yard with spiders and cut-up pieces of newspaper. The small dining and living room had no window, the only light coming from a window in the scullery. Upstairs my grandparents slept in the front bedroom, their two unmarried daughters, Lil and Hilda, shared a smaller room and my six-footer uncle, Abie, slept in the tiny cupboard bedroom with his feet hanging out of the window because he was so tall. Riches are relative and I only knew we were all poor because my mother said so. Compared to the tenements nearby where many families had to share one loo, we were well off and I hated it when my mother kept going on about it. She thought of herself as the spirit of progress – which I suppose she was, poor woman.

We of course had a tin bath and all the men were sent out of the house during the ablutions of my aunts and grandmother. You couldn't play about with respectability in London's East End. If you strayed outside it you fell into a bottomless black hole unsupported by any welfare system. So the respectability was rigid. The strategy of bathing in such a confined space often proved too much, so like our neighbours in the little street we all lined up at the Municipal Baths on Friday late afternoon for our Sabbath scrub. All this may seem primitive but to my granny our shaky house was a marvel of technology. You only had to push a little stick on the wall and 'Lo there was light.' Also milk could come out of a bottle as well as a cow. Round the corner was a little dairy with its own cow.

I realised very early on how relative riches were. Until I caught my mother's success fever, I was indifferent to them. In the cut-price grocery shop in Stepney Way I was happy buying broken biscuits and cracked eggs. It didn't occur to me to buy any other. A weekend roast could be a browned roast lung. It was a like a savoury bolster, textured with holes like a meaty version of some kinds of chocolate – but the slices on our plates were massive and that was the important thing. My grandmother also made wonderful grated potato fritters, *kartoffelnpfuffer* in German, *latkes* in user-friendly Yiddish. In desperate times we ate them on toast or with chips. It was a good way of eating potatoes with potatoes. We used to sing a Yiddish song called 'Bulbe' (potatoes) of which the English was: 'Monday potatoes, Tuesday potatoes, Wednesday potatoes, Thursday potatoes and on Friday and Saturday for the Sabbath, what a delicacy! A potato pudding!'

Now there are many types of responses to poverty – resentful, angry, accepting, funny, mystical, jokey. Ours was a warm poverty. Provided you didn't fall foul of those *éminences grises* – the bailiff or the rent collector – in our life, it was in many ways a good and a pious one, and my problems really only developed when I had to leave it and was evacuated to an alien world. I know of course my psychological problems must have been there already lurking in my mind's darkness, but I was only aware of them sporadically. (I played 'Doctors and Nurses' with gusto and curiosity, together with other little boys and girls, as is normal.)

When I think back to Winwood Street where Granny Goldstein lived (or was it Windward Street? I no longer know), I remember families sitting outside their donkey-stoned (i.e. cleaned with a piece of sandstone) doorsteps, calling out to each other in a goulash of rich Russian, cockney and Yiddish, and passing each other bits of carrot candy and chunks of pickled cucumber. It was our parliament where we discussed Hitler and Mosley and shivered, and the boarding house we might get into next August in Margate where they came round to ask you if you wanted another portion (fancy!), and where Dad ate bacon though no one mentioned it. Marriages were planned there and the marriage broker was consulted there and taken into a parlour (the posh room) if everyone meant business.

Because people came to sit and talk in my grandpa's cobbler shop, I also got to know the non-Jews who passed among us and liked us and fought alongside us during the Mosley marches, and over the years came to be part of us. There was the gasman, a thoughtful idealist anarchist like Grandpa, who taught me to tell the time, and a drayman who taught his horse Yiddish so that the Jewish children would not be frightened of it. It was true. When the drayman said '*Shteh*' (Stay) the horse stopped and when he said '*Geh*' (Go), the horse plodded onwards. They taught me never to be frightened of non-Jews and I recognised them as family too. There was also the lamplighter guarding the frail mantels on the gas street lights, which we children tried to smash as soon as he went on his way. And there were the *Shobbos goyas*, the poor gentile Sabbath ladies, whom life had brought low and had ended up lighting the Sabbath fires of poor Jews who were ritually forbidden to do so on the Sabbath. There were also Ernie and Dave, the outriders of the bookie who stood on the corner of the street, who gave me a penny if I spotted a policeman heading towards them. There was also Stencl, one of the greatest Yiddish poets. He slept on a park bench nearby as his public dwindled and was finally extinguished in the gas chambers.

Sometimes in sentimental Jewish plays a matriarch whose family has made it to the heights of Hampstead would happen on a piece of carrot candy and suddenly wanted only a return ticket to Whitechapel – and she ups and goes back to Petticoat Lane and the warm poverty she once knew. Well, I'm not like that. There isn't any going back. You cannot unknow what you already know. If you try it, the result will be only banality or hypocrisy. With all the problems of my later evacuation and Oxford, I would still reject the return ticket. Though I resented my mother's push, in my heart I knew she was right. Ours was a doomed world and the sooner we got out of it the better. It was too narrow, too poor and too limited and, without intending to, it destroyed people.

Vinvoo – the Buried Street

I tried to find 'Vinvoo Street' (or was it Windward or Winwood?) on an old map of Jewish Stepney but it was too small to have a name. It was a very little street, as I've said, which ended up in Stepney Way opposite the new sweet shop which opened in 1937. On a recent recce for a TV film I tried to find it, but was told the little street had been burnt by incendiaries, then obliterated by a land mine, and then a modern block of council flats had been built on top of it. So now, like the ancient Roman catacombs and medieval London, whatever remained of it lay buried beneath my feet.

The little street was poor but *edel* – genteel – and only two streets away from the dreaded tenements. A holy man lived in our street – a rebbe (rabbi) and a mystic. His light burnt throughout the night because he never stopped studying, writing and reading. My granny bought Cabbalistic charms from him, which she tied around my neck, and then burst into tears when my father snatched them away before I went to school. Our part of the family, I boasted to the other kids, were 'moderns', who didn't go along with the old superstitions.

At the other end of the street lived the woman whose brains had been shocked in a dreadful pogrom in the old country. She used to compulsively wash away the horse manure which enriched our street and sometimes tried to wash away my father who had come to collect it. I used to take little parcels of cake to her from my granny, who said it would help her brains and sweeten her memories. When I said I was frightened of her, my granny was shocked. 'A big boy like you frightened of doing a good deed for a poor woman with weak brains and who loves you so much! Ts . . . ts . . . ts . . .' The mad lady did like me, I knew, because she gave her poor husband a rest from her tears and sorrows when I crossed the street to her and she fed me in return with Rumanian syrup cakes and crooned all her grief out to me.

There was also a stable in our little street – hence the horse manure – and a grocery shop with a barrel of fresh green pickled cucumbers in brine, and two ladies who used to donkey-stone their doorsteps in time with Granny. The street was our theatre. Little processions of socialists, communists and Zionists all wearing different coloured shirts marched through it. But the black shirts of Oswald Mosley never dared. Street musicians either alone or in little bands played their way through it. For a ha'penny they would serenade you with 'A Brievele der Mamme' ('Write a letter home to your poor mother in the old country') or 'Bei mir bist du shane' ('To me you're beautiful in every language but best of all in Yiddish'), 'Yiddel mit dem fiddle, Yankel mit dem bass' ('Judah with his violin and Jacob with his double bass') and of course 'My Yiddishe Momma'. The audience could never get enough of that one and the whole street would join in sobbing it out, some in English and some in Mameloshen, our Yiddish mother-tongue. It was sentimental, sure! But the sentiment was true. I think it was the same in the Irish Catholic streets, though with different songs and another mix of languages, but we never really knew them until in the Blitz the bombs blew us together.

There were also beggars who had an honoured position among us. We all knew that one turn of the wheel of fortune or another rise in anti-Semitism and we could all be beggars too, in another land if we were lucky enough to get out in time. (My granny held that meeting a beggar was the nearest we would ever come to meeting God in this life.)

Then there were the domestic dramas. My granny, like the other pious ladies, used to cook her Sabbath cholent, a stew, in the baker's dying oven at the corner of our street before the Sabbath started. But often the labels got loosened and as soon as the lid was lifted off, we knew the smell wasn't right. In the street my mother, who was a lawyer's secretary, negotiated the exchange of pots while Granny wept and Grandpa cried out to a heaven – in which he didn't believe, being an anarchist.

In my living room there is a painting of the little street that was done just decades later. I had enrolled with my friend in an art class in the 1970s. We all set to work on the standard studio nude, who was our exercise. My dud picture of the nude turned into a landscape, then into a mess, then into a procession moving down a small street. It is Vinvoo Street, and since Vinvoo Street no longer exists, it is the only record of it. It was buried deep in my unconscious memory as well as under concrete.

4

My Lady Poverty

In 1950, when I was up at Oxford, I read about the mystic marriage of St Francis to My Lady Poverty in Dante and was deeply moved. But then I thought back to my own childhood. My own family was married to poverty too but it wasn't a mystic marriage, just a shotgun wedding. We couldn't help it. Poverty for us was no lady but a slut and a destructive one. My parents' marriage was a mismatch, no economics could alter that, but they would have come to terms with each other sooner and better if Dad had not been forced on the dole, which destroyed his pride and turned my mother willy-nilly into the breadwinner of the family. She got a job, graciously offered by an old boyfriend, which my father resented.

My mother's family were poor folk who came from the little Jewish villages of Poland and White Russia. Like thousands and tens of thousands of others, they were fleeing the poverty and persecution of Tsarist Russia in the last decades of the nineteenth century. Most were travelling in steerage heading towards Ellis Island and the fabled golden country of America.

It is appropriate that the lines on the Statue of Liberty they longed for should have been written by a Jewish woman, Emma Lazarus:

> Give me your tired, your poor,
> Your huddled masses yearning to breathe free,
> The wretched refuse of your teeming shore.
> Send these, the homeless, tempest-tossed, to me:
> I lift my lamp beside the golden door.

Many, like my grandparents, never made it to the Golden

Country at all. They only got half way there and ended up in the tenements and little back streets of London's East End.

I cannot tell you much more about the origins of my grandparents, because the world they came from was extirpated in the Holocaust. My grandfather, I know, was a young lad fleeing conscription in the Tsarist Army (a brutality that could last a lifetime), and my grandmother was an orphan, only a young girl when her village clubbed together to buy her a ticket to London where it was rumoured she had a rich uncle. They tied the ticket round her neck and sent her off. Perhaps the two met on the boat, lied about their age to get married and set up house together. My grandfather became a cobbler, and my grandmother hardly ever left her kitchen, still frightened of pogroms till the day she died. It took her a long time to realise she was in London not New York, since both spoke the same foreign language.

I never found it easy as a child to work out what language my grandparents spoke. They communed with God in eloquent Hebrew and even Aramaic (the language of Jesus) and with each other in fluent Yiddish. They made love in Yiddish – I heard them – but they swore in Russian, White Russian or Polish as their fancy took them. They also learnt cockney English as the outside world gradually seeped into their home, even into my grandmother's kitchen.

But the old ways remained and until 1939 and the evacuation, it was much like living in a hamlet near Vilna, Minsk or Odessa. Our society was traditional, with its own standards and its own celebrations of ancient fasts and feasts, the ban on bacon, ham and pig, and its spotless doorsteps, which you leapt over so as not to dirty them. They were for gentility rather then utility.

In our kind of Jewish family, children were both loved and spoilt, but we were not protected from the realities of life. We learnt early on about the pawnshop, lining up for the dole, and going to Christian missionaries for free medical aid. (You said a prayer but when you got home you washed your mouth out.)

From what my mother and my Aunt Lil whispered to each other in Yiddish – which I understood better than either realised – I learnt the economic facts of life from the rise and fall of their brother Abie, my favoured uncle. Besides being good-looking, God had given him all the graces. He was a superb dancer, a lady charmer and also a brilliant drawer, painter and designer. He made portraits of all the street, but he really got engrossed in drawings of me. He couldn't stop drawing me because he loved me like the rest and I puzzled him. He saw as good painters do beneath the surface of kiddie cuteness to something that contradicted it. 'Be careful of that kid, Hetty,' he used to warn my mother, who never listened to a word.

Someone sent his drawings to a famous art school, which offered him an interview and scholarship. But my grandfather wouldn't let him take it. He had to go into the sweat shops and design and cut cheap clothes. He didn't forgive my grandfather, but left home and fell into a down-at-heel bohemia. His promise was wasted and during the war he died of TB and an unmentionable illness, which my mother and Lil barely whispered to each other. Even during the Blitz they braved bombs and flack to visit their brother Abie on alternate nights. He had lived with a non-Jewish girl of whose existence my grandparents were never told. She had had a baby by him and, after my uncle's death, she and the baby were supported by Ma and Auntie until the baby died too and his unfulfilled history came to an end. All that remains of his talent are one or two drawings which survived the Blitz.

That is what poverty did to promise that was never fulfilled.

I too, when I was older and almost a grown-up, wandered into a bohemian lifestyle but, having learnt from my uncle's life and death, though also tempted to throw everything up for love or romance or Marx or Jesus, never did. Although I had no particular liking for the bourgeoisie, if you let go of them you could fall into a very black hole with no bottom.

Other members of my mother's family were also the victims of 'My Slut Poverty'. My youngest aunt, Hilda, lost a lung through working in a sweatshop and Aunt Lil's children were stillborn because she had to work too hard and too long. I liked the Marxists because they didn't want to mysticise or romanticise poverty but abolish it. It wasn't beautiful but ugly.

Later in life I thought about Poverty a lot. I didn't like to admit it but perhaps the religious reactionaries had a point because beautiful things bloomed in it. Now that I am ensconced in the suburban twenty-first-century middle class with money in the building society, I can gild the picture.

On Thursday nights my grandmother and some other old

women (they were just in their fifties or early sixties), in their black shawls and boots with slashes in them to ease their bunions, used to take me with them at dead of night. They put little parcels of food or some small coins through the letter boxes of families in the block where the men were out of work. They did this at night so giver and receiver never met and they did it on Thursday nights so that people who lived in the lean-to houses and tenements could also celebrate a Sabbath. I never thereafter had to believe in slim fashion-plate angels with wispy drapes. These solid and dumpy women were my angels. I recognised they were messengers from God – if I had allowed myself to use such a term. A lot of religious iconography is kitsch or pap and often a laugh. There's not much Jewish iconography to laugh at because of the problem of graven images but what there is, is also stereotyped – dancing Polish rebbes and rugged prophets and visionary pioneers.

I have never since met such generosity of spirit as I experienced in the back streets behind London Hospital in Whitechapel. My mother gave her only winter coat to the coughing cleaner who lit our fires on the Sabbath. My father brought in every mangy dog for anointing and feeding. My granny who feared the non-Jews around us peered at some disconsolate demonstrators from Wales walking in the rain who couldn't afford a visit to the pub, and invited them all into her holy kitchen to dry off and drink her soup. She too had a revelation of class unity. 'Poor like us,' she muttered in Yiddish.

In our different ways we all tried to escape into alternative reality to ease our poverty. At six years old I would escape with my 'girlfriend', Alice, whom I had met at the cut-price grocer's where our families had sent us to buy yesterday's cake for a treat – 'stale yockers' I think they were called, but what that means I no longer remember.

We used to stare through toy shop windows and I would say magnanimously, 'If I had a half crown, Alice, I'd get you that sleeping doll and its change of clothes.'

'And Lionel, I'd get you,' she replied passionately, 'the Meccano set with the nuts and bolts.'

We stared at each other, overcome by our generosity, and held hands.

All the men in my family dreamed their escapist dreams like

Alice and me. They dreamed of a worker paradise in Stalinist Russia or in Zionist collectives or in Trotskyite or anarchist theories. My mother, who secretly made fun of them, also escaped into her own private celluloid reality three times a week when she could afford it, where she danced in dreams with Fred Astaire in *Top Hat* or was clutched in breathy embraces in jungle or South Sea island romances. These dreams stopped us getting poisoned by our own bitterness. We also once a week, every Sabbath afternoon, inspected the photos in the window of the photographer Boris near Aldgate because he made 'every Sadie a lady and every Jake a gent'. It was as if we were in the 'pictures'. He gave us our glamour.

My granny had her own way of escaping poverty, once a year. She couldn't take a seaside holiday because at first she didn't have the money and later on was frightened to go too far from base, so instead she looked up rooms to let on the heights of Hampstead and Golders Green. Though she didn't want one, nor could have afforded one even if she did, she still wanted to visit them just to see how rich people lived. So with me in tow because I could speak proper English, we set out on our expeditions. What those upper-class people made of us, I don't know. But I think they recognised my granny's innocence and played along with her fantasy game courteously. Some even gave us tea and biscuits.

I made my own little forays into 'the big time' too. With other kids I dressed up smartly and dropped into Sabbath celebrations at posh synagogues for tastes of sweet wine and almond biscuits. We also tried to sidle into wedding parties on Sundays but got chased away because they weren't weddings at all but confirmations and wakes.

After such a childhood, I identify with the down and out – I don't just sympathise with them. When I pass a derelict outside the supermarket with her worldly possessions stuffed in two plastic bags, I feel close to her. I have a strange desire that must be a hangover from childhood. I would like to go to a down-at-heel town I knew nothing about, and look in the windows of corner shops for cards advertising rooms to let with evening high tea. And then I'd turn up and rent one and relive the respectable poverty of my childhood again, reading the free papers in the library and cadging cups of coffee in churches. It would be a relief. I'd be back home again and no longer have to put on the style.

Granny actually made life tough for me because she taught me that the closest I'd ever come to God is by acknowledging the soul of someone begging on the street. But since her days, beggars as well as bankers have become worldly-wise and tricky. So now I no longer give coins but sandwiches, the same that I make for myself. They're usually well received. I've only had two rejections. But then street people have been rejected so often they're entitled to do a bit of rejecting themselves.

5

Ideologies

If you were poor in the years following the depression of 1929, you lived on dreams and visions of escape. Some families had selfish dreams of just being in the money and driving down to Brighton in a posh car with a dickey seat. They wanted to race round the admiring alleys of the East End to show off their 'caboola', their greenbacks, and sharp suits with flapping lapels. My mother's family never did have enough of the old caboola to possess dickey seats. So their dreams were more refined, secular maybe, but unworldly.

In the mid-1930s, sitting at the Sabbath table as a small child, I listened awed by the dreams, visions and ideologies of my uncles and aunts and cousins as they crowded into my grandparents' windowless living room and took their places in the light of the Sabbath candles.

Not until the rituals ended (Granny saw to that) and after our transcendental guests had been welcomed among us – Queen Sabbath, our guardian angels, and the Shechinah, the presence of God – my extended family would recite the articles of their secular faiths rather like modern contract bridge players making their calls. It was obvious to me even as an infant that their individual articles of faith were incompatible with each other's and this made me worried and insecure.

I can just remember a quiet couple of family friends, 'honorary cousins', always courteous and kind to Granny, who dreamt the gentle, idealist, anarchist dream of Prince Kropotkin, who in the Siberian forests demonstrated that the species co-operated with each other for survival – there was more than just nature red in tooth and claw competing ruthlessly. They tried to interest me in a world without flags, passports, banners and soldiers. States declared war on each other, they explained, but not individuals. I think that is why many years later the idea of the State of Israel did not take hold of me, as much as the well-being of its inhabitants. My cousins certainly convinced me of their goodness, whether they believed in God and rituals or not. I could feel their spirituality even if they were atheist; they were among the most spiritual people I knew and the closest to my pious granny. Of course I couldn't put this into words at the time – I was too young – but children are perceptive and I venerated them. They returned to Russia a year or two later to convert that ruffian Stalin and were never heard from again. No one knows the gulag they were murdered in. They were not official martyrs, of course, and the only one who remembers their nobility now is me . . . and perhaps through this book a few of you. I don't light candles for them because they would have been shocked by such superstition.

Another cousin mocked them. He was young, a paid-up, full-blown Stalinist, who carried the red banner at communist marches. When a police whistle sounded, the procession melted away through the doors of sympathisers, of which there were many. But my idealistic cousin couldn't make it. Though he was short, his banner was big and wouldn't go through the small tenement doors. So he was shut out and wandered down the street wondering where to park his precious banner. He was the one who got nabbed by the police.

I admired him because he tried to give his life for his cause too. He volunteered to serve with the Republicans in the dying days of the Spanish Republic in 1937, but he got taken off the train at Dover. He had lied about his age and was too young to travel without his mother's permission. But he was accorded hero status locally.

Some wore the red shirt of communism and others the blue of Zionism. I was firmly told to stick to the school blazer my father had run up for me, otherwise I'd be put back in knitted silk suits. I learnt a lot from them all: from the Fourth Internationalists, whose leader Trotsky (Lev Davidovitch) was murdered with an ice pick by a Stalinist agent in Mexico in 1940, and from my traditionalist conservative father who believed in Baldwin and the Family (our family?). I never sorted them all out in my head but I was proud of them.

My mother made fun of them and when they got going round the Sabbath table she used to wink conspiratorially at me. But she didn't live in the real world either, though she thought she did, given that her heaven was Hollywood.

Until I was about five or six I sided with my pious granny. From her I learnt that if I prayed for something unselfish with my whole heart God would grant it. Being a pragmatic child, I prayed for the speedy demise of Adolf Hitler and our own Sir Oswald Mosley ('May their bones rot' as the rabbis used to say!). But their bones did not rot because I saw pictures of both of them in the newspapers I bought for Grandpa and they were both flourishing like the proverbial bay tree. It was obvious that granny's juju didn't work so I marched with the Reds instead, piping up 'Redfront!' between the slogans. They gave me biscuits afterwards. They themselves were scientific, they said, and I went along with Marxism for nearly fifteen years. Some of it still remains with me, the source of inconvenient thoughts. Even now when in a monastery retreat I suddenly wonder how St Teresa of Avila could possibly understand the Reformation she had crusaded against since she didn't understand the economic forces that drove it along.

This rich ideological muddle certainly increased my insecurity. 'Lionel, buy me a *Herald*!' shouted Grandpa, sunning himself on the Sabbath morning at our front door. 'He means a *Daily Worker*,' said my cousin, winking at me. 'The *Picture Post*!' shouted my mother. 'He shouldn't buy any paper on the Sabbath,' mumbled Granny.

I knew none of their dreams would come true. In my heart of hearts I believed Hitler would take us over or our government would sell out and that would be the end of us. Where could poor Jews flee to? Early on I came to terms with the brevity of life. History was against us.

When I said this to my grandfather, who mended shoes in his open-windowed front room in Vinvoo Street, he told me not to say such things out loud and 'help the devil'. He was a handsome man of strong physique who cobbled away, bargaining through a mouthful of nails, over whether it was worthwhile repairing such cheap shoes. In his workshop he kept the black and red flag of anarchism flying, together with the drayman who had taught his horse Yiddish and the non-Jewish gasman and a broken-down old synagogue cantor who also caroused with him in the local pub when my granny wasn't watching.

Grandpa taught me not to be exclusive about Judaism. More fundamental than being a Jew was being a human being like the gasman and the drayman. I have never forgotten this lesson. Exclusive Judaism I find mean.

6

Life with Mother and Father

It's a sad story and the one who comes out of it best is my father, though it took me a long time to realise it. I only realised it in fact after he died in 1965.

We were a dysfunctional family, and it was not until I left home in the 1950s that my parents started to get their act together. In my wisdom I had always thought I kept them together, but I was quite wrong.

My mother was the local beauty but she was over-confident, and blew her chance with the womanising intellectual she really loved while watching *La Bohème* in a box in Covent Garden. They had a dreadful row in public because to create attention she arrived deliberately late after the opera started, but he was absorbed by the singing, not her new frock.

My granny had always distrusted him and was delighted to arrange a marriage with my father for her on the rebound. Though older than my mother, he was a man of respectability, a bespoke tailor who lived in a tall fine house on a better street with his parents, brothers and sisters. He wanted her badly, and so did his mother, and he lured her with a flashing diamond set in platinum, which she showed off nonchalantly to all her friends and foes.

After they were married in the early 1920s they set themselves up in a corner sweet and tobacco shop. But they were not competent. Ma ate more sweets then she sold and became very fat. Dad invited a local market man to come and inspect the shop and then recommend it to his friends. He did but some of his friends were herders leading their animals, which followed their masters and trooped into the shop with them. The resultant wreck was not insured and this was the first time – though not the last – that my parents went broke.

Then came the slump of 1929 and the dole broke his pride. They were about to split when I arrived on the scene. Because of me they would stay together and, like a mini-messiah, I would one day lead the family out of poverty and the dole and the menace of the rent man to the promised land of north-west London.

They had one thing in common: they loved me with a most unselfish manipulative love, and before I could even squeak they had made deep plans for me. My mother, who was the most purposeful, wanted me to be a sharp lawyer, and Dad a famous boxer. My mother's mother favoured a scholar who would read the Talmud with the same ease as the *Dandy, Beano* and *Radio Fun.* Suffocated by all this, I sometimes wondered if I was God and felt guilty because I couldn't fulfil the role. I was so confused by so many hopes I wasn't really sure.

At first there were intervals of peace when my mother was in hospital for long periods of time. I remember being allowed to peer at her through a tiny window into a long hospital ward and waving to her. I myself was quite happy. I liked being worshipped.

Then in 1934, my mother was finally released from hospital and I was no longer allowed to play with the children on the street because I might pick up a cockney twang. Dad wasn't allowed to talk to me about boxing and other low sports. But I was introduced to the local library and I thank my mother for ever for letting me loose among books. She also told me to listen to *Children's Hour* on the wireless. I began to enjoy it, strange accents and all. It was such a weird world in which the Brown family had maids and cooks, but I never got the hang of *Swallows and Amazons.* Was it true or wasn't it? But I did like Dr Dolittle, who could have been Yiddish he was so humble and loving. Under the supervision of the BBC, I began to improve my accent and my awareness of the English class system, though I couldn't work out where I fitted into it.

I thank my grandfathers' friends and especially my father for teaching me generosity without realising it. Sometimes it led to trouble. My father saw a foreign sailor being thrown out of a pub. He sailed in all fists flying. When the barman came to, he looked at my father through his one unblackened eye, exhausted. 'Hershel,' he whispered (which was my father's Yiddish name), 'I only threw him out because he was making anti-Semitic remarks.'

My mother, who had dressed up in her best to saunter down Whitechapel, shouted, 'I told you so, Harry! I told you so!' and burst into tears.

I watched such scenes trying to work out the rights and wrongs but they were beyond me, and my parents. My father was a traditionalist who expected his wife to serve him his nightly meat and potatoes. Ma rushed home at eight in the evening from work and frantically stirred the stew, the tail of her fashionable fox swinging into the gravy. My father objected and said his mother didn't do things like that. Whereupon my mother, after a bad day at the office, poured the contents of the casserole over him. He, goaded beyond endurance, boiled over when she raised doubts about my paternity and hit her. While they were both rolling on the floor, I packed my little case and marched to my granny who was guilt-ridden at the mess she had helped my mother make of her life.

My family had an awful habit of taking more responsibility than they could bear, and this megalomania has continued in me. Only in my seventies am I detaching myself from it, separating my responsibilities from those of the Almighty, who is supposed to handle such things better.

All three appealed to me, their midget messiah, for support. I sort of loved them too but sometimes I fantasised about trading them all in for another set. It was their inexhaustible capacity for self-sacrifice which shattered me most. I remember once when times were really tough, I stupidly admired a cream cake in a baker's window. Without a word they went in and bought it for me. But I knew straight after they bought it they had used up their supper money that night. I nearly choked over that awful cake.

It's more difficult remembering the good times, but they were there. I remember walking through the red dawn fog holding my father's hand. Before breakfast he dropped in to a house synagogue, called a *stiebel* by us East European Jews – a small holy room – to say memorial prayers for relations he remembered that I never knew. After the prayers we shared a glass of tea with the taxi drivers and pious factory workers who prayed on their way to work. As a little boy I was proud to move in such exalted male society, and it had a long-term effect on me. I can still see through the rat-race of modern religion, the modern prostitution

24

to a holy numbers game, and the endless appeals for money for fine buildings, to a poorer Judaism, more limited but more decent and certainly more religious.

Occasionally my parents acted together and I was really proud of them. When Mosley tried to march through the Jewish streets of East London, my family formed itself into a little brigade and went into action along with the tram drivers, tailors and factory girls – Catholic, atheist and Jewish. Grandpa landed in jail, Dad in hospital, and Ma made sandwiches and passed along buckets of water to throw over the blackshirts and their establishment protectors. I was responsible for supplying mugs of tea. It was one of the happiest days in my childhood and I asked myself why it couldn't always be like that.

I also remember Dad taking me secretly to a strictly non-kosher male pie and eel shop to escape 'the monstrous regiment of women' which he suffered like John Knox. This was Dad's blow against the matriarchy that ruled the Jewish world. But in the end this freedom could only be an interlude. Practically speaking, the only choice left to him was subservience to his determined mother or his obstinate wife. I perceived this quite early on and left him to his fate. To survive in this world of mixed-up adults, charging around like confused elephants, I had to look after number one – myself.

7

Maps in My Mind, Maps of My Life

In the occasional sunlit periods of domestic peace or armistice that broke out between my parents before the Second World War, Dad, forbidden to teach me a low sport like boxing, taught me geography and map-reading instead. He had discovered a love of maps during his days in the Royal Flying Corps in the First World War, and with my mother's consent this he passed on to me as well as swimming (though not boxing). He never realised how he had opened not just my mind but also my soul to far horizons.

He had an atlas and a book entitled *How Much Do You Know?* which he had saved up and sent away for, and under his tuition I learnt the list of every country in the world and its capital city. This knowledge my family expected me to show off to their friends, who had to look suitably impressed.

But these maps came to represent more urgent life in me, and my inner thoughts and preoccupations still hang upon them to this day.

My first map was a pragmatic one. How did I get from infant school to the safety of my grandparents' home? 'Here Be Dragons' blocked straightforward routes. Dad explained to me the geo-political facts of our existence. There were Jewish streets and Gentile streets, he said, and problem streets where Jews lived on one side, protected by the *Mezuzahs* (little boxes of Bible texts) in our doors, and the Christians on the other side, some with haloed saints cut out from pious papers stuck in the window – serving much the same purpose, I assumed. I was a knowing kid, but then you had to be in London's East End if you were not a member of a gang which would support you – and I was totally and absolutely forbidden by my mother to join any gang, not because of their violence but because I might pick up their nasal cockney accents and the vocabulary of Stepney gang warfare or dirty the knitted silk suits I was forced to wear and deliberately unravelled. She was probably quite right because they used me to steal at Woolworth's. Some got sent to Borstal schools but I was let off, classed as 'infantile' not 'juvenile' (I was about five).

After 1936 the gap between the two communities widened. The Jewish houses were for the Spanish Republic and some of the Catholic ones for Franco. But we joined together once again in the Battle of Aldgate when we actually stopped Mosley himself. Practically speaking, this meant that I had to reroute my way home many times, constantly considering the changing realities of life among London's immigrants. So the first maps in my mind were about getting home, spotting and avoiding the traps, decoys and guerrilla warfare, only breathing freely when I made it to the Cohens' Jewish sweet shop, after which I was home in my own territory, luxuriating in the comforting Yiddish and the Jewish smells of cinnamon, egg bread and poppy seed.

My mother also left a map in my mind. It was based on her London Underground Map that she used for her office work concerning property in London. Its scale was too vast for me to comprehend but I learnt its message as I was meant to. Cousins and family friends, who had done well and God had rewarded, had escaped from Whitechapel and moved east along the Central Line to Leytonstone and later to Ilford, and even off the map altogether to Westcliff-on-Sea where gentility resided and riches told. They were above working in factories and shops. They owned them.

Another line – a black one – more mysterious than the straight red one that led east, tangled at Euston, bifurcated around Camden Town and then the trails led to the heights of Hampstead and Highgate. Some of my mother's friends who had made it lived there, and they not only had money but class. I could personally confirm this class connection because I accompanied Granny as she peered nervously into rooms to let on those heights.

Many years later, in 1944, towards the end of the war, my mother did make it to the north-west London suburbs with Dad and me in tow. My father liked it because she liked it and for the first time in his life he had a garden. For me it was a desert, just like the leafy lanes of the awful countryside I was expelled to during the wartime evacuation. But eventually I too eventually managed to make my way out of it to the Old Kent Road, where I set up my rucksack with my Union Jack and joined the line of students and displaced people making for romance, passion and Paris.

Jumping ahead once again in this geographical story of my life, there were other maps too which took over my mind and imagination at special times. In the 1930s even before the war I plotted Hitler's path as he circled ever nearer me. I didn't think I'd escape. After war was declared I learned to live for the day, and wondered and waited for the end. Then one day I heard the fool had invaded Russia. Being utterly selfish, I thanked God for the postponement of my coming execution. There was nowhere to flee to, and I decided I would do as much damage as I could before the Nazis got me. I didn't expect much out of life, certainly not longevity. Let it be short but destructive in the cause of righteousness.

In the children's library in the East End, which my mother took me to, there were framed maps of fairyland. These intrigued me – but I dismissed them. I was a natural materialist and preferred people with two feet on the ground and without wings. Later on in adolescence I never took to Chagall's floating lovers either. I preferred Dad's soft porn, which seemed unhygienic but explicit and credible – though startling.

And later during the evacuation years another map lodged in my mind at school, and it lodges there still. I began to chart the journey of Christian in Bunyan's *Pilgrim's Progress*. Though I was not a Christian, this did not seem like fairyland. With some difficulty I grasped the reality/truth of Doubting Castle and Vanity Fair. Bunyan's chart has been a lifelong indicator and I am still studying how to cross the Ouse, the River of Death that is, and I sometimes think I see the shining of the Celestial City. (*Pilgrim's Progress* remained as a guidebook even during my Marxist years, and I consulted it at any big turns in my life's road.)

But I am not Christian (nor even christian). When I peered over the bank of the River Ouse itself in Bedfordshire to reconnoitre the terrain Bunyan described, I nearly got bitten by a swan, and I had to remind myself that it was an inner map I had read, not an outer one, however practical, detailed and seemingly real.

Since Dad's instruction, companionably lying beside him in bed with his book and atlas, I have always experienced this life as a journey. It is not a destination nor even a resting place. Much later on, I decided the real rest comes from that other life I am journeying towards, that other dimension part of me already lives in, which is Heaven, my home.

8

Evacuation

At the end of August 1939, peace juddered to a halt and expired and preparations for war (not yet declared) began. All the families at my school received the same stern note. We children were to report on a certain morning in the playground with a rucksack (preferably) or a case with straps. We would not be going to lessons at our school that day or even that year but were going with our teachers to the country.

The contents of the rucksack were carefully stipulated: pyjamas, a face flannel, etc. Nobody of course took any notice of these instructions except my conservative father, with his knowledge of English Flying Corps life during the First World War.

Granny Bluestein, always concerned for my health and the Jewish food laws, stuffed my rucksack with a kosher chicken, a kosher salami, an apple strudel and a bottle of new green pickles in case I felt peckish at night. Step-granny Goldstein, my grandpa's second wife after my real granny's death, wedged in prayer books, my praying shawl, my skull cap and assorted Cabbalistic charms against catching a cold and the 'evil eye'. She was so like my real grannies in her love for me that I couldn't tell them apart.

When my father hoisted the rucksack on me, it was so weighty I fell flat on my back, and two uncles, one on each side, supported me to the school, where the harassed teacher threw out the chicken, the strudel and my pious Jewish prayer straps (which are used like a rosary for morning prayers). My father called her a fascist, which was nasty of him, and he apologised fulsomely and insisted on giving her the chicken, heaping it on her pile of papers.

Our procession was just beginning to move off to I knew not where, when I saw all the female members of my family running towards me to rescue me. I didn't want to be rescued, I wanted to leave the lot of them, I wanted to be with my school – but once again nobody asked me.

My family keened and slobbered over me and told me I was going on a ship to Canada, to join the family of my mother's boss. The ship was a phantom ship as all the ships came under heavy attack from submarines, so I never made it to Canada, only to Devon in the direction of Plymouth where we could or might embark, and then it was back to a bombed-out London during the Blitz. An invasion was daily expected. My parents meant well but were not consistent with children. They either did too much or too little but never left my life alone. They meddled and worried too much.

I waited for the phantom ship in a superior kosher hotel in Torquay, courtesy of my mother's firm, and was then removed to the care of a kindly lady who couldn't walk but lived in a bungalow in the depths of the Devon countryside with her son, who was polite to me, but made it quite clear that he had his mates and I wasn't one of them. I longed to be with my school wherever it was. I sat in that empty 'country' wondering what one did in it or with it, and I can still only take the 'country' in small doses. It had no stalls, no fish and chip shops, no beggars or bookies, no gang warfare between blackshirts and redshirts. There were no cinemas either, and I missed the 'Dead End Kids' and my latest passion on the silver screen, 'Horace Debussy Jones'. I did however enjoy watching the sea, which was only a short walk away in a cove. I couldn't read anything because our cottage contained nothing to read. Coming from a Jewish household, I was startled – I had never come across a bungalow before. Perhaps bungalows didn't have books. I was confused.

Then my mother descended again and I found myself in Exeter with a family I really warmed to. I took to 'Auntie' Poppy and 'Uncle' Harold and they conscientiously tried to educate me and teach me manners. At the beginning we just didn't understand each other. It had never occurred to me that children went to bed at fixed times, not just when they were tired. I was also scared of the bathroom. We had never had one in the East End. I think I scared them too. To my surprise, I learnt that children were to be seen but not heard. I couldn't believe it! It was the opposite of Granny Goldstein's house in London, where I was rewarded with chicken giblets if I made set speeches 'To the working class' or about 'What Trotsky should have said to Stalin' (this was my speciality) or 'What I would tell Hitler'. All my speeches started the same whether in Yiddish or English. 'Workers, revolutionaries . . .' I piped up reprovingly. But in Exeter I declaimed my piece, shot my bolt, got no giblets and was promptly sent to bed.

I learnt a lot at Exeter. I did learn manners, which were much admired in the ghetto when I got back later. I opened the door for ladies, and was specially polite to skivvies and charwomen. I doffed my school cap. It was at school I learnt about John Bunyan's Doubting Castle and Giant Despair. Was it true? It took me some time to figure out. This knowledge was not received with great acclaim in the ghetto. I learnt to play six-pack bezique. I marched in Rechabite processions against 'the Demon Drink', singing:

> My drink is water bright, water bright, water bright
> Water bright from the crystal stream.

Also:

> Hurrah for the pump hurrah,
> Her blessings are pure and free.
> I visit her every day
> And she's the old dame for me.

During the Blitz I sang these words to my grandpa Goldstein and this enraged him more than the Nazis, he being a whisky drinker and nowhere near a Rechabite.

In Exeter I also learnt to tap dance. I was getting obese on a self-chosen diet of *faux* doughnuts with false cream. The school doctor suggested rugger or running from lamppost to lamppost. But Aunt Poppy said there was a Jewish family in Exeter, and their daughters ran a dancing academy. So I became a hoofer instead and shuffle-hopped along with the chorus, occasionally tripping up the whole line because like the people of Nineveh in the Bible I didn't know my right from my left. I also had a special turn, and a sweet plump girl called Sarah with a very nice nature was appointed my partner as we shuffle-hopped across the stage warning rabbits in song to 'Run, run, run! Now that the farmer's got a gun, gun, gun' and advising everybody that 'You can't black out the moon'. We were called The Wonder Girl and the Wonder Boy and, wearing dinky gas mask cases over our shoulders, we tried to wow hamlets on the fringes of Dartmoor. There was a war on and people had to take what they could get in the way of entertainment and we were passable, especially when she dropped into my nervous, shaky arms, wondering with the audience what on earth would happen next.

The popular songs then began to get more ominous. We sang 'In an old Dutch garden by an old Dutch mill' as Holland fell and Rotterdam was dive-bombed. And then as Paris fell it was replaced by 'The last time I saw Paris'.

London could so easily have been invaded after Dunkirk. I expected the Nazis nightly. This daily expectation of an invasion also meant that there was no evacuation ship that could now break through the German U-boats and E-boats, so my parents decided that I should leave Aunt Poppy and return to London or what was left of it in the East End. When I got back I realised it wasn't home any longer in the old way. I had lived among Gentiles so long, a full year, that they had become my world.

9

Blitz!

I enjoyed the Blitz. It came as a kind of relief. My parents had brought me back from the country in 1940, thank God, because after the fall of France it was best if we stuck together. Dad would fight on while Ma and I would flee. Though where, nobody knew. I discussed this with other bewildered children who had got yanked away and then crept or were yanked back like me. There wasn't any place left. I was given another rucksack with emergency rations in case the invasion happened and told to keep it by me. At night I kept it wherever I was sleeping together with my gas mask case. The Blitz was a relief because I was back in a proper town again, even if it was getting more and more blown up, away from the dreadful 'country'. And I was also back with Ma, Pa, Lil and Hilda, their brother Abie dying in hospital, and Grandpa. They all functioned very well together in an emergency and I liked them a lot.

My day went like this. When we emerged from the shelter after the night raids and the All Clear, we went back to our homes to see if they were still there and to have breakfast if they were still standing and habitable. Dad, who was a fireman, arrived back, black with soot and burns from putting out fires in the docks. He had some sleep while Ma tried to find a way to her office through the fresh rubble. I went to school for two or three hours until the next wave of bombers came over in the early afternoon. Sometimes the sirens sounded before I got home but somebody would always grab me and take me into their Anderson shelter and I became part of their family till the All Clear.

When the All Clear came again, Grandpa and I lined up outside the local brewery with our family's bedding to get a place in the vaults so that we could all get a night's sleep (except Dad or if you were doing air raid warden duty). Sometimes we were lucky and got a good patch below. Sometimes we found that good patch and only Grandpa noticed that he could see stars and that we were under a great big bomb hole. Ma sometimes made it only just before they closed the gates. Once she arrived too late and you could already hear the ack-ack. I kicked and bit the gatekeepers till they had to open them a crack to let Ma in. They weren't cruel men but just doing their duty. Only so many allowed in. There was a war on!

The shelters were the best school I had at the time. We were all equal there as the revolutionaries said and we loved each other as the religious lot said. We used to share each others' rations and it was the first time I ate sausage roll. It's all bread, said Ma, when the pious objected. And she was probably right. No hammer fell on me and I finished with the food laws once more. Jews slept next to Irish and our families joined together and when the bombs became really bad we all started singing to drown out their noise. Songbooks were popular at the time and that's how we made our entertainment.

While the women were clearing up the bits from our midnight feast, my political education began again in earnest with an even greater intensity. I already knew about Stalin, Kropotkin and Trotsky but now I was educated in the history and assassinations of the IRA and the differences between Fianna Fáil and Fine Gael. Other names like Casement and O'Connell entered my mind. It was after the time of the Molotov–Ribentrop pact and we were silent as the old-time reds tried to justify the past while London was being bombed. There was such relief when Churchill replaced Chamberlain. We needed to keep things simple under a bulldog leader. Chamberlain was too nice for our time.

Once an old man broke down in hysterics because he was worried about his barber tools. If he lost those, he lost his living. To quieten him, Ma somehow got out, walked through the shrapnel and came back with them. She was really a heroine and I held my breath while she was away. Was I as brave? Probably not, but I was getting there. Everybody was.

When the gates were opened after the morning All Clear and we went home, I used to prowl around the ruins because like all the other kids who still remained I was making my own collection of shrapnel. Once I found a lovely piece and put it on the mantelpiece. Dad took one look at it when he got back from the fires and the next thing that happened was that he threw Ma and me through our back window. I had brought home a live incendiary bomb. It was eventually turned into a cigarette lighter. It disappeared during one of our many moves after our house was flattened. Ma got a barrow and took what was left to the lock-up for bombed-out people. It was Dad's family who took us in that night and looked after us.

There weren't many of us at school but the teachers were a wonderful bunch of retired oldies who never minded if we asked questions. They often rambled on about their lives and taught us tantalising bits of culture, which was very helpful. After school I met other children wandering in the rubble. Some were lost or abandoned or didn't like being shut up in shelters and played truant, choosing dangerous freedom. Being a kid with a family, they didn't allow me to join them though they weren't nasty. People were nice then. At the time I am writing this story, in the twenty-first century, our society is going through waves of paranoia, worry and fear once again. Perhaps because we own too much and have so much more to worry about. But it's good to remember a time when anything that moved would stop to give you a lift and I was told to take the hand of any adult I saw if a raid came unexpectedly.

I was sorry when later on in the war we had to move from the East End for the last time as my parents had found lodgings in the safer suburbs. I had tentatively absorbed one lesson during the Blitz. My 'real' home was not our lovely lean-to in posh Jubilee Street which we had moved into about 1937, after Dad got a regular job as manager of a floor in a steamy factory, but the cheerful space in the shelter where we sang to each other to keep up our spirits and there was a lot of supportive kindness.

10

Damp and Cold and Grey

After this war is over,
When all the bombs have dropped,
Then comes that wailing warning
That Hitler's pranks have stopped.

But then the ack ack roars overhead
And the sirens sound once more
And many a heart will be breaking
Long after this war.
(Lines we used to sing in the shelters)

When I was evacuated from London for the second time, because
our home had gone in the bombing, a strange few years began in
which I was parachuted into other people's households, lives and
religions, while waiting for that non-existent safe convoy to
Canada. It was the U-boats' deadliest time. It was also the time I
was approaching my first serious state exam, and at Blitz time the
educational system staggered along but only just. I was sent to a
school in one town and then quickly transferred to another with a
different family, life and religion. En route I picked up different
accents, scraps of evangelism and peeks into the strange tangles
adults got themselves into.

In some I found genuine friendship and even love, which
surprised me, because even at that time I was a problem child.
Before the Blitz there was 'Aunt' Poppy and 'Uncle' Harold in
Devon who were the real thing and after the Blitz there was
beloved Mrs Holt in Surrey whose husband had disappeared
many decades before. Perhaps he suffered from amnesia, because
she was a gem. I was at last convinced that Gentiles could love

children just like Jews and that their love, though less demonstrative, was also less manipulative than ours.

I remember becoming addicted to wireless religion when I lived with Mrs Holt. At that time the *Today* programme and Radio 4 weren't even twinkles in the eyes of a BBC producer's mother, and we only knew the Forces Service which we sang along to or the Home Service in which we hopefully 'Lifted Up Our Hearts' to God. The news was often so bad there wasn't much else we could do.

We lived in a little terraced house in Guildford, and in the early morning all of us rushed downstairs in our overalls and hairy flannel pyjamas and sat in a solemn circle round the Bakelite wireless, drinking in every word over mugs of boiled tea, my evacuation auntie Gertie Holt, her daughter, grandpa, the cat Binkie of uncertain gender, and sometimes even my own mother who'd bolted for a night away from London on fire and a proper sleep. Listening was our patriotic duty and our psychological necessity, because times were grim. One country after another was falling under Hitler's heel and until he invaded Russia we could be the next that night. One convoy had made it through the U-boats. We couldn't help thinking about the sailors on the ones that hadn't and praying for them silently.

But morning wireless put new cheer into us. Our retreats were always strategic and their advances, did they but know it, over-extended their lines. Then we gave a sigh of relief and had another gulp of tea as we got reviews of films on release and the ladies fantasised about clutching Clark Gable in a New York night club. After that Gert and Daisy recommended an imitation mashed potato and mangelwurzel roast you coloured with browning and beetroot if you liked your roast rare. The preachers reassured us that God was on our side and would even bring good out of the evil around us. Nightingales sang in woods near London as well as in Berkeley Square. Looking back, it was one of the nicest times during my second evacuation.

We all needed a little love at that time to warm us up because the world around us was cold and grey. The wool we wore was always damp, coal on short rations and shell eggs unknown. We were fed yet still hungry. We shivered around small fires, wrapped in our bed blankets as we tensely waited for the six o'clock news. The Fire

Service told my father they were going to issue him with a pike – a bayonet on a paling – because guns were in short supply.

And even in evacuation territory, we rushed to the shelters muddling our gas masks in the panic, and listening for the ack-ack and the crump-crump of the falling bombs from German planes as they got rid of their loads before their return.

There were compensations, of course. Everybody bought the latest songbooks and we bellowed out 'Under the Spreading Chestnut Tree' with actions which made us giggle and 'We'll Meet Again, Don't Know Where, Don't Know When', which didn't.

In some homes – billets we called them – like many evacuees, I did not want to go 'home' after school to meet 'uncle' and 'auntie', and they didn't want me for 'nephew' either. 'Uncle' and 'Auntie' were neither nasty nor sadistic, but conscientious, hard-pressed, working people who needed the frigid handout of the state, especially when it was sweetened by my mother's extra. These were the days before national insurance and the social services. They needed me, problem child or not, to survive.

I had had to leave lovely Mrs Holt because it was thought that I had passed my scholarship (the system was in chaos) and a new school in a new town had to be found for me. At my new billets I made myself scarce. After a half-day school, I bought a stodgy doughnut and disappeared into the library and read books at random. I plugged away at *Jocasta's Crime*, bewildered because I couldn't identify the crime or the criminal. Many years later I realised I was reading a psychoanalytic classic, not a detective story. Then I disappeared into the cinema as in the old East End and watched Carmen Miranda, Dorothy Lamour, Horace Debussy Jones in the *Dead End Kids* and Bob Hope over and over again till it was time to go 'home' to soup, a sandwich and sleep.

I got myself to sleep by reading Angela Brazil's schoolgirl stories from end to end by torchlight, knowing only that I preferred them to boys' school stories. I was puzzled but I couldn't ask anybody about it. All this may sound very barren and indeed many of my 'homes' were barren, without the kosher cuddles and kisses I was used to. But 'there was a war on', as we were told time and time again, and were consequently expected to put up with things without asking. I used to sing quietly to myself:

> Bless 'em all,
> Bless 'em all,
> The long and the short and the tall . . .

and this was the nearest I ever got to a prayer.

I felt very proud to be British then, and this pride has never left me. It was one reason why I studied British history so hard. At night when the bombs were coming down, and the ack-ack was going up, people turned up trumps. They shared their food and their houses, or what was left of them, with strangers like me.

I needed this elation because being evacuated I was sometimes the only Jewish child in a country school. The lads in one attacked me in the playground and pulled me to the ground, searching for the stumps of horn in my head. I think they got the wrong end of the stick, so to speak. I wasn't hurt but mortified. But there were some nastier manifestations of anti-Jewish feeling which unfortunately I took to heart and made me retire inwards. I was retiring inwards now at quite a rate. Normal boys don't fall in love with members of their football team. I did. Like all love, it was painful. I also found out I had to pretend to fit in to survive. At the library I pretended the schoolgirl stories I took out were for my non-existent sister. Reports about my bizarre reading even got through to my mother, who whispered her worries to my dad. My turning inwards picked up even more speed as I tried to puzzle out the problems of puberty. If life was going to be like this, how would I survive?

It was at this time that it began to dawn on me that I was in real trouble, that I was made very, very different. (It only occurred to me many years later that perhaps it was society that was ill, not me – I just suffered from its illness.) I began to realise that I was becoming the strange one in my class at school, the odd boy out – every class has one. I couldn't talk my confusion over with anyone, if it could ever be talked over, but I was beginning to lose my hold on the outer world and living more and more in my inner world. The latter was beginning to feel more real than the former.

These were the signs. I couldn't walk on the cracks between paving stones. I had to compulsively touch things to shelter me from the 'evil eye'. When they visited me I had to ask my mother and sometimes my father strange ritual riddles and pored over their answers, looking for flaws in their responses. Even when I returned to London, I needed to sleep with them in the same bed until I was nearly fourteen. The emptiness of my own bedroom, the remembrance of early infantile fantasies in which a cold white moon climbed through the window, and its strange cold face peered into me, these stopped me sleeping alone.

I lived in stories, usually with a changeling theme. These stories were accompanied by waves of insecurity concerning class, caste and relative riches. I pretended when we got back to London at the end of 1943 that our ordinary rented suburban house had two bay windows at the front (it only had one) and then trembled lest anyone find our house and explode my pretensions, giving away the key to my hidden inner world.

Masturbation discovered me and it became compulsive. I didn't use it for pleasure but for oblivion. The loo, any loo, was my retreat from outer reality. I even managed to masturbate myself into fantasy in libraries or in the welcome darkness of cinemas. And with all this was an overwhelming, unmentionable longing for sex with someone like me, a lover! I realised many years later that if someone had come along I wouldn't have known what to do with him, and my 'lover' would have scared me out of whatever wits I had. I was frightened of getting diseases from lavatory seats or giving girls babies by a kiss. I went to a VD clinic at fourteen, sure that I was infected. They were pleasant people, though a little puzzled by my age. I was puzzled too when they asked me what had happened. I kissed a girl, I told them. The nurses stopped whatever they were doing to listen. 'And why do you think you could get VD from a kiss?' they asked. 'Because she wasn't a nice girl,' I replied. They tried hard to keep a straight face and comforted me with tea and biscuits. I didn't dare tell them that I would have preferred to kiss an experienced chap. In the 1940s they put you in prison for that sort of thing.

All these embarrassments carried on after the evacuation years had ended. But even during them I wondered how long I could carry on and whether I would have to terminate the show. The hand dealt out to me was too difficult to play.

But I carried on playing because I became addicted to knowledge. Some corny, the leftovers from my father's early instruction, like learning by heart the names of capital cities and populations of every country in the world, and some more seminal and enterprising. At thirteen I had started to engage with Spengler, Marx, Macaulay, Milton, Gibbon, Rider Haggard and Sax Rohmer. I enjoyed doom and gloom so much I learnt big extracts by heart. I began to learn lots of poetry and began to get addicted to grammar and pure maths because they were pure mind exercises. I was an omnivorous reader and consumed books indiscriminately: George Meredith, Tarzan, Dennis Wheatley and the Dimsie stories, which were schoolgirl stories that were more modern than Angela Brazil's. I chortled about the japes of Rosie of the Lower Fourth and got starry-eyed over the Chalet School.

I knew instinctively that I had to be careful about religion because there were so many marvels and miracles in it, which could pander to and expand my neurosis, not cure it. I had to be careful I wasn't taken for a ride. So though I occasionally tried to be religious by confusing mythology and fiction with fact, thank God I never succeeded. There were so many fantasies already going round in my mind, I couldn't take another lot. So pious fictions never got any welcome from me. Though a very few gave me uncommon insight which seemed to work on the material level too, I was cautious.

So even in my Christian days I was not seduced by the 'magic' in it. My nativity story had no wise men, nor shepherds nor kneeling animals, nor guiding stars. There was just a woman with child, who wasn't quite married. My religion would have to get by on that.

But to return to my puberty years, I knew I had to form my own strategy to survive because I didn't really believe in such sillinesses as souls, and I had to keep my body under lock and key – in a closet, in fact, though I had never heard the word. Only my mind provided some common ground between me, my parents and society. It was then that I developed a bitterness about society which wouldn't, couldn't let a confused lad like me speak about his thoughts and feelings. Would this go on all my life? I cursed the world around me for locking me into a private hell.

I suspected that there must have been more than a few boys like me, and girls too. There were signs. But because of my constant moves and my single-child situation, I never got to meet them. I only knew from puzzling over graffiti in loos that I wasn't alone. My mind couldn't make sense of the terminology but my body could. How could I meet one of the authors of those graffiti?

There must have been even Jews among them. Irrationally, this shocked me.

I did try to talk to a teacher at school about all this, but he chose not to understand. When several years later I approached a rabbi I got thrown out, and Christian clergymen disappeared so fast over the horizon you couldn't see them for dust.

So by the time the war ended, I was a fifteen-year-old dysfunctional member of a dysfunctional family, firing on only one cylinder – my mind – and with a deepening frustration which I couldn't and daren't express because I was sensual, horny and ripe for love. I was also self-centred and wondered if I was unique. Sex seemed such a strange business. I got it confused with the black magic stories that I was reading at the time.

The hell of those years came back to me many decades later when I heard 'pious' bishops and traditional lords promote Section 28, which effectively prevented the discussion of homosexuality or letting some light into the subject in schools. They never thought about the gay child seeking his or her facts of life in a heterosexual society. But then no establishment, religious or political, likes minorities. Whether they're Jewish or gay they demonise them. That isn't piety, it's populism; not religion but respectability – and damn them all. If reincarnation turns out to be true (and most rabbis in the Middle Ages believed in the 'transmigration of souls'), I hope the judgemental lords, ladies and ecclesiastics are born again as lesbian cross-dressers.

I steadily became more revolutionary. I had it in especially for the House of Lords. It had opposed the Reform Bill of 1832, emancipation from slavery and Home Rule for Ireland, which might have saved both our islands a century of civil war, mounting bitterness and terrorism. With such a track record, why keep it? It had served the class interest of wealthy landowners for too long.

A note! This was how I thought. Now I am older and more comfortably off myself, I don't see it the same way, of course. I toy with the idea of an established Church and even a House of Lords without, please God, hereditary peers – *À bas les aristos!* Which just goes to show what a conventional chap I am. I do just the things a sociologist would expect of someone of my age, class and disposition. I am conditioned by my environment just as Marx said I would be.

11

I Educate Myself and Discover Alienation and Sublimation

Having got through all the material grimnesses such as always feeling cold and wearing damp clothes and staying with foster parents who weren't real parents, I began to deal with my mental grimnesses. Here there were a few rays of light which made me feel that I hadn't fallen into a world cooked up by a sadist. They may seem small but they were wonderful for me at the time.

One was the unknown lady who wanted to give me a bookmark like a cross in church, and when I told her I was Jewish, promptly withdrew the cross and found a card with a picture of Abraham. 'Take this, dear,' she said, 'and I'm sorry for what your families must be going through under them.'

These kind words presented me with a dilemma. Yes, I did have some family 'under them', though I didn't know much or anything about them till years later. Some distant cousins in the Ukraine managed to get their children on one of the last trains going east. My aunt Lil who couldn't have children discovered them through the Red Cross, and wrote to them in an orphanage in Central Asia. She wanted to adopt them. For a while there was a dribble of cards from them, but then these abruptly stopped and she was told not to try to make contact again. It was dangerous to have foreign contacts in the latter years of Stalin's Russia. A small family tragedy but a real one – an ordinary bit of fall-out from the war. Most Jewish families had experienced worse.

No matter how bad things were for me, I told myself, for my cousins and the Jewish millions who had not got out in time, mainly working class like us with no money or connections, the

44

world I lived in would have seemed like a paradise. This stopped me in my tracks when I couldn't cope and wanted to end it all. The same strategy helped me years later in hospital. However ill I was, there was always one patient in the ward worse off than me. If all else fails, this grim line of reasoning still keeps me going.

A half dozen of the villages and small towns that I was evacuated to didn't have libraries. There were only the small penny ones at the back of tobacco shops. But their selection was limited and I discovered junk shops with discarded, torn books – usually a ha'penny each or five for tuppence. And I started to make my own library and not just use the official ones. This was a new thought!

That is how I discovered lines and sentences in books which I underlined and which changed my life. Two stand out and I consult them today. One was the sayings of Marcus Aurelius, the Roman Emperor (AD 121–80), who disliked the new Christianity marginally more than the old Judaism. He lived mostly on horseback, trying to hold back the barbarians from the Roman frontier. In his occasional moments of free time, he jotted down his thoughts. He knew no miracles, neither had I. He wasn't a ritualist, neither was I. (I had succumbed to heady smells of fried bacon rind long ago.) He was a universalist, so was I, and above all, he was honest, which I was trying to be to keep my sanity.

He opened the door of religion slightly for me. 'If there is a God,' he wrote, 'follow him. And if there isn't, be godlike yourself.' Though I'd no chance of being godlike, I could swallow that. He also said, 'Tell yourself each morning: today I shall meet an envious chap, an ungrateful one and a bully, and if I had their life I could easily become one too.' For a while I started rehearsing in the morning the situations that I would face that day and working out how I would deal with them. I never asked any god for help, but it was the nearest I got to prayer before I was overwhelmed years later at a Quaker meeting by an experience of Whomsoever Whatsoever. But more of that later.

The Emperor also said that I didn't have to bother about outer temples (in my case synagogues and evangelical chapels), because there was a place of worship already inside me. Which is why, when sometimes I pray in a rush, I even now throw my shirt tails over my head turning them into a prayer shawl whose whiteness helps me locate a reference point of purity within me. I didn't at the time succeed in this. I tried to think about purity but all I got were images of legs, hairy ones or smooth muscular ones.

The second book that touched me was one we read in RE classes. My parents had wanted me to withdraw from them. But I insisted on going to them and also to Christian school assembly. Jesus was wounded and tortured and so was I. I had no feeling for the Almighty Father who had dealt me such a difficult hand. I could feel more for someone who had suffered the world, not created it. I liked the lover part too. 'Jesu, lover of my soul, let me to thy bosom fly.' I shivered with uneasy feelings as I puzzled over it.

The book that we read aloud in old-fashioned RE was my 'special friend', John Bunyan's *Pilgrim's Progress*, the standard volume in the sparse libraries of my billets. When I was introduced to the class, they were listening to the tales of Vanity Fair. Once again it was not too distant from my own experience. I'd met all the characters in the East End, in Petticoat Lane market, and in my inner turmoil. Yet it was considered a marvel that I, an 'unbelieving Jew', should know the book.

I bought my own copy in the jumble shop for a penny and couldn't resist dipping in. It made some sense of my grey evacuation years, after the trudge from one 'aunt' and 'uncle' to another. I grasped the important fact that life was a journey, an idea which I was at home with, because of what Pa had taught me about maps and my own family had, like all migrants, wandered to whichever country would let them in, just as I was dumped every few months into another family which would let me in.

And I started a new game of character spotting. I began to identify the people in the pages of the book in the changing people around me. Vanity Fair and Doubting Castle were real places because they were everywhere. I was hindered by two truths I had to face up to. The quotes from scripture meant nothing to me. I didn't recognise scriptures. They were only old books. Their validation was not a text but their relevance to the realities of my life. The second difficulty was that in my own eyes, I was no innocent pious pilgrim but a beady-eyed youngster, older than his years, who knew too much for his own good.

That is why I did not identify with Christian as he prepared to cross the river of death (the River Ouse) to attain the Celestial

City. Not believing in a Celestial City, I could only identify with Mr Despondency and especially with his daughter, Miss Much-afraid. I considered this passage many times.

> When days had many of them passed away Mr Despond-ency was sent for. For a post was come, and brought this message to him, 'Trembling man, these are to summon thee to be ready with the King, by the next Lord's day, to shout for joy for thy deliverance from all thy doubtings . . .'
>
> Now Mr Despondency's daughter, whose name was Much-afraid, said, when she heard what was done, that she would go with her father. Then Mr Despondency said to his friends, 'Myself and my daughter, you know what we have been and how troublesomely we have behaved ourselves in every company. My will and my daughter's is that our desponds and slavish fears be by no man ever received, from the day of our departure, forever; for I know that after my death they will offer themselves to others. For, to be plain with you, they are ghosts, the which we entertained when we first began to be pilgrims and could never shake them off after. And they will walk about and seek entertainment of the pilgrims, but for our sakes shut ye the doors upon them.'
>
> When the time was come for them to depart they went to the brink of the river. The last words of Mr Despondency were, 'Farewell, night; welcome, day.' His daughter went through the river singing but none could understand what she said.

I felt like her because people were beginning not to understand me either. I was taking the first steps away from the reality of society and common sense towards the reality of myth and nightmare. That kind of journey I later found out is called alienation, and it sucked me more and more into its strangeness, until it culminated in breakdown and thoughts of silly suicide.

But though my feeling and imagination retreated from the world, the clever part of my mind did not, but used ideologies to make the world a more understandable place and therefore more bearable. I had spotted alienation though I had never heard of the word. Again I had discovered something else equally important, though again I only knew its name much later. It was called sublimation.

Ideologies would have to stand in for the lovers that were forbidden, for the brothers I never had, for the friends I hardly knew how to make. The ideologies I tried were Marxism, Zionism, Anarchism, Christianity and Judaism. And later on I added some eastern ones. Each deserves separate treatment because though I was using them in the wrong way they all were true pieces in my jigsaw puzzle. But perhaps I was not using them in the wrong way either. I was only using them in my way out of need.

Marxism, my first love, is no longer fashionable particularly since the collapse of the Soviets but, to my credit, I never identified it with Stalinism and refused to join the Communist Party and even earlier the Young Communist League. I was content until 1948, a little before I went up to Oxford, to be a fellow traveller. My gritty preference for truth prevented my becoming a true believer, just as it would later on prevent me from becoming an Orthodox Christian or an Orthodox Jew or indeed an orthodox anything. I would remain forever an outsider in an insiders' world – a subversive, if you like. Even in Judaism, my home for many years, I remain a window which lets some outside light into an introverted world. I do it for my religion as well as for myself.

Because I was semi-aware of my own irrational motives, I spotted the rise of irrationalism in politics and religion earlier than most. I began to realise in a hazy way what the learned adult hardliners I met wouldn't face up to – that sexual and personality problems were closely connected with theological and ideological ones. This limited any strength and support they could give me. Occasionally I did bump into a source of inner strength but I didn't know what to call it. Conventional labels didn't bother me and I eventually decided 'Soul' was as good a label as any.

12

I Escape

Returning permanently back to London in 1944 just as the war in Europe, apart from the new doodlebug bombs, was drawing to its close, I had to live with my mother again. I left school at fifteen but, after over a disastrous year as an articled clerk in my mother's office, I returned to school in 1946–7. As my mother was pretty overwhelming, when I was sixteen I made a bolt for freedom and escaped from her, Dad, suburbia, the lot. Though I recognised England as my home, I also knew another home from the moment I first saw its thin horizon from a North Sea ferry. I recognised it, I did not learn it and do not understand its roots in me or the reasons why they went so deep. I only know that I have loved Holland from the first and that its raw rain-washed skies unknotted me spiritually and artistically ever since (sexually too, but that came much later – when I discovered that there sex could be acknowledged in its own right without closets stuffed with excuses, fibs, little white lies and big black ones). Like the modern Dutch poets Marsman and Bloem, I loved the dark waterlogged fields reaching to far horizons. I was thrilled by mighty skies and cloud castles lowering on top of busy, busy pygmy towns, with their crowded cafes whose clients munched, munched, munched, like their own cows, and then some.

The salty North Sea purified me from the hypocrisies of lower-middle-class England to which my own family belonged. Holland became thereafter my place of pilgrimage, more life-affirming for me than an old stone wall in Jerusalem that once surrounded a sacrificial cult or the ornate baroque of Rome that reminded me of Lyons Corner Houses in London. In Holland honesty was accorded the same status as manners in England.

My education started as soon as I got there, or even before. After the war in Europe had ended, my school had arranged for a party to tour the Netherlands. It must have seemed a dull sort of place, and after the occupation it was indeed a very poor place, and fighting a bloody war it was bound to lose in Indonesia. Anyway, two weeks before our party left, a letter arrived informing my parents the tour had been cancelled through lack of support. They would try to set up other arrangements. Youngsters wanted Paris and cancan girls not clogs and cows. I never told my parents about the hand-delivered letter and just kept it. I subsequently waved goodbye to them at Liverpool Street Station, telling them I'd meet the rest of the party in Harwich. To my relief they left, and I was on my way alone to the mysterious continent which had survived the nightmare of Satan.

In Rotterdam, I was introduced by a Dutch student to a Dutch family who invited me to tea. I have long since forgotten their name but I have never forgotten the platter of cream cakes they passed towards me. My God, the cows of the country must have been working overtime, and cream for me was a memory, something I hadn't seen since my infancy when war began.

Being polite, when they offered the platter to me, I said, 'Really, I couldn't,' waiting for them to press a little harder, and then I would help myself to the biggest and creamiest. But they didn't press harder. The platter with its treasure moved to the top end of the table, and I was left bereft and creamless at the bottom. I decided from that moment on to go Dutch, to try to eschew role-playing, bourgeois hypocrisy and *perfide Albion*, and begin to say what I thought, though not quite what I wanted – that was the most forbidden fruit which still bewildered me. I didn't even know what to call it.

I travelled around Holland as the guest of Dutch students who finally put me in various vacant student flats in Amsterdam, leaving me to make what sense of the city I could. I couldn't at the beginning because I got flu and fever, and was stranded on the fourth floor of a tall Dutch house with steep crazy steps I couldn't stumble down. I just had to stay put till my temperature returned to normal.

The unknown student whose room I was in must have studied literature because, with the aid of his dictionaries, I started to try and make sense of the feast of Dutch poetry that overflowed his shelves, without knowing how on earth the language sounded. It was lovely, like opening a box and finding it full of blissful chocolates all with different fillings.

Sometimes my guesses at Dutch led me astray. I started on the moody marvel of Gorter, thrilling to the opening lines of 'Mei', his great epic. 'A new spring, a new sound . . .' I could manage to translate that but a few lines later there was '*In het huis was het donker*', which I translated breezily as 'In the house was a donkey'. So it was an animal poem. Now I liked donkeys and flipped the pages of that misleading epic but could never find out what happened to my donkey. (NB: As Dutch students will know, *donker* means 'darkness' not 'donkey'.) That was one of my failures! Not bad, though, with a temperature. But I did make some sense of another poem which gave me pause, in which a messenger from on high tells the receiver, 'Clear away all the silliness from your life and one day you will see Him in peace'. The bells of the nearby Old Church playing the great hymns of the Reformation underlined this message. I discovered that though a Marxist I had a puzzling religious bent and understood them.

I needed a bit of divine love badly, because while I was suffering, declaiming and masturbating on the fourth floor, a student with two girlfriends was making love twice over on another floor. I swooned as I strained to hear their grunts, groans and grinds. And in a house nearby were 'the ladies', who heard about me and filled my basket with necessities and then hauled it to me on a rope. They were very loving in their own way too!

I began to realise I was just the hungry filling of a sex sandwich. I cried in self-pity. My temperature got down to normal, but still there was nothing I could do about my love needs. But a middle-aged cleaner in the house surprised me with a hearty kiss, and I still remember the soapy cleanliness of her creamy breasts. If only a wicked old man or predatory *femme fatale* had found me, my life might have been very different. But they didn't – sniff, sniff – so I had to make do, as I have said, with mysticism and imagination. This was a mix I had to make do with for many years, until my late twenties when I suddenly saw the homosexual world that God had put in front of me and which had been waiting for me all the time. I never found the opening at that time. Perhaps I was unlucky, perhaps I was too scruffy, with bitten nails and showers of dandruff, perhaps He had reserved me for higher things. (Be careful, Blue – sublimated mega-lomania!)

When I got better, I tottered to the Old Church to hear concerts on its great baroque organ. I discovered Sweelinck and Buxtehude there, and thought about the Jewish life that had been deported for murder a few streets away in the Hollandsche Schouwburg, an empty theatre taken over for the tragic assembling of the victims.

In the mornings I cycled out into the flat country of Northern Holland. I could never have enough of the looming skies, which comforted me because they dwarfed the problems of my own adolescence. In the afternoon I sat at a sandwich stall in the flea market on the Waterlooplein, drinking coffee and munching and staring (I had caught the Dutch habit).

When I arrived back home in England, my parents fell upon me. They had heard about the cancellation of my 'safe holiday' to Holland. I no longer prevaricated. I told them straight out – Dutch style – that I was never going to go on holiday with them again. They had their life, I had mine. They could lump it or leave it. I mollified my mother with a bottle of Advokaat and my father with a packet of Dutch bulbs. From now on I was going to be my own man – if I was a man, God help me!

13

Going My Way?

Holland had shown me the way. Now there was nothing I could not do. On the last day of term, I staggered to school, looking like Rumpelstiltskin under the weight of my enormous Army Surplus rucksack, festooned with rolled blankets, mess tins, enamel mugs, and a spare pair of boots tied on by their laces (which a thief snipped off as soon as I was on the road). The moment the school holiday bell was rung I made my way to the Old Kent Road and joined the long line of other young hopefuls, all hitchhiking along Chaucer's old pilgrims' route to Canterbury and the coast. After Calais, I would make for Paris, then for Cannes and then for Venice, whose dream-like sadness matched my mood and drew me on. I had just discovered by chance in the library creepy Baron Corvo, alias Pope Hadrian VII, and I identified perfectly. I wasn't a Catholic, but I would have liked to be a Pope.

I slept in hedges, youth hostels, lorry drivers' seats and priests' garden sheds, and got crucified on the back of gravel lorries, in the back seats of sleek cars of Belgian profiteers, once in a hearse, and even on the back of a motorbike. One Belgian profiteer's blonde 'bit' offered me chocolate and called me 'Monsieur', which cheered me up no end. I remember a honeymoon couple who took pity on me and took me half the way across France. They slept at night in a tent for two and I found a haystack. I must have been a smelly, unappetising car companion. The honeymoon wife introduced me to chips with mayonnaise.

Half the time I hitched alone, but I did hitch with an American girl, I'll call her Sue, who had a hidden pepperpot to guard her honour, though not from me. Once I met up with a worker priest who showed me how to serve him at Mass. He asked me if I'd like to communicate too. I said 'yes' and meant it though

I was not a Catholic or even a Christian. But beggars can't be choosers and I felt very good afterwards. He told me communion wasn't a prize for good behaviour like the ones they gave out at school, or a cherry on the religious cake, but a way to goodness. I certainly needed something and I felt very refreshed afterwards. It didn't quite take, however, because I wanted it only from him.

My journey through France was spiritual, not sexual, because I think I must have looked too off-putting. But with divine love I was way ahead. I lurked behind a hedge while Sue the American girl tried to fascinate lorry drivers by waggling her skinny brown legs and bottom. I would lie in wait to jump out and join her when anything stopped. During the long periods when nothing happened, I pondered *Pilgrim's Progress* once again. Vanity Fair and Doubting Castle were wonderful introductions to life on the road. Like Christian, I was also carrying a pack that was too heavy for me but the contents weren't the same. I tried to puzzle out how such a valiant man could believe in witches and their horrid tortured end.

I met good folk who gave us lifts and even sandwiches, nasty ones who slowed up to inspect us and then put on the accelerator, giggling, watching me fall flat on my face behind them, hypocrites who gave a sign they were full when they obviously weren't, and an occasional courageous lady driver who tut-tutted and poured out a cornucopia of handy hints neither Sue nor I could understand.

I half made love to Sue once and brought her to a multiple climax (fingerwork) which surprised me even more than her because I had hardly any knowledge of the female body or how it operated. I didn't know what went into where. I must have reached bull's-eye by instinct.

She left me near Avignon for some other American. I was a drag, she said, puffing her Gauloise into my face. But I then met up with an engaging thief who stole my tin plates, again by cutting the strings while I was asleep.

I also stayed with some Capuchin friars as displaced as me, who had returned to their native Italy from a liberated Abyssinia and felt lonely. They wanted to learn English and I tried to teach it to them from a dog-eared copy of *Ulysses* by 'Yame Yoiche' – James Joyce to you. This disconcerting book made us all merry and fall about with laughter, though I don't know why. But it was pretty absurd.

At that time just after the war so many people were on the move. I was one atom among them. Ukrainians trying not to get sent back to the Workers' Paradise, where they said they'd be shot, and I reluctantly began to believe them, Jews making for Marseilles and a boat to Israel, displaced people looking for their families, refugees of many races, young Germans trying to escape from the shame of defeat and get away to South America, and adventurous worker priests. They all needed to talk in a babble of languages and like the wedding guest in *The Ancient Mariner* (which was our set text at school) I had no choice but to listen.

I'm pleased I did. I got pally with a young German, in a youth hostel communal kitchen, the last of the Nazi Youth to battle on until his home was occupied. His father had died on the Eastern Front, and his mother had married someone else who did not want him. We slept outside for two nights, and hugged before we left. He vowed that he would never be against Jews again. Promises! Promises?

I learnt so much while hitchhiking that now I am over seventy I still go over in my mind what was said to me by the people I met on the road, not only by mouth (a lot of their polyglot I couldn't understand) but by their gestures, pleadings, an occasional kiss, some smiles and curses.

The Book of Life that the Jewish liturgy talks about was becoming an open book. I could read it but I couldn't yet understand it.

14

The Wrong Side of the Rainbow

Sooner or later I knew I'd have to make another journey and cross over the Iron Curtain to see for myself how the other half of Europe, the communist half, lived. I needed to check theory against reality. That other side began between Lubeck and Rostock and cut through Europe like a piece of cheese down to Trieste. I had hitchhiked through Western Europe about three times. I had 'done' it. Now I had to get to Eastern Europe, to find out what was fact and what was capitalist fiction there.

Not having any contacts, before I did my National Service I joined a student party that was going to build what turned out to be a badly planned and constructed socialist highway from Zagreb to Belgrade. Our brigade met before we went off. It was led by communists, mainly middle-class ones, who taught us jolly songs to sing when we got there about fat capitalists watering the workers' beer, and about how old age was always respected in the Soviet Union, and lyrics greeting Marshal Tito, our little red flower who had liberated or was going to liberate Trieste. In my cups I sang it in a Trieste cafe and was thrown out just before I caused a riot.

But nothing went right. Tito got slung out of the Cominform before we got there, which caused consternation among the communists. Was the Marshal still a little red flower? They had agitated meetings about this, or so I heard from a girl member who had a sense of humour. But it was too late to cancel now. Chugging through Italy, we then heard that Togliatti, the Italian Communist leader, had been shot, and there were rumours about gunboats on the Grand Canal in Venice. I got holed up in a hostelry attached to a convent and existed on mounds of tomatoes stewed with stale bread in olive oil.

We got to the Yugoslav frontier in closed carriages that crept around the Adriatic to the frontier. At the frontier we stampeded towards the loo. There were two doors whose Serbo-Croat inscriptions no one could read. So the men charged through one and the women through the other and we all met at the same cabin with the same hole. So why two doors and only one hole? It was 'kulturny' (cultured) said the frontier guard.

On Ljubljana station platform I met a lady communist with a trunk or two of the latest new-length dresses, so she told me. I offered to heave them. She was grateful. We found we had friends in common, and we joined up for the rest of our stay. It was only weeks but it seemed like months, and I was determined to get back on my return from Yugoslavia to effete, crumbling Venice, even if the gunboats had grown into battleships.

For most of the time our brigade inhabited what I later realised with horror must have been a cleaned-up concentration or labour camp. Luckily, our thoughts were not on ghosts but goat meat. We longed for some and heard how some brigades who had over-fulfilled their 'norm' had earned delicious roasted slices of it. We did not even fulfil our norm, being such a confused freewheeling lot, so all we got was ersatz coffee, gritty black bread, tasty tinned grapes to keep us regular, which were good, and UNRA (United Nations Relief Agency) jam which was probably meant for other more needy mouths than ours. I think we also got tobacco and free cigarettes, or perhaps we just bought them – they were so cheap it was almost the same thing.

My famished girl friend and I lured a young lad into a maize field where he produced his hidden tin of real sardines. But we were discovered by his friend Laura just as we were finishing the last drop of oil, and she was indignant because the soft chap had also promised a sardine to her.

I took to Laura because she was so direct and honest and thought straight, and she became my friend for life. I apologised for the sardines. That was indeed a sin and I wondered how noble I would have been in a concentration camp. Obviously not very. She was a tall, big-busted girl who led her group to the workface singing 'Bang Away Lulu' and other soldier and rugger songs. She studied literature and wrote sensitive short stories.

She met a lovely Dutch guy called Johannes who loved her as much as I loved him – though of course I couldn't say so. He was strong and gold and like a child. He had run away from Holland to avoid conscription to Indonesia, and that out of time war, so he couldn't go back there. He could only go on and was looking for a boat in Rijeka that would take him to the pure socialism of the USSR, not the flawed one of Yugoslavia. He wanted to marry Laura. But Laura regretfully said no because he was a sailor, and she told me that marriage for her meant being faithful and she would never be faithful to a husband who would be away from her so often and so long.

I think Johannes got his boat, and I still try not to wonder what happened to him under Stalin.

It was in Yugoslavia that I encountered two earnest little Albanian students who, now that Tito had offended Soviet orthodoxy, were going to be moved to a more ideologically correct country. They were so sweet and earnest, and tried to bring back a lost sheep like me to the Stalinist truth. But they didn't succeed any more than other Marxists, Anarchists, Orthodox Jews, Anglo-Cats, etc., etc., etc.

After I got back to England I received a letter from them. They were now in Prague, burbling on about the pure beauties of the system there. Surely, they wrote, it was time for me to recognise the truth. (Lots of people have since said the same thing to me, but I remain an unbelieving Jew and free.)

I answered stupidly and thoughtlessly. I sent them back a polite letter stating the reasons why I'd remain a heretical social-democrat and my opposition to the East European personality cult. It was a dangerous letter, not for me but for them. I realised this afterwards and just a bit at the time. It was certain to have been opened by the Czechs and they might pass it on to the Albanians, whose mad paranoia I only began to learn about later. How would they have regarded their two students with dangerous foreign contacts? What might they have done with them? I should not have sent that letter, being honest and virtuous at other people's expense, to young people like myself, who had done me no harm.

I remembered the prayer of that worker priest, 'O Lord have mercy on us! Christ have mercy upon us.' But no prayers wash out the past, or make it to have never happened. All you can do is never repeat your mistake, your sin. That, said a rabbi, is repentance. I agree, but no Day of Atonement washes that sin clean. But perhaps I blame myself too much, as later on my therapists said. Perhaps my little Albanians got good marks for trying to convert me. Perhaps they got a medal for resisting decadent western ideas. I hope so.

15

'The People's Flag is Palest Pink!'

I was no good at love affairs but fortunately I discovered that ideologies were also a turn-on for me and served as emotional substitutes. Alone in Amsterdam or lurking behind hedges, I had taken stock of my position. Only rarely did I make contact with people. They were wary of me because I wasn't a complete person, just a disembodied and soulless mind. So instead of making dates in dance halls, I dropped in instead on ideological meetings in more austere halls, where I sat at the back sucking toffees, listening to Mr Palme Dutt, the communist ideologue (whom I didn't trust) ranting on and on, all the while considering, considering . . .

But I was not bloodless, and my feelings seeped out or burst out while marching, shouting slogans, and arguing passionately into the night. I learnt the trick of polemics and could do it well. It was the applause of a crowd which gave me tingles down my spine, not twanging brassiere straps in the back rows of cinemas like the other boys I knew.

I was attracted to Marxism for many reasons. The war had just ended. If Germany had not invaded Soviet Russia in 1940, I would have been a whiff of smoke from a concentration camp crematorium. I shuddered to think what would have happened to my family. And who among our non-Jewish neighbours would have sold us down the river to save themselves? And would I have done the same? I was an honest child, and knew I didn't know the answer to either question.

I chose Marxism because I had begun to understand its theory. From *The Theory and Practice of Socialism* by John Strachey, a Labour Minister, I had progressed to the 1848 Communist Manifesto, whose passion and clarity exalted me. The slogan 'From each according to his abilities, to each according to his needs' still does (and I am pleased that decades later I managed to insert these words into our traditional prayer book) though it bemused some conventional colleagues. And then I struggled with *Das Kapital* itself, marvelling at what I could not understand. One thing seemed clear to me. Marx and Engels had turned history into a science. By studying the past, scientifically, I would be able to predict the future and prepare for it. All previous history seemed just like stories, still at the level of King Alfred burning the cakes. I decided to study history in depth at Oxford because I wanted to play my part in the coming revolution. But when I finally attained Oxford, I was shocked how history there hadn't progressed much further than Alfred burning his cakes.

And yet I was uncomfortable. Because it was not only reason that thundered in me as the 'Internationale', the communist anthem, said. There was also anger at being a poor relation, envy of richer relations, hostility to the poverty that had wrecked my own family, dislike of sexual repression (even worse in the USSR than in the decadent West, Reason whispered in my ear), dislike of the myths, whether Nazi, national or religious, which stood in the way of my own happiness. The truth was that I was sitting on a cauldron of repressed feelings, which made me want to blow up the world with me in it. In feeling, I anticipated the adolescent suicide bombers of the next century. But I was not in love with death or martyrdom and never quite lost my cockney common sense.

But I chose Marxism too because it was the only ideology which seemed to explain my own time – how excess profits channelled into capital had led to a conflict between supply and demand. This had led to the expansion of empires and the annexation of sources of supply and markets, which had led to world wars, which had led to the horrors of dying capitalism, which had spawned fascism and Nazism to protect itself, which led to mass murder. I still think this analysis of one period of modern historical development is substantially correct. But Marxism was itself a child of its time and never foresaw the eruption of the irrational into political life. How could it! Marx was a generation before Freud. Nor did Marx foresee the welfare state nor the rise of Stalinism, when the revolution was hijacked by the personality cult, the love of power and the attraction of an elite.

For a while I said to myself, 'Marx, I believe, forgive mine unbelief.' But you cannot unknow what you do know, whether it is religion or ideology, so I gritted my teeth and read all the books good communists keep away from. *The Managerial Revolution, Animal Farm, Myth and Violence* . . . I started to read the idols of my grandfather and his anarchist chums – *Mutual Aid* by Prince Kropotkin, and the autobiography of the radical anarchist Emma Goldman. Anarchist 'scriptures' impressed me. They had gone one stage further than the others. They were the only ones who talked about sexual politics and freedom for youngsters like me. But it seemed to me the stuff of dreams. I wrote them off too easily because they didn't seem successful. The mafia of Stalin ruled the roost among the revolutionaries. I remembered my idealistic family 'cousins' who had gone to Russia so many years before to tell him so.

I had now argued my way out of Stalinist purity and knew the fault was fundamental, not just a chance hiccup. So in the late forties while marching in a procession which was shouting itself hoarse reciting the names of Stalin's mafia like a litany, I abruptly left the procession and have never rejoined. My mind couldn't take it. I missed the thrill of marching for the masses, but Stalinism was idolatry and the death knell of true Marxism. Instead I retired to an Indo-Pak restaurant and over a burningly hot Bangalore curry, which purged away my false over-easy beliefs, and a beer to cool down my raging emotions, I considered living in a world without an ideology. I felt naked.

In this I was more advanced than my upper-middle-class fellow travelling students and lecturers, whom I met a few years later at Oxford. Coming from the working class, I was tougher. I could see the implications of Stalin's treason trials in the thirties and persistent reports of the gulags. Not as sadistic as Hitler's camps, but just as indifferent to individual suffering. And almost as mad.

I waited to see what would happen next. I knew a breakdown was in the offing but my ideological adventures hadn't finished yet. In this I was quite right. My life's journey then 'progressed' through Zionism, Quakerism, Anglo-Catholicism, and finally to suburban Reformed Judaism, where I still am, an honoured eccentric, 'idiosyncratic' they say politely. As the great-aunt of my second partner Kim used to say, 'Odd I don't say, queer I grant you!' She spoke wiser than she knew.

16

Dancing into Zion

I began to get caught up in Zionism when I was about fifteen, just as I was beginning to have doubts about Stalinism. I came to it not through my mind this time but through my guts and dancing feet. My parents had bullied me into joining a synagogue youth club which without sex on my part was a boring, bourgeois irrelevance. We assembled in a dreary synagogue hall where I had to drag a girl around in time with the music from a radiogram. She knew that there was nothing in it for her, poor lass, and I was sorry because she was an insecure refugee from Germany and deserved better.

Then into the hall from a classroom, a band of youngsters suddenly jumped out, energised with ideology, who burst into strange tribal passionate circle dances, shouting what seemed like political slogans, but in Hebrew, of which I hardly understood a word. My roots were in a Yiddish culture, not a Hebrew one. Two of the dancers recognised me from school and to my astonishment held out their hands to me, welcoming me into their magic circle. I was bowled over since I had no friends, my alienation had gone too far. I bounded into their ring and decided whatever they were dancing for was for me. And whatever the shouted slogans, I'd go along with those too. It wanted me, it would get me. Revolutionary liberty and equality were cold virtues compared to the intense fraternity of newborn nationalism.

Also a part of me which I had suppressed was released. I was brought face to face with my own Jewishness, and the Holocaust, which I had intellectualised – because the horror was too much for me. I kept it in another world far from the ladies and gentlemen of England. But with the help of the new nationalism, I was willing to face the memories and tales of poverty, persecution and anti-Semitism in Poland and Russia from which my family had fled, even the Nazi monster and the killing camps that had succeeded them.

I discovered that the dancers also had a dream just like the Marxists, but a dream created by Jews, for Jews. Together we would drain the swamps of the Promised Land and bring water to its deserts. The wilderness would blossom like the rose, and we, together as a group, would by saving the land save ourselves from all the inner twists and scarring defamations that the anti-Judaism of two thousand years with its ghettos and Jewish badges had inflicted on us. Together we would build peaceful agricultural co-operatives and collective farms, and live socialism, not just theorise about it, leaving capitalism to the Sodoms and Gomorrahs of the cities. Together we would gaze sun-tanned into the future surrounded by our simple bucolic progeny. I am not speaking fantasy. This was reality for many members of my group who dedicated their lives to this ideal.

The effect this vision had on me was curiously like that of the pictures of simple righteous folk in illustrated Mormon Bibles and in the frescoes in Mormon temples. I desperately tried to imagine myself like them. But how could I when what I secretly yearned for was a little bit of Sodom and a whiff of Gomorrah too? Golders Green on the Med had no attraction for me.

So I was living the same lie as among the Marxists. I did everything I was supposed to do by my group. I rejected ties as bourgeois, favouring Aertex open-necked shirts, 'pioneer style'. I spurned ballroom dancing in which I had to hold the girl for a unisex muscle-to-muscle folk-dance. I was perfectly willing to share my pocket-money and possessions. I wanted to share all of me, because I didn't like me much. I wanted to get rid of me and this was an acceptable way to do it.

My Zionism gave me back my roots, as I've said, a modern Jewish education utterly unlike the medieval one I had once endured in Hebrew and religion classes – also an exhilaration as I rejoiced in the new folk song, dance and literature. I was reborn with my people.

But you can't ditch the past so easily or free yourself from its cruel claws. Well, perhaps you could, but I couldn't. I knew jolly well there was no place for a homosexual in the beautiful pastoral vision, which was actually becoming fact in front of our very eyes. (The State of Israel was proclaimed in 1948.) I tried to explain my situation to a Zionist youth leader. But either he didn't understand or he didn't want to understand. It was not my fault that I felt a fraud, a deceiver of my group which had given me so much.

The end to my dream came abruptly. Our youth leader told us suddenly but firmly that he was going to disband our group. Some, the elect, would start to train for an agricultural life. The rest of us would sort ourselves out as best or as worst we could. The state was important and its needs were urgent, our fate was not in the same league.

I was shattered. The group life was my only defence against the alienation which was catching up on me like the Erlking in Schubert's song which I got to know later at Oxford, accompanied by his outriders – despair, introversion, anxiety and deep, deep depression. I thought I had already plumbed the depths, but I hadn't. I hadn't begun. I was crippled by it. Living with my parents, I often couldn't get out of bed till lunchtime. I couldn't answer a telephone or even draw a curtain. And this state of affairs carried on patchily even after my later analysis. If you have never experienced such states, you cannot understand what they are like unless you have great imagination. If you suffer from depression you will understand my oddities only too well, like not being able to answer a telephone, post a letter or open the curtains. These were of course hangovers from early childhood insecurities. But they are acutely embarrassing when practised by an obsessive near-adult.

But back to Zionism. There were other omissions besides my own sexuality.

Although we studied Jewish life in Israel from every angle, we passed over the Palestinians. Some said breezily that they would adapt, and their refugees be taken in by surrounding Arabs who had just hit the jackpot with oil, the black gold. The Marxist in me was worried. More fundamental than being a Jew was being a human being, and a worker (though at that time I lived on my parents). The Zionist classics – *The Jewish State* by Herzl, *Auto Emancipation* by Pinsker, the essays of Ahad Ha'am – seemed thin compared to the solid and weighty Marxist tomes. It was only the baleful light of the Holocaust that played around them which gave them a greatness they did not really deserve.

I kept these thoughts to myself, of course. I couldn't see the point of resurrecting Hebrew. Herzl – the author of *The Jewish State* (1846) and founder of modern Zionism – himself had thought the language of the Jewish state should be German, the language of culture. I thought it should be English, the language of the new technology. Hebrew seemed to me a sentimental mistake and, with its own alphabet but with only an imperfect vowel system, not fitted for the task. In this my opinion goes against the group opinion of most Jews who venerate Ben-Yehudah, who brought the language back to life by refusing to speak any other. He was the pioneer of modern spoken Hebrew, before dying in 1922.

But deeper, I suspected a covert sin in all nationalism. You loved your own more by loving others less. Nationalism didn't have to be like that, of course, but it nearly always was. A culture, a common history and literature, a landscape, wasn't enough. A flag, a passport, an anthem, and the raw feelings and slogans of football supporters' clubs seemed to be necessary too, a stray gentle anarchist 'cousin' had warned me.

Before I went up to Oxford, I thought that communism for good or bad was the ideology of our century (the twentieth). But it wasn't. It was nationalism. This was the culprit which had brought on the bloodbaths of two world wars in Europe, and there might be more in waiting.

I kept on seeing Zionism in different lights. Sometimes it was the fulfilled vision of the prophets or the dream of modern Jewish idealists. Sometimes it was the last wave of East European nationalism, owing more to Rousseau than Micah, Isaiah and Amos.

17

'My Parents Didn't Understand Me.
They Were Bourgeois!'

Or perhaps they understood me only too well. You are a better judge than me.

Externally this is what happened. I had stayed at school till I was fifteen, top of book studies and bottom of life studies and steadily getting odder. I then left school in 1945 at my mother's behest. She had sworn lifelong loyalty to a work friend, who in return would make a solicitor of me, and then a partner, and later he would transfer to me a small but strategic building society, just right for the post-war property boom. I was accordingly articled to him and in 1945 studied law at King's College, London, while working at his office during the day. It was bleak.

After over a year I walked out of my LLB finals in the middle of an examination. I had had enough. I loathed law, the office and everything about them. They were dreary and dismal and going in each morning felt like another death. My mother had hysterics and said her lifelong work was in ruins. I told her I was pleased as I wanted to blow up the lot. She said she was going through her change of life and needed special consideration. I told her she could stuff the emotional blackmail because I thought I needed special consideration too as I thought I was homosexual. She and the solicitor sent me to an expensive psychiatrist, an analyst. He asked me to draw a symbol. I drew the hammer and sickle. He said that meant buggery. I was shocked. And told him he was a dirty old man. My father's only contribution to this interchange was 'Listen to your mother, boy!' – which I ignored.

My mother, and my subservient father, finally did a deal with me. I would graciously agree not to go as a pioneer to Israel (I had no intention of doing so in any case). In return I could go back to school (humiliating) and try to get into a university. After I got a degree, I could go to hell in any way I liked. So, after I had returned to school, I sat in the local library and wrote steadily down the list of Oxford and Cambridge colleges. Girton, Newnham and Lady Margaret Hall wrote back to Miss Blue encouragingly. But when I got accepted by Balliol I stopped because a master at school said it was the best. Whether it was the best for me, I doubted.

After I was accepted I did National Service for six weeks. In that time the chap I loved (he didn't know it) wrote to me that he was getting married. And a girl I was just beginning to enjoy sex with told me she'd found someone far better. She could hardly find worse so I didn't blame her. The double whammy led to raging headaches. I was referred to the eye doctor, who recommended me to the camp psychiatrist, who recommended my discharge. A homo had no place in the post-war new model army. I was lucky I wasn't incarcerated in Colchester military jail.

I was discharged, returned home, and informed Balliol I was now free. I didn't specify why and they didn't ask. I finally went up to Oxford a few months later in September 1950. I did well at first, then I fell into a nightmare and attempted suicide, had a religious experience and then a Freudian analysis. This was very humbling but I was no longer as fake as before and I did get a distinction and a special grant in my first year before the breakdown broke. I remember worrying obsessively that I wasn't entitled to wear a scholarship gown, just the ordinary commoner 'bum freezer'. This of course was insecurity. My state school thought I was wonderful getting into Oxbridge at all, for I was their first.

Oxford did not seem as strange as I thought it would be. Unexpectedly it reminded me of the East End of my childhood. From the railway station I contemplated the Oxford skyline punctuated by church spires, just as every small East End street had its formal synagogue or informal pious prayer room. Once again I was in a holy city – a curious Anglican one. It brought out my religious streak which Marxism had covered but not collapsed. What went on in those chapels, what curiosities? What could scholars, real scholars with degrees and titles, actually believe in them?

Did I have any homosexual experience before I went to Oxford? Yes, one. Before I went to Oxford an old middle-aged man picked me up outside a loo and did It with me behind a tree in a park. I wanted to talk to him but he then rushed away, frightened stiff that I could identify him. I wanted to talk to anyone who could enlarge my knowledge – whether they were dirty old men or *femmes fatales* was irrelevant. Sexually the episode was too basic to be of any use to me. But I did feel for him, poor sod. What a life, reduced as an oldie to a ghastly grubby teenager like me. The result of my first erotic experience wasn't passion but compassion. Religion again! That was the way the signs were pointing.

18

My Family Values

A necessary note on my family, a retrospective, because it explains a lot of what happened to me before Oxford and in Oxford and even after. Now people talk a lot about Family Values and even (God wot!) about Victorian Family Values. They bear the same relationship to the reality I knew as *Fiddler on the Roof* to the modern Jewish households of north-west London. Before I went up to Oxford I began to consider my family more charitably than before, because I was just about to distance myself from it and felt less threatened by it and all that sticky love.

Now at the religion classes my family sent me to after state school, doubt and dithering were not welcome. 'The Jew does this,' the teachers said firmly. 'The Jewish family keeps that.' 'We believe this . . .' And we were shown little diagrams of The Jewish Family at the Sabbath table. Mother dimpling at one end, Father patriarchal at the other, and the children odiously clever and clean in between.

I was a young unbelieving Jew and I wanted to meet The Jew and The Jewish Family but couldn't find them. I certainly never met them in my family circle who, though pious in patches like most Jews, doubted, dithered and compromised like mad. I decided the prophets and saints of my teachers only had a half-life like Shirley Temple, Tarzan or Mickey Mouse.

At home I asked my parents straight out whether the Red Sea did or didn't stand up like a wall at the Exodus. They were beside themselves with pride at my juvenile intellectualism and boasted about my cute questions to their friends. But they never answered them because they were as bewildered as me.

My mother never sorted out the religious business, though she lit Friday evening candles more often than not because her

mother had trained her to, and she fasted on the Day of Atonement – but in bed not in synagogue (she needed the rest). Years
later in 1953 I rang her from Oxford to tell I had decided to
become a rabbi. There was a pregnant silence at the other end
and I assumed she was so choked with pious emotion words
failed her. When they came, they had a steely quality. 'Lionel,'
she said, 'you're doing it to spite us. All our lives your father and
I have worked our fingers to the bone to get you out of the ghetto
and now you're at Oxford all you want to do is jump back into it
again. You're doing it to spite us.' With a click she slammed down
the receiver.

But she was a shrewd cookie and after she was assured I was
not going to grow a big black beard she got interested. She
suddenly asked me over a curry (non-kosher but non-pork) if all
this religion I was learning would make me nicer. It was an
honest question so I gave an honest answer. 'Religion can make
you very nice or very nasty,' I said cautiously. 'I think on the
whole it's going to make me nicer.' 'Hm . . .' she said thoughtfully
over her gin and tonic which was her curry tipple. (She liked her
kippers smeared with butter and jam just as I enjoyed and still
enjoy munching raw onions like apples.)

I understood her doubts because in the beginning it did make
me nasty. My grandfather had to smoke in the loo on the Sabbath
and my dad couldn't go secretly to his eel and pie shop, his token
revolt against the restrictions of his family, faith and matriarchy.
In contrast I became unnaturally pious. I became very nasty also
because he could no longer garden on the Sabbath so as not to
offend this newfound piety, though he needed the fresh air after
the steamy hell of factory life. But he was not articulate and I only
got to know and appreciate him too late.

When I was thirteen I fell physically in love with him and tried
to touch him all over in the narrow bed we shared in a crowded
boarding house in Bournemouth in 1943. He looked at me
compassionately, kissed me and turned over. I couldn't sleep for
shame. Unfortunately we couldn't talk about such things. Old-
style Jewish life was far too inhibited and this was in the forties –
pre-pill, and pre-homosexual because the very concept didn't
even exist for most people. I went through all the emotions of a
rejected lover. I knew it was unfair on him but that's how it was
with me, and he died in the 1960s before I understood my

71

relationship with him and my own feelings of rejection. There are fashions in sexual problems. Today the publicised sin is child abuse. An elderly experienced nun who once ran schools told me that in her day it was incest – mainly between fathers and daughters. Fathers and sons produced no babies so any horsing around between them wasn't worth bothering about.

Ma eventually told my father that I was homosexual when I left that awful solicitor's office in 1946. He never mentioned it or criticised me. He was just kind and helpful to the exotic company I sometimes brought home. He only said, 'Find someone decent, Lionel, that's all.' Thanks, Dad!

Theirs was in part an old-style arranged marriage. I suspected that in sexual matters he was a bit of bull in a china shop while she craved for cinema romance. Until he got a job again in the late thirties and was rescued from the humiliation of the dole, it seemed a mismatch. As a child, I sometimes wondered if a divorce might not be best for both of them and for me. But the old pieties were too strong.

All families are complex and when we simplify them by smooth talk about Family Values and Victorian Virtues, we unwittingly falsify them or, more likely, we want to deceive ourselves with a never-never land located conveniently in the past. I do it myself. Those current shorthand phrases like 'The Jew' or 'The Jewish Family' don't do the confused reality justice.

The values I got from my family as a child were the importance of love, however manipulative or misdirected (I don't think you can recognise love in later life unless you've experienced it as a child). We didn't put on the style, accepting the world as it is and not as we would like it to be, we knew how to make up after rows however bitter, and how to feel at one with people worse off than you. They're not the values those clever clean children in the picture were supposed to study, but I have no complaints.

I must add one note. 'Ah,' I can hear you say, 'all that broken family stuff must have made him gay. It stands to reason, a forceful mother, a defeated father – why look any further?' But life isn't that simple. I've met young men with much more complex broken backgrounds than me who are raging heteros or fine family men, American Midwest style. So such 'explanations' are too convenient and too easy. Religious people of course favour them. They would do, of course. There are many other factors that condition or determine a person's sexuality and gender. Clerics pronounce on such matters without doing their homework. After all, what was the family life of the Holy Family like? How homo or bi was David? Who satisfied St Joseph's love needs? Was lesbian love rampant among the many wives and concubines of early Hebrew religion? Is St Paul's dictum 'It is better to marry than to burn' good family guidance?

19

Bright Boy at Balliol

Oxford was the place where it all began to happen for me, where I tried to end my old life literally, where I began life again and the chains of causation were subtly falling in place which would eventually form a new future for me, one which I even now inhabit.

I arrived at Balliol with my possessions in cardboard boxes, looking wild and unwashed – a mess. But Balliol was unfortunately in a mess like me, though a superior one. I learnt that it was an intellectuals' college, open to Scots, Jews and Blacks (when they played the African war canoe scene from *Sanders of the River* in the local cinema, the audience shouted out, 'Well rowed, Balliol!'). This was fine by me. My emotions might be in a tangle and my sexuality muddled and my body unused and misused, but I still had a good mind. I was a bright Jewish boy.

But there were more ingredients in the post-war Balliol mix. There were still the class bits from before the war. There were bright Fulbright scholars. And older men whose education had been interrupted by the war and now came back to Balliol on government grants when they were demobbed, their years and experience well beyond that of the head boys and prefects from minor public schools.

The dons were equally disparate. The Master, Sir or Lord Somebody of Somewhere, didn't take to me and I didn't take to him. He was a conservative choice after a succession of stylish liberal Masters who had brought lustre to the College but hadn't balanced the books. We had to read essays to him. Mine was about how we, he and I and the world, would have to change if we took Christianity seriously. My Master was aghast!

Then there were the Marxist dons such as Christopher Hill,

whom I liked very much, and his followers. Many of them, including Christopher, left the Party I am pleased to say after the Hungarian Uprising of 1956. Many of the students, especially the public school lot, were enthused by them, and used to drawl out, 'Go home, Yankee!' during ceremonial visits by American bigshots. But what was exciting for them was not exciting for me. They were coming to Marxism, I was coming out of it. I respected Christopher Hill. He had actually read one mouldering volume after another of sixteenth- and seventeenth-century sermons. This is what made his work on the 'English Revolution' i.e. the Civil War, so solid. I was asked to become President of the Karl Marx Society but, though a Marxist still in many ways, I declined. I was moving in the other direction.

All around me at Balliol were reminders of another faith. I came on some by chance, some by searching. The Victorian chapel had one of the coldest atmospheres, though it was not the oldest in Oxford. It was on the road to spiritual nowhere. I wanted to ask the chaplain about it, but I kept away because I didn't want to overwhelm him, poor chap. He was a shy person with his own brand of introversion.

The other reminders of religious passion were less obvious than a chapel with a chaplain. There was the massive burnt door that got burnt, I was told, from the fire which burnt Latimer and Ridley at the stake when Mary Tudor's Catholicism was in the ascendant. Ridley was worried about his truss but then felt he would burn better and more painfully with it, so he welcomed it. What on earth were these Gentiles burning and being burnt for? Even now, I think it was all a terrible mistake, like the tragic rebellions of the Jews against Rome in the first and second centuries which resulted in the murder and enslavement of almost an entire people. That is how such heroism will always look to an outsider.

Outside the chapel was a short memorial to Balliol Germans, among whom was Adam von Trott, a devout Christian who after compromising with Hitler had then unsuccessfully tried to assassinate him. It was too late in the war to make much difference but at least the German officer corps acquired a saintly man and a martyr. He was a Lutheran and a friend of Dietrich Bonhoeffer, the theologian who was executed after the plot against Hitler in 1945 and who was a special martyr of the German resistance.

And in the library above the chapel I rummaged around and discovered an English history I had never even guessed at, though I had got an A and a Distinction in the official exams. There was Bede with his parables of what happened when Anglian warrior kings caught religion. And there were books about very curious and dicey mystics. I didn't know why nobody had ever told me about Julian of Norwich, Margery Kempe and the Cloud of Unknowing in school history lessons. Instead we got the misdeeds of the aristocratic mafia which, stripped of their Roses, provided unimaginative repetitive exercises in ambition and assassination – like a late medieval Chicago or Palestine and Israel today.

In Balliol there was one scholar who could have opened up this world to me. He had the scholarship, he had the faith. But it takes two to tango, as I've said, and I was retreating from the real world too fast to stand still and be taught. Still, I remembered Dick Southern, and later on when I had left Balliol I read his writings on the Middle Ages again, and again – and now they stand beside my copy of Helen Waddell's *Wandering Scholars*. I had found a new world which would redress the balance of the old, and help give me back my soul.

The Dean of Balliol made a deep impression on me. He was a bluff naval man, a military historian and a most unlikely friend. But unlike Lord Somebody and the dialectic-worshipping Marxists who were too busy standing Hegel on his head to bother about a mere individual like me, he was kind. He said he was going 'to pump ship' when going to the loo. I was quite pleased when he called to me across the quad asking me if I was becoming a clergyman. I nodded self-righteously, and was appalled when he artlessly bawled back, 'Which religion now?' Later on he kindly gave me permission to go to London each week for my sessions of psychoanalysis that I started in the second year.

In Balliol for one year, I had two enormous unheated rooms on the ground floor, in through which illegal late-night entrants tried to climb. I also had a 'scout', who had scouted for students of real class and distinction. He nevertheless doled out my meagre rations of coal and laid small fires, served me sherry on occasion and brought me buttered crumpets. High life! (I had a grant from the council or government, and the solicitor I'd been articled to supplemented this with a small allowance.) My set of rooms had two outer doors. When the very outer one was closed, I was supposed to be working and should not be interrupted. In fact a closed outer oak door meant sex, but sadly I never made much use of it.

I occasionally condescended to invite my parents up to Oxford to show off. They didn't visit together. I even put Ma up at the Randolph Hotel, no less. I told her grandly I could not accompany her one night as I had been invited to a very swish party. I arrived at the party late to make an entrance. 'Oh, Lionel,' the host whispered in my ear, 'you must come and meet a most extraordinary woman Jeremy picked up at the Randolph Bar.' I was then of course introduced to my mother. We looked at each other balefully but as she was in possession and I was becoming a gentleman, I retreated to a pub and then to a burning curry. In a Bengali restaurant I ostentatiously tried to read Jean Genet though the important forbidden words weren't in my dictionary so I didn't understand much and I nursed my wounded pride.

20

Balliol in Retrospect

Even though I'm seventy-four I still haven't fully thought through my Balliol years from 1950 to 1953. They're still a muddle in my mind. I still haven't worked out what really happened in them. What I do remember is despair and masturbation and breakdown. I also remember stepping into another dimension, a spiritual one, and falling in love with Love, and beginning to be honest about my body.

And yet I have lived on both the pluses and minuses of those three years ever since. I no longer believe that many of the problems I endured were of my own making, such as putting on the style or coping with the class system in decline, or academic sniggers about counselling, therapy and analysis, or the oppression and demonisation of sexual minorities.

Our moral tutors were supposed to deal with 'that sort of thing'. I can't remember who mine was, or whether I met him. Other 'services' which were supposed to be helpful didn't know in my case what help was. There was a university office to help me think about my future career. Now I wasn't exactly straightforward, I admit, being still in the throes of a breakdown, but the only opening they could suggest to me was the prison service. Was I meant to view the prison system from within or without?

There was a disappointment for me in Oxford. I expected the wrong things. I went up hoping it would help me sort out my ideological tangles. I watched, fascinated, as the Oxford intelligentsia twisted and turned like corkscrews trying to come to grips with the Lysenko affair! This is an almost forgotten scandal and sensation of those years. Not being a scientist I never understood exactly what it was about. On the surface it concerned plants, genetics, crops and their effect on agricultural production of which

I knew nothing. What was important to me was that world scientific opinion went one way and the Stalinist establishment another. My communist acquaintances looked worried and whispered together and had private meetings I couldn't crash into. There were defections and schismatics because communists thought of themselves as very scientific. It was a wonderful example of an orthodoxy that couldn't cope and got its knickers in a twist. I later saw the same thing happen among funda-mentalist Jews and Christians and Zionists.

Nevertheless, Oxford did help me in an elliptical way with my ideologies. In the modern Diaspora, Jewish nationalism is so entangled with religious Judaism that a great effort is required to distinguish between the highest common denominator of indi-vidual perception and the lowest common denominator of tribal feeling. They both seem to have their source in that 'power greater than ourselves' that alcoholics call to their aid to release them from their addiction. It is important to sort this matter out. Otherwise we can easily confuse the power generated at a Nuremberg rally or a march-past in Red Square with the attraction of spirituality and God and his goodness.

Zionism did not work for me because when I hitchhiked to Israel during a university vacation, I felt more in exile there than in Oxford or Amsterdam. There was no place for homo people like me in the collective ideal, in the kibbutzim, at that time. I did drop into kibbutzim certainly, both preparatory ones in England and a few in Israel where I had friends. I could see the advantages. Collective living could rescue me from the rat-race which I was unfitted for, and being neurotic I needed a set-up that could provide a structure to my life. But I didn't like country life whether in the English Home Counties or in the Middle East, and as the monotony of agricultural work bored me stiff I knew I could never endure it. I decided I preferred monasteries. But then I had only endured Sir Oswald Mosley and his fascists, not the real Holocaust! If I had, my views might be very different. Also, kibbutzim were probably wonderful place to bring up children – but that was not my problem.

I would have to sort out my ideologies myself, which I did – not at Balliol but in a Quaker meeting house which was only a stone's throw away from the college.

21

A Friend in Need, a Friend Indeed!

I found a lifelong friend at Oxford. We were put together to share two rooms by the powers that be, either by accident or because we were both Jewish. There our resemblance ended. In addition at Oxford I also acquired a deep love of England, its religion and its mysticism (before I went up I never realised it had any), a girlfriend who loved me and who taught me how to become a gentleman, an Oxford accent, which made me acceptable to the Anglo-Jewish upper class, a respect for genteel poverty and a deep suspicion of celebrity success.

My friend was very important because I met him on the day of my arrival and this slowed down my flight from reality into inner fantasy.

His name was Robin. He was 'class' and an Anglo-Jewish gentleman, which is why he put up with me despite my abstracted use of a pickled herring as a convenient bookmark in one of his beloved books, and nearly wrecking his new gramophone by playing all the long-playing records at 78rpm, pleased though startled by the brilliance of their sound. I had no feel for machinery and at that time little for music. He was the type of young man my mother used to drool over.

I confessed to Robin straightaway that I was beginning to get curious about Christianity, and I pinned a picture of the Virgin over our shared desk in the same experimental spirit with which I had eaten my first pork pie during my evacuation to see what would happen next. Robin, who had been to a Quaker school and knew something about Christianity, obligingly lent me his copy of Victor Gollancz's *Year of Grace*, and I began to wonder as I read through it if perhaps religion and spirituality weren't fairy stories but the heights of human achievement and a bit more. I was getting high on those heights myself, and gave a sigh of relief as I read that wonderful Gollancz anthology, and discovered one jewel of a life after another, who had all got illuminated and above themselves, and how this didn't make them ordinary fools, but fools for God, which were a special kind of fool. These were all very new thoughts for me.

Quite a few people were pleasantly amused by me, but Robin actually put up with me. Crazy people liked Robin because he was sensible and sympathetic and clean-limbed and pleasant-looking. He introduced these crazies to each other, but we didn't get on that well. He was the daddy we wanted and we were too competitive for his attention. Though I was one of the dirtiest and most demanding of his friends and followers, he later arranged a party for me where I met Leslie Shepard, my Reichian analyst. It was also through Robin that I hitchhiked to Israel with Colin Winter, the future Bishop of Damaraland in exile. But in our last year at Balliol, Robin slipped away from me and went to share digs with his more normal mates. He needed a break but this nearly broke me, because after years of alienation I had few connections with the real world. But thank God by then I already knew Leslie in London and had acquired some insight into my own condition, and also began to mix with the wise and witty remnants of the Weimar Republic that Leslie had introduced me to. They and the Quakers were my lifelines to reality.

Robin had had to put up with a lot from me, apart from my unkemptness and disorganised laundry and my clogged electric shaver which it had never occurred to me to clean. I assumed that electric things cleaned themselves. He also had to put up with my new patronising 'nose in the air' piety, which really got under his skin. No decent chap, he remarked very reasonably, could live with that. Looking back, I must have felt singularly insecure to pull spiritual rank in that way.

He also had to put up with my lying accounts of my love life (with girls). But one midnight we both confessed our real inclinations to each other over cocoa and sherry. Unfortunately, by that time we knew each other so well we could only be friends, not lovers. Nobody wanted my soul or my body and I felt aggrieved. I could never do right.

We bonded without sex. We're no writers of letters, but

whenever we meet we just catch up. He educated the Jewish youngsters in Aden and helped organise the Exodus of the Jewish community from Yemen and Ethiopia. He's gone from conference to conference and never lost his Jewish humanity nor his English rectitude and politeness. He's one of the great English-trained Jewish international civil servants.

He doesn't think much of all of this because he still wants to be a writer. But he worries about his writing too much to succeed. He's destroyed by his own perfectionism. He expects the muse to sail through the window and touch his work with a magic wand. He is probably not egotistic or nasty enough to be a writer. There isn't enough aggression to express, sublimate or cover-up. He also hasn't got the ego most writers require, or enough pressure to pay the bills.

He was the biggest plus for me from Balliol. And my mother used to drool over him. She said exasperatedly that she could teach us both sex. Did she mean it? Don't ask!

But he's become a good, honest, incorruptible and efficient administrator and more people owe their lives to him than he realises. I see this so clearly. He doesn't.

I tried to repay Robin for his kindness to me. I tried to find him a partner. Some years later I arranged a blind date with him with one of my closest Amsterdam friends, deciding they should spend a day in the Dutch countryside together. They both sat stony-faced in the car as it departed, as far away from each other as is possible without falling out and left exchanging no word, just a look of such distaste that I shivered, and had a Dutch brandy in a cafe as soon as I'd got them off. I heard later that they hardly said a word to each other all day.

Robin then decided to forage for himself. One of his friends was so attractive and high-minded that he was beyond my ken. But Robin assured me they weren't so high-minded when and where it really mattered, which relieved me.

And then a friend – André, a single-minded respected artist – found Robin, and they're good for each other. Robin and André have both been ill and this has made them both cared for and carers. We're all getting old together and ageing is educational. André brought Robin fine art and fine cookery.

Good friends are the treasures of life and Robin is the only one that remains from my Oxford years. He was also important because he was a gentleman and the first person I knew who taught me to be one.

And it was Janny, who I met a few months after I met Robin and who was my girlfriend and a true lady, who continued my lessons.

22

The Biggest Might-Have-Been
of Our Lives?

The biggest might-have-been in my life was Janny. Robin had shown me what a gentleman should be. Under Janny's influence I started to become one. We came back together at the end of her life but there was not enough time and it was too late.

This is how I met her. Another chap on my staircase was forming a party for the Balliol ball and asked me if I would squire his fiancée's best friend. I felt flattered and agreed, though I only had black boots to wear with my 'black tie'.

My 'blind date' partner disconcerted me, she was so much a lady, but I was not gentleman enough to match it. I had never met anyone with such courtesy, integrity and goodness – these were unfashionable words even then. There was no need to play-act on my part, which was a relief, because she was in love with a young man who was going to marry someone else. I don't think she ever told him the depth of her love, but hesitantly she told me – to quieten me, I think.

I told her my own problems which she listened to pleasantly and interestedly. I had found in her another friend and prattled on freely, enjoying the cups of quality tea poured from a real silver teapot in her college room. I later learnt she was bewildered, shocked and horrified by my confessions, which must have surpassed St Augustine's, but she never showed it.

She also never showed me or complained of the bruises on her shins while I hopped and kicked dancing the Charleston with her in my black boots. I had proudly bought my first shop-soiled, reduced-price evening suit but I couldn't run to evening shoes which seemed to me unnecessary. She also taught me to be a 'gentleman' just as Ethel taught Mr Salteena in *The Young Visiters,* another book to which she introduced me.

The most memorable lesson took place at another ball. It was the time of strapless evening gowns. During a fast Scottish dance, a young lady twirled but her strapless dress didn't. Quickly throwing a scarf over her shoulders, her partner led her quietly off the dance floor and out of the room. Nobody looked or remarked on the incident except me.

'I'm so sorry for that poor girl,' I said unctuously.

'I don't know what you mean,' Janny answered.

'You must have seen what happened,' I said, puzzled.

'A lady only sees what she's supposed to see,' she replied tartly, 'and being a gentleman, I suggest you do the same.'

I was puzzled. She had never spoken in that tone of voice to me before. The gentleman business was the most valuable lesson I learnt at Oxford besides religion.

We gradually became close friends and something more, though what it was I was never sure. To go beyond 'close', took one (it was always 'one') into sex, and homosex, and religion and class – none of which were easy to talk about in England at that time.

We both left Oxford with lots unsaid. I hesitantly suggested to Janny we make a stab at pre-sex, but my proposal was not inviting and I was too sensitive to rejection in that area to press my suit. I didn't know if I wanted to or was even capable.

We lost and renewed contact a number of times in the after-Oxford years. We occasionally talked about marriage but so unrealistically I wasn't sure if we were discussing a hypothesis, an escape, a fantasy, but I knew it wasn't sexual reality. But at the same time I also knew Janny was beginning to love me – and she had a tremendous capacity to love, and I was coming to think she was one of the most wonderful people I had ever met. We were out of step, though, because I had just had a first taste of real homo sex (something more than a nervous encounter in a park) with a handsome chap a little older than me who did not love me but loved someone else.

Oh what a tangle! A loves B and B loves C and C loves A. It became a constant pattern in life.

One day Janny came to me and said she was marrying someone else. I was puzzled, I was at a loss, she cried and left. I left too, confused but relieved, because I was just about to go to Amsterdam. She would be happier with anyone other than with me, I thought. But this was cowardly wish-fulfilment. She wasn't. I think she loved me so purely, I panicked. I put her on such a high pedestal it made workaday (or night) love impossible.

One evening several years later I returned to the little house I shared with my first partner, JB, which without love no longer felt like home. It was my birthday, a date unrecognised by my partner-no partner. I rang Janny to ask her and her husband for a drink. I got a strangely cautious reply.

Later on, Janny told me she was getting her marriage annulled. It was no marriage. We started meeting again after the annulment came through. We could talk more easily and our words could even match some of our talk.

I would soon be as free too because I was leaving JB, who had met her and disliked her. But instead I met Kim, my second partner, and went off with him not Janny – why, I didn't know. And I don't know now either.

Whether we would have made a success of marriage I also don't know. Would it have been a prison to me? How much hurt would she have suffered? How did other couples fare in situations like ours? They certainly weren't visible at that time. Was it right for her to become Jewish? (She was the most Christian person I have ever known.) She was sensitive – would the prejudice against converts in Judaism worry her? Would my first partner, JB, have bashed me to bits? Again, I do not know. I only know that we were very close to each other and I passed it up partly because I was a coward, partly because I was cautious. I was still struggling out of my 'slough of despond' and didn't know if I could carry her problems as well as my own.

Later on we resumed contact and got to know each other once more in the years she became ill. I persuaded her to write a book. It is called *A Book of English Belief* and it is a kind of testament.

Janny continues to live in me since she died, as people you have loved do if you give them room in your mind and heart. Her voice says to me, giggling, 'Lionel, you can't do that' or seriously, 'Lionel, you mustn't do that – it's not fair!' or we just hold each other in our imagination arms.

What a fool I was – I think!

23

Curiouser and Curiouser

Curiosity had drawn me to Christianity at Oxford in the first place. But this Oxford Christianity was really new to me. The only new thing there. History had been a disappointment – a few more facts, another list of dates, only English history allowed at the time I had discovered Europe. It didn't take me long to suss out that Oxford was a holy city as stuffed with religion and piety and narrowness as the East End of my childhood. It was an Anglican holy city just as Stepney in London was a medieval Jewish one. I could read the signs. I felt quite rightly that unless I could come to grips with the Christianity of English history, I would only be able to analyse it from the outside and reduce the living story to a few more facts and another list of dates.

Next to Balliol was an Anglican church which boasted to all confused tourists that it was not a Protestant church but a Catholic one. I was puzzled but sat in it sometimes, testing it out, not sure if it was the kitsch or the Catholicism of the interior, coloured like boiled sweets, which took me out of myself and made me feel as if I'd touched heaven.

I didn't analyse these feelings. If the magic worked, I was with it. It was a pretty desperate time for me and beggars can't be choosers. I was on dangerous ground because in religion truth and factual honesty aren't the same.

I had reservations from the beginning. After all, Christianity had preceded Hitler with ghettos, Jewish badges and demonisation (demonisation of homosexuals too). Also, I didn't understand how serious people, even scientists, could believe this pantomime stuff about virgins giving birth to babes, wise men pursuing stars, disappearing bodies, miracles two a penny and a cast of angels, devils, burning hells and some awful whoppers.

Crikey, what a mix! After closely argued Marxism and relatively sober Judaism, people could get high on this stuff. It was like alcohol or opium. It could give such wonderful quick fixes to shaky neurotics like me – but would they last?

I tried to explain this fascination to a Marxist Zionist who come up to Oxford from London especially to lead me back to sense. I didn't know how to explain all this muddled mythology to him and he left. Keeping his temper, which was good of him. Though I could see his truth, he couldn't see mine.

From being curious about Christian places, I then became curious about Christian lives. Though I was neurotic, I was still pragmatic and the proof of the pudding was in the eating. If needs be I was prepared to swallow an angel or two – though not a disappearing body or pregnant virgin. These were too much.

So I started to get to know Christians. I was surprised by the warmth of their welcome, because I was so bad at relationships. I was invited to cocoa parties, where I was Exhibit No. 1, to intimate study groups, soul-searching over Marmite sandwiches, to silent meditations and to some very sincere friendship and goodness. Some of the last I discounted – the conversion of a clever Jew could earn you top marks in the numbers game and most were so interested in my soul, they couldn't be bothered about my agonised, frustrated body. But I had to admit the generosity of spirit among them and an openness I hadn't experienced since the death of my grannies. When you meet real goodness, you don't forget it.

Judaism like Christianity is also a generous and warm religion in patches. But because of its history it has turned in on itself and, although polite and pleasant and long-suffering, is hesitant about strangers. After all, you do not need to be Jewish to be 'saved', whatever that may mean in Judaism – or Christianity for that matter. Anyway I found the Christian universalism and outreach refreshing (like Marxism after Zionism). Whatever their motives, the saints were marching in and I was welcomed into their company. What I did get out of Christian churches was the quietness in which I could listen.

My curiosity had another motive. My studies of history drew me to a study of English Christianity. Marxism had given me the key to European history and the capitalism of the late nineteenth and early twentieth centuries, but it had not given me such a key to the Middle Ages or the birth of the new Christian Europe. I examined those Dark Ages curiously, and they were not as dark as I had supposed. The darkness was studded with a milky way of saints. The glow of the Jewish mystical Chassidic rabbis shone out of Bede's stories of Celtic saints converting tough Angle and Saxon kings to holiness. I had not expected such a wonderful kickstart to the history of this country. I was drawn to be one of their wayward company.

I frolicked around the edge of this most peculiar religion. It was dotty but so was I. I wondered if I could become, after my forthcoming breakdown, an ornamental hermit. Perhaps I could become a real one in an awesome cave, high up on a cliff.

All this asceticism was a turn-on and new to me. So was the magical liturgy when things turned into what they weren't. I didn't take that one seriously. I did feel sorry for Jesus. He reminded me of me.

I enjoyed Christianity, preferring a son to a parent God. I had no wish to project my family problems on to the cosmos. Also a god who suffered with me made more sense than one I only read about and discussed on committees. I occasionally talked to Jesus in Christianity mode and I didn't get anywhere. At the beginning it was all one way, though the silence wasn't empty but drew me into it.

I know I was using Christianity to evade and avoid both my sexual problems and my work problems. I tried to work in every library but all I could do was masturbate furtively in them. I was brought low.

And so it remained until something happened one November Thursday morning in 1951 when Christianity came alive and a voice spoke to me and turned me inside-out.

24

Meeting

There were two events at that time which turned me round –
away from a living death in a psychiatric ward with ECT or a
lobotomy, or a real death in a badly judged half-hearted suicide
attempt – and the Quaker meeting was the first.

This is how I fell into the Quaker meeting. I was trying to make
mad passionate love at Lady Margaret Hall with Janny but it was
hopeless. She had a dripping cold and could only sniff while I
pretended passion. I didn't think I could go on pretending much
longer, though I liked her a lot. I was even beginning to love her
though I wasn't sure what that meant outside literature. She was
a lovely person but I couldn't simulate erotic desire. I would have
preferred to talk about it over a cup of tea and a biscuit, not to do
it.

I came away feeling grey inside and the weather was grey
outside. On the way home the rain came down in buckets and I
sheltered in a doorway. The door opened – a lady (Miss Joachim,
I learnt later) opened the door and beckoned me in to a quiet
Quaker meeting for farmers, who testified soberly and con-
vincingly. And then I stepped in and helplessly testified Jewish
style from the depths of my tormented being. They didn't sit up,
and I didn't care if they did or didn't because I was beyond
exhibitionism. I was in a Dostoevskian nightmare, known to many
in a severe depression. I asked a deity in whom I didn't believe to
make some sense of my misery.

The Quaker farmers must have thought this great stuff, because
I received an approving accolade at the end and Miss Joachim
asked me to tea.

But what was more important, the deity, in whom I didn't
believe and I couldn't name, granted my prayer and a message

did get through to me from outside me or perhaps it welled up from deep inside me. The first explanation felt more right. The message was muddling yet clear. I should turn my miseries upside-down, invert them and then look at them in another light, a heavenly light.

I started doing that during my explosive testimony and continued to do so silently. I surprised myself by thanking that God I didn't believe in for all my problems! Without them I would be a self-satisfied prig or a sharp suburban solicitor. With them I could learn mercy and self-honesty and what it was like to be at the other end of the stick. There was no other way I could ever come to such wisdom. My problems might be in fact a grace of God if he existed and not his punishment. This made me feel very chosen and very important. One of the nice things about Christianity was that it made much of an individual and not just another member of a collective. It was a private one-to-one relationship between me and Whomsoever Whatsoever – let's call him WW or Fred or Smokey the holy ghost.

A shift took place inside of me. I recovered the pleasure of giving. After the service was over I started giving away things, mostly my own things but some of Robin's too. The 'Jesus thing' had got to me, I decided, and had turned me inside-out, and topsy-turvy. What I was experiencing was a rebirth of my soul, which I had lost or dismissed in London's East End at the age of five. I was no longer a mere mind – I could now proceed from a feeling centre. It is true it was a bit atrophied but new life was pumping into it. Robin approved when I told him about it though he was rightly apprehensive about my wild dispersal of my possessions and his too, to whoever asked, and I surprised fellow students who didn't approve because it wasn't just topsy-turvy, it was also over the top.

But I left that meeting light and soufflé-ish giving away even my precious velvet tie to a surprised acquaintance, not knowing what had hit me.

This revealed itself not in a church but a cake shop. I was queuing up for my slice of Fuller's Walnut Cake, idly listening to the background music. The words of the song actually went 'Falling in love with love is only make believe' but I heard it as 'Falling in love with Love *isn't* just make believe' – which is quite the opposite. I had fallen in love with Love and it was reprogramming me. If you think that this is Christianity, well, I was in, but if you think Christianity is attachment to creeds and surplices and scriptures and institutions, then I wasn't – I remained an outsider.

But what I did get was that I could fall in love with Love as I've said and that love could have a human face, and the kernel of it all was generosity.

Something else did happen at the Quaker meeting. I started to speak to an imaginary figure, which was no big deal as I'd been inhabiting a fantasy world for years, both mystical and masturbatory. But there was a difference. In this new fantasy world the Jesus (or WW or Fred) figure spoke back, but his answers and concerns weren't the ones I expected.

He popped up at the Quaker meeting but at first I didn't take him seriously. Droopy chestnut-haired men with constipated looks are not my line at any level. In my imagination he didn't stay that way for very long. But however he looked and whatever he was, he became the human face of my religious life. He was the Virgil or the Beatrice to my Dante. He showed me heaven, and heaven was here within me (and in you too) and always had been.

25

The Bishop of Damaraland (in Exile) Passes the Toothbrush Test

Oxford was a small gossipy ghetto and it quickly got around that a clever Jewboy Marxist from Balliol (where else?) was having live visions in dead C of E churches. That's how it got to Colin Winter and an amused acquaintance of Robin's arranged a meeting, for Colin was not only C of E but the highest of high Anglo-Catholics. ('So high you could scrape him off the ceiling, dears,' commented a camp Catholic.) Colin and I had more in common than we expected because to earn his way through Oxford, he successfully flogged nylons during the vacation in the East London markets, where he met my grandpa's boon companions. Colin was a genial chap who could sell anything, nylons as well as religion, indeed anything except the Thirty Nine Articles.

He received his call at Loughborough where he had trained to be a PT teacher, so he didn't make fun of mine which was a relief. From his gym work he had a well-honed body and oodles of charm especially with young women who only wanted his nylons and nobody else's. He was consistently chaste, though eventually he decided 'to marry rather than burn' which was wise of him because his sensuous lips were an indicator of seething passions near to exploding like mine.

He became my guide into the Christian mysteries. I said the Offices with him, whose regularity I appreciated because of my own life's lack of structure. He taught me the mechanics of 'Anglo-Cat' prayer and I enjoyed the click of rosary beads, the bendings, bowings, bow-wowings, scrapings, crossings and genuflections that came with them. (When Colin was away I never bothered with them much.) I learned from him the great truth that a friendship with a see-through being required the same sacrifices as a friendship with an opaque one, i.e. attention and time. So I got into the habit of dropping into empty churches and chapels of which there are many in Oxford. At first I just regurgitated routine niceties to my see-through visitant but then realised it takes two to tango, so I relaxed and let him do the work – I just thought my Friend present to me and he was and left the rest to him. We imaginatively held hands and I felt at home in his company. Sometimes he led me into another dimension whose logic was not just imagination but hard uncommon sense.

Now Colin believed the lot, and I tried to believe like him because I was attracted by his belief. He taught me why Mary had to be a virgin before, during and after, why the Archbishop of Canterbury was a proper Patriarch and that the Church of South India needed my prayers. Poor Church of South India! Occasionally he laughed at his own enthusiasm as I egged him on to even more mysteries. I was getting high on them. I tried to believe them all. I shut my eyes, swallowed hard and then retched most of them up. I was sorry about this because these rites or myths helped me see the world in a fascinating way, and this different vision has changed me not just for an Oxford term or a year but for keeps.

Even though I couldn't believe like Colin did, his belief gave me a lot. The icons, the incense smells, the jazzy colours and the click of beads might seem kitsch to the outsider, but a spiritual experience need not be an aesthetic one. Good taste can get in the way of good religion. I still appreciate such religious paintings as 'The Presence' in Edinburgh's Episcopal cathedral and 'The Prayer' by Gerard Dou, a lesser follower of Rembrandt, aesthetically not the tops but experientially helpful. Michelangelo's ceiling, on the other hand, left me cold. It was as secular as Lyons Corner House and in the same style.

I of course had my problems, not all of which I could tell Colin at first because I was too inhibited. After my experience among the Quakers, I thought I had found the way, the truth and the life and all I needed were more doses of prayer-induced courage to leapfrog over this world and jump into the next. But it didn't work like that – I wondered indeed if anything had changed in me at all. Though I now meditated in churches and prayed myself into ecstasy, I still masturbated in loos on the way to those churches. I still couldn't produce an essay on time or ever. I still couldn't dress myself properly or shave or wash. If I let myself think, I wasn't sure what I made of all this religious business – it was too bizarre. I knew I wasn't being completely honest and felt a traitor to Judaism, Marxism and the Enlightenment. 'What is truth?' said Pontius Pilate. I knew just how he felt. In my heart of hearts and my intelligence centre I still knew I was heading for a breakdown or a feeble suicide attempt – run-of-the-mill religious experiences and tuppenny-coloured conversations with my Visitant notwithstanding.

In desperation my parents gave me some money to hitch to Israel to cleanse me of Christianity. I agreed, provided Colin came too. As with many holiday companions, we never had a quarrel but somehow separated en route. It was impossible to quarrel with Colin, he was so Christian and forgiving. He was the only Christian or non-Christian I knew who automatically shared his toothbrush with me when I lost mine. It never occurred to him to do otherwise. Not many religious or non-religious pass the toothbrush test!

I resented that he closed his mind to Marxism and all the ideologies which were still fighting a rearguard action in my own mind. (This was indeed a joke, considering what happened later.) He was so sure of his localised Anglo-Catholicism that I became exasperated. I must have annoyed him too because I couldn't settle on anything whether it was saying my beads or bloody revolution.

This was a typical incident on our jolting journey through France. On a country bus Colin noted with approval a country priest fervently reading his missal. 'Now that's real religious attention,' said Colin to me smugly and I felt abashed. But then the priest turned over his missal and it wasn't a missal at all but a crime story tucked away in missal covers. I didn't crow, just looked superior. If Colin had allowed himself to swear he would have done so. Instead he turned towards me with a look of such radiant forgiveness I wanted to hit him.

We separated as we got to Israel itself. The last part of our journey was accomplished by Moroccan immigrant boat. We were technically in the same steerage class as the ululating Jews who were like no Jews I had ever met. But being European, we were accorded honorary first-class status on board which delighted me but made more Christian Colin uneasy.

When we docked at Haifa, I sauntered down the posh gangway and was handed fresh orange juice and polite greetings. At first I couldn't see Colin but then noticed him coming down the Moroccan gangway battered by bags and parcels and pushed aside by excited ecstatic women. He was at last among the poor whom his religion said he must love. Just before he landed, a nozzle was off-handedly put down his neck and like Moses he disappeared in a cloud (of DDT). After this disappearance from my sight I never saw him much again either in Israel or in Oxford when we returned home. Marxism he could abide, psychoanalysis he thought more dangerous. Holidays, which are meant to draw you closer together, so often reveal the distance that separates you. This is what happened with me and Colin.

I didn't see or hear from him again for many years, but out of the blue many years later I received a letter from him asking me to see him. A wave of gratitude and fondness for him engulfed me and I dashed down to the country where he was recovering from a heart attack brought on by overwork for his people oppressed by apartheid. I had of course heard about him and his mass meetings in support of the ANC. I had seen the mass he celebrated outside South Africa House on TV and the congregation which filled Trafalgar Square. He was the Bishop of Damaraland (in Exile) and I was honoured to know him.

When we met he got straight to the point without sentimental reminiscences. He had work to do. He had just arrived back from the German Democratic Republic and wanted me to help with some liberation theology broadcasts, Marxist style, which could help his cause. I told him my views of the post-Stalinist set-up in the East and the gulags, prison and torture which were anything but liberation. I told him I would help him but it would have to be in my own way and on my own terms which were not Stalinist. Politically we had exchanged roles.

He changed the subject and gave me his blessing and the standard broad Christian smile which meant we had little common ground. We were fighting different battles though under the same slogan, 'Let my people go!' We couldn't help each other. So we had a polite cup of tea. He had a nice wife and children. We didn't speak about ourselves or Oxford. On my way back I brooded over all Colin had given me – how his toothbrush had pointed me to the core of Christianity and he had later on introduced me to my first monastery experience. Now I knew that monasteries with all their faults pointed in the right direction and would remain part of my life. I would always be in his debt. Later on, I heard from an Anglican priest that he had died of a heart attack not long after our meeting. He was a good guy who followed his Christ.

26

Conversations with Colin

After Colin died, I continued to think about the conversations we had had together when we first met. They weren't exactly conversations because I, being very Jewish, did most of the talking and Colin most of the listening.

We hadn't wasted time on Oxford teatime pleasantries. I plunged straightaway into the problems left by the fall-out from that Quaker meeting and he was the first person who listened and took me seriously. This was my first cause of gratitude to him.

I told him that I had begun to discern a glimmer of light from religion. The Quaker experience had suggested that there might be something on the other side of problems and failure, that some strange light might be shining secretly in my mental darkness, though I didn't know how or what. Colin said that lights shining in darkness were a religious speciality – look at the gospels, look at St John of the Cross, look at The Cloud of Unknowing. My own light had certainly had an effect on me but it was a muddled one, I told him, and needed thinking through. Whereas before my experience I had been unbearably nasty, now I was unbearably nice. Robin, my sensible and sensitive room-mate, couldn't stand my newly acquired hypocrisy and self-righteousness.

What stopped me giving up was the Inner Voice that had spoken to me, within me, at the Meeting. He, She, It, wasn't just escapist fluff. Who he was or what he was I didn't know. I also didn't know whether I should think of him in psychological terms or theological or mystical ones. Colin knew or thought he knew but was tactfully silent.

On some important matters the Voice was wondrous vague, on some small ones he got het up and quite specific. I asked him for example if he was Christ and whether I should become a

98

Christian. On that he was wondrous vague. What labels and categories I used were my business, he seemed to say. He wasn't going to get involved. No comment from Colin. But one comment Colin made was helpful. If I kept on praying, my voice would reveal its hand and so it did. It never told me the secrets of the Universe, just what I should do next. It also gave me some extra strength to do it. That was quite enough.

It got quite excited about whether I should show a little more understanding to Dad and Ma, though it pointed out that small family problems were more difficult than cosmic ones. My Voice just shrugged its shoulders so to speak about my worries concerning self-honesty. That, he suggested, would sort itself out by itself. (Which it did.) I couldn't tackle everything at once. He even suggested I should enjoy a bit of mythology, whether of my own private sort or the established public sort. I'd given myself a hard time and some opium of the masses was deserved. This shocked me. My voice also wanted to see a lot of me. I amused him. So I got into the habit of sitting beside him in empty chapels – there we held hands as it were and enjoyed each other's company as it were. He liked me as I was, just like my granny and perhaps my father, though I never knew if my father understood me. He was a man who couldn't express his feelings to me.

Colin was bit stumped by all this so he sent me to a monastery up north. He thought quite rightly that a bit of spiritual stability and genuine modesty would do me good. I shall always be in Colin's debt for the introduction to contemplative monasteries. The life in them has drawn me ever since. Practically speaking, I always work better in a structured environment which is why I like hospital life, and the ministry and therefore monasteries and why my present worldly partner is the tidiest person I ever met. I was very happy regulated by bells and the pre-Vatican II regime suited me fine.

The great plus of monastic life for me was that it was looking away from the Vanity Fair of academic life towards the Celestial City, to the 'Beyond Life' that was revealing itself to me every day, to the 'country far beyond the stars' of the poet Henry Vaughan, to my true home. In its light I saw this world undistorted by the rat-race or the success cult. Because of this I could cope with its pettinesses and peculiarities. (Though, as I have said, for short visits only.) If only I wasn't such a sensual youngster I could have been quite content in a monastery but that isn't the way I was made. For the sake of integrity I couldn't leave my member out. It was also part of my truth and life. What was the use of a monastery without the truth? Colin rolled around with laughter but refused to carry on with this conversation. Later on I met a monk who was very practical. Only enter a monastery, he told me, if you can sublimate a lot, have a low sex drive and/or an accepting disposition. It would obviously be as unsuitable for me as a kibbutz. Bang went another illusion.

But whatever its problems, I still go on retreat to monasteries over half a century on, and I don't forget that it was Colin who launched me into them.

I would like to discuss my doubts yet again with Colin. Our conversations were more valuable than I realised at the time. They helped to cure me at least of religious romanticism. I just wanted to enjoy religion. I didn't want to examine it. But the honest part of me knew that a religion which costs you nothing, gives you nothing. Very reluctantly, after I gave up and broke down, I tried to put my mind and soul together but Colin couldn't help me because without a row or a cross remark we had somehow parted company.

I began to formulate the truths of my religious experience. This took me many years and I was only a reluctant student, but this is when I started out on what seemed a stony road. A bit of me was prepared to go forward, and the rest of me, which would have to catch up – in a year or a lifetime or more than that – I didn't know. I did know I didn't want my newfound spiritual awareness to lead me into Cloud-cuckoo-land.

During all my spiritual contortions my friends (because to my great surprise I had made far more than I realised) worried about me and in the vacation, to cheer me up, they took me along to a neat dingy council flat in London's King's Cross for a party. The host, whom I did not know, was a friend of Robin's and also a friend of a strange non-Jewish lady, who infiltrated neo-Nazi and Fascist headquarters in order to feed back information to counter-racist squads. I met her and tried to ingratiate myself with her, but it was so obvious she didn't like me I gave up. I couldn't blame her either, because I didn't like myself – I loathed me. I felt deformed. This didn't stop me feeling hurt because she slept around with everybody except me. Though she has been dead for many years, this rankled for a long time. Male vanity!

The party for me was not a party, just a non-celebration of my decision not to return to Oxford. All the striving, the sacrifices of my mother, the hopes of my father and Ma's boss would go up in smoke. Another bright Jewish boy had peaked too early. Only my oddity would be left. I wondered if they would come around and collect me and put me in an asylum. In my despair I called unto the Lord, Jesus too and Whomever Whatever I had bumped into during the Quaker silence. They started up the action!

27

Leslie

I think of Leslie Shepard as the most important person in my life. I met him at that party during the Oxford vacation in 1951, thrown by friends in his King's Cross council flat. They were good friends who had thrown the party partly to cheer me up for I was a weight on their spirits and a drag. But I wasn't sure of returning to Oxford again for the next term or ever. I only felt my isolation more keenly as I heard their laughter in another room, while I listened alone to Bessie Smith on the gramophone, wailing her 'Down and Out Blues', and I accompanied her, adding my wailing Yiddish depression to her black sadness.

It was then that a shadow materialised from a corner and a slender mousy man materialised out of it. He told me pleasantly but brusquely to come and see him next morning at ten. He was my host, the tenant of the council flat I was in, my analyst-to-be and my saviour, the mysterious Leslie. He was also the most significant person in my life in that he turned my life around from destruction to reconstruction. Despite my experience at the Quaker meeting I was still on a psychological knife-edge and without him could easily have called this life a day and headed again towards death.

Leslie was a psychoanalyst, a Reichian and a radical Freudian, mainly self-taught, though later on I learnt that he had been a pupil of Derek Eastman, the early follower of Reich. We wasted no time. I lay on a couch and to my astonishment and annoyance he proceeded to massage the muscles in my body instead of listening to the neurotic patter I had carefully stored up for him – mainly accusations against my poor parents (already told ad nauseam).

That could come later, he said firmly, but first the muscular tensions. They were basic and, unlike words, at which I was adept, they didn't lie or play games. I was scandalised that he discarded my well-honed mind and my burgeoning soul in favour of my slob body.

His touch was light but the tensions increased though I couldn't work out why and I burst into tears. From then on I couldn't say words, only utter baby sounds. I had reverted to a time before speech. His massage continued and the great ball of pain like a cancer in me began to shift in me and then move out of me, like a monstrous painful birth. I lost myself in early nightmares and mishaps. I had pre-birth experiences too. My muscular tensions were a map of my unconscious.

After the pain slid out of me and the muscular tensions of my body began to ease, I was allowed to talk and he listened. This was another new experience. Nobody had ever listened to me like that before. He didn't offer solutions. He just wanted to know what the world was like to me. I didn't have to compose my story or calculate it to fit in with any theology or ideology. I didn't have to buy approval by compliance. Truth was coming out with all the muck of repression and the truth made me free, as the gospels said.

Eventually I stopped, exhausted. I felt ravenous just as I do after prayer and meditation. In his kitchen he gave me a steaming mug of tea. I was too shaken to talk. After the tea I went back to the couch again, though our session had already lasted five hours, but it started up again as before.

Once again an explosion of memories, baby sounds and pain rose to the surface and three hours later I went very silent. I was really exhausted now. My voice had gone quiet and I was quiet, the first time in my memory.

My first session had ended. I felt like Bunyan's Pilgrim when he is released from the back-breaking rucksack of woes and sins as it falls away from him and he takes his first unburdened steps.

At King's Cross station I puzzled over my body, my poor rejected body, with its piss and semen and smells. I had thought of it as a dirty smelly body shaped like a monster's. Before a mirror Leslie had patiently begun to convince me that I had a perfectly normal body with two arms, two legs and the usual bits. It was even a nice body, he said. But I was not ready to take this on board – yet. It took decades before I really had any confidence in it.

This was my first step towards becoming a whole person. For a while I shot through traumatic hoops, the prize analysand, and was released. I was already of course a mind and something had woken my soul. Now for the first time since the evacuation years I began to take pity on my body. How it had suffered, poor sod, from ideology and spirituality and religion and mental games! I had never recognised the honesty of its reactions. It had never occurred to me that it could do even better than my mind or soul.

This recovery of my body made me real – honest, even. During the year that followed I came down every week from Oxford for another all-night or all-day session. Those sessions were my lifeline to rebirth and sanity.

Two others started analysis with Leslie at the same time as me. Both broke it off in mid-course. One committed suicide and the other was left in a negative transference (his words) which was a brake on him for years afterwards. I was the only one who continued to the end, not because I was courageous but because I was desperate. Freedom was worth the pain of memory. I was a prisoner in *Fidelio* struggling to the light. I had to reach it – there was just no other way.

I asked Leslie about my religion! He was short about it and wouldn't be drawn further. Would my religion survive such an analysis? Insofar as it was neurotic, it wouldn't. Insofar as it wasn't, it would. End of question! I asked him about Jung. It takes longer to get to the point than Freudian analysis but you get a more interesting ride.

I asked Leslie about my homosexuality! He thought I was bisexual, which was probably true. Homosexuality, he said, was a more difficult fit physically, socially and psychologically but both homo and hetero forms could achieve the same results. There was no 'ought' about them and they didn't remain constant through life. Sex was also not the purpose of our life on earth and both porn and Christianity had blown the subject out of all common sense.

A lot of neuroses he considered as the problem of the surrounding society, not those of the analysand. A woman had come to Reich with a problem, he told me – her lesbian longings. 'So what is the problem?' asked Reich. 'My lesbian longings,' said the bewildered woman. 'So what is the problem?' Reich asked again. The woman looked bewildered. 'Here's the phone number of a lesbian acquaintance,' said Reich brusquely. 'Ring her up!' End of problem! This left Freud far behind, closed in his bourgeois shell.

Was Reich expected to adjust someone to a happy life in a psychopathic state like Nazi Germany! I began to get some self-respect as a homosexual, though it was still criminal in its expression. (This happened long before the Wolfenden Report, the Quaker document on sexuality and finally in 1968 the first step towards gay legal freedom in this country.) Perhaps the religious establishments should be undergoing analysis rather than those who are persecuted by them like me. (Just as the Holocaust was not a Jewish problem at all, but a Christian problem, and it was the anti-Judaism of Christianity that needed analysis.)

I was trying at this time to put together the truths I had encountered in psychoanalysis and the truths I had also encountered in religion. I think Leslie was trying to do the same, though I did not realise this at the time. I was too preoccupied with my problems to consider his problems. I did however realise that Leslie had a genuine sympathy with Judaism (though not with Christianity) and when I later became European Director of the World Union for Progressive Judaism, and the World Youth Director in 1962 (long title, limited resources, little money), I introduced him to our youth conference. What I wanted from him was the truth, the kind of truth that sets you free, the obvious truth – not the communal and nationalist kitsch that was being served up to young people, 'the kids', by the 'progressive' as well as the orthodox establishment.

This he gave. Young Jews led by him in a series of conferences examined the realities of the world they would live in and the forces that moved it such as ambition, money, the rat-race, sex, status and the media. As I had hoped, he stated the obvious and the obvious had as much effect on a group as it has had on me personally. Some 'chose' God and discovered vocations for the rabbinate, many put aside the rhetoric which always accompanies religion to examine the metaphysical basis of the fragile new Jewry in Europe that was emerging. Many of course could not cope with this injection of truth, and spiritual energy was converted into sexual energy as an escape. Many people got engaged at those conferences, often unsuitably.

I doubt if Leslie's contribution to the rebirth of European Jewry and the development of Reform Jewry will ever be acknowledged in the official reports of Progressive Judaism in post-war Europe. He will probably not even merit a footnote as a maverick eccentric figure whom Lionel brought along (if he is mentioned at all). Official accounts are always part cover-ups. But some of the most creative rabbis today will not, I think, have forgotten him and his spiritual plain speaking. I must also add that he never made a fast buck out of me, nor a slow one either because he never charged me a penny. It was all for free. I have never found his like since.

But I am going too far ahead and must return to the Oxford years. My analysis ended in abrupt fashion. I phoned Leslie from Oxford to make my next appointment. 'There won't be another next,' he said. 'The analysis is finished.' I panicked and could scarcely take this in. 'But I've got finals coming!' I shouted through the receiver, hunting for coins to feed into the machine. (It was the phone outside the Balliol Junior Common Room.) 'You can't let me down like this.' But he could and would and did. 'I'm not able to cope!' I shouted back, listened to by an interested line of fellow students waiting to use the phone. 'Yes, you will. You're a toughie,' he said. 'You can't make analysis a substitute for life.' I shouted again, the coins running out, a rugger type violently shook the telephone box and Leslie disappeared – incommunicado as I expected. He only let me resume contact after I had sat my exams. He stopped me becoming dependent on him.

I did take the finals. I got a lower second and a nice letter from my tutors saying they'd hoped I'd get a first. But for me it was a triumph to have sat finals at all. And I was no longer pretending to be a doormat, which was another triumph. At last I had allowed myself the luxury of a temper! I could even swear.

About Leslie's private life I know little. He was heterosexual and had been married to a lady, who left him for someone else. They had remained friends. The strains of 'love on the dole' had destroyed his relationship as it had destroyed my Uncle Abie.

He went to an ashram in India and is a Vedantist. Since his visit he no longer practises analysis. He introduces Hindu gurus to the

West. His selection is good. A few gurus, he said, are phoneys and many are self-hypnotised phoneys, but with discrimination you can discern the rare real thing.

He is the only man I know who has composed a whole encyclopedia (three volumes on the occult and paranormal). He is a collector of street ballads and incunables (early printed materials) and an expert on Bram Stoker. He devotes his life now to restoring forgotten masterpieces of the silent screen.

He lives in Irish suburbia, respected by neighbours and scholars, because he has few pretensions. He has retreated from society, he says, and is now a hermit. (I find him entertaining and even loquacious when I meet him.) He is as he was – a tidy shabby OAP but courteous and tenacious.

Both my parents trusted him. He understood them and explained my homosexuality to them. He gave them peace of mind and brought me back to life.

28

Irena

Leslie did not in fact abandon me and I did not return to the horrors of the loneliness and solipsism of the time before I met him – which was what I was really afraid of. Because of my analysis and my newfound soul, I had had a shaky rebirth. I was not the same person I was before, though I still endured the same symptoms. I still lived a lot of the time in fantasy because I was still scared of opening letters. I was still fearful of anything to do with sex and went white thinking about all the diseases I could get from a lavatory seat or the babies I could inadvertently father while sitting on one. I still used masturbation as an escape and tranquilliser. But joy was beginning to come back. I was ready for things to happen.

It was at this time that Leslie took me to see his friends Irena and Harry (and their six children). He left early in the evening but I stayed worshipping at their shrine. And they were well worth worshipping.

First of all they broke a myth – that all the victims of the Nazis were Jewish. Irena and Harry were neither. They could have accommodated with the Nazis but chose not to. They had their honour as intellectuals and atheists or agnostics, and did far better than many of the religious lot who no longer knew how to see the evil that was thrust before their eyes. I had met many clever people at Oxford; some were truly brilliant, but most were part of the academic industry, fighting in the rugger scrum for places, positions, recognition, titles and tenure. Ordinary trade unionists with academic techniques. But Harry and Irena were the real thing – true intellectuals.

Harry and Irena were poor and lived on handouts in a Hampstead basement, and they never got naturalised – though like me the immigration officials were enchanted by them. They were both prodigiously talented. Harry had come over here as a student of Bertrand Russell, but he politely parted company from the great man because he thought the prevalent logical positivism as fruitless as the old scholasticism. He preferred to keep his integrity as an occasional night telephonist in a Jewish old people's home where he had time to think and philosophise. He wrote little and was not concerned about publishing it.

Irena his wife amused him as she amused me, and I pieced together their story in part. Harry was the handsome son of an operatic diva brought up in the free heady atmosphere of German theatre. He was the serious philosophy critic of the Ullstein Press in Berlin when he and Irena stumbled across each other. She was almost twenty when she was appointed 'Auntie' to people's problem letters. But being so inexperienced, she didn't even understand what the problems in their letters meant, though she was naturally sympathetic, an original wise woman of the woods, though a young one. She got into the habit of running down the corridor to Harry's office, asking him to enlighten her about these strange terms (lesbianism, dyslexia, anal pleasures, Cabbala and so on). Harry carefully explained everything to her accurately and without condescension. She trusted him.

Her trust proved itself after the Nazis came to power. She told me about that terrible time. A relation was hounding her, accusing her of mixing with homosexuals, Jews and communists, which was damning. Everybody, she said, compromised with power – businessmen, bishops, professors, artistes – some sooner, some later. (I wondered if a lot of rabbis would have joined them if only they had been offered the opportunity, but they weren't.) They went down like ninepins. Irena's innocence saved her. She could recognise the whiff of evil. Only her Harry had never compromised and with their child they had to make it hotfoot to England, which they liked enormously and found curious and funny. A comfortable country!

Of course they had to get married first but Harry had to be divorced first. They had a divorce party in a famous Berlin restaurant – Harry, Irena, Harry's first wife and her present intended. They followed the traditional procedures of the place. Harry publicly insulted his first wife by throwing a dish of pistachio cream at her – her favourite flavour. The rehearsed waiter then rushed in and recorded the 'insult'. They were all now virtually free and affectionately enjoyed their last good meal together in Berlin. I was in seventh heaven as I listened. You couldn't get farther away from lower-middle-class suburbia than that. At last I was living! Irena also introduced me to a lovely lady writer who lived with two men in a pleasant threesome. They shared one double bed and one single one. I wanted to ask more but I was too shy. At Oxford some lecturers and students occasionally exchanged wives but this was much more interesting.

My friendship with Irena was a great education, and made Balliol seem pretty sterile by comparison. On Saturday nights we hung around London pubs and off-licences with our bottle of cheap Spanish wine. When customers came to buy better bottles to bring to a party, we asked them if we could come too and shook our bottle hopefully. Hampstead was a free and easy place. We looked a curious, harmless pair and were usually told to come along. In that way we partied with the Socialist Party of Great Britain (no, not the Labour Party, quite *autre chose!*), with the Trotskyite Fourth Internationales, with the Anarchists who reminded me of my childhood, with debs who had gone slumming, and curious yogi-bogey groups who showed us the latest miraculous manifestation (it looked like dry rot). Early next morning we poured out our findings to Harry, who was charmingly cynical but tried to be fair, as a true philosopher should.

My Inner Voice approved of Irena and Harry, even though they didn't believe in him. There was after all a level of goodness in Irena that I knew I could never attain. A Chinese sailor who knew hardly any English had turned up in her life in the way derelicts do if you are open to them or see God in them. He was dying. Irena, who could hardly communicate with him, sponged him down and spent the night holding him to her while he trembled with the fevers of his wasting illness. She went to him every day and many nights till he passed away, holding her and confusedly thanking her. I was touched. It merited a bead on the rosary a Christian had given me. I wasn't interested in all the Virgin prayers. They seemed over the top and soppy. Instead I dedicated each bead to a memory of God manifesting himself in my life. Another bead is devoted to the times she accompanied me to tests at a hospital's 'Special Clinic' which I patronised because I used to get neurotic fantasies about the consequences of sex, or in my case no sex. She was a real pal and yet another bead on that rosary.

Sometimes I wanted to shake both Irena and Harry because they had been given so many talents but, as soon as they were successful with any of them, they promptly stopped and turned to another. They were two clever children cocking a snook at the world. I was not so talented but under Irena I learnt to paint, just as under Leslie I started to write poetry.

As a child, I had been thrown out of the art class at school because I couldn't draw daffodils for toffee and all my water-colours ran into each other. Irena taught me that my first dull wooden painting was only the start. Then she made me pour turps all over it and then scrub the canvas board with a rag. Then I should look into the resultant mess like a child peering into the flames of a coal fire. What did I see in the mess? she asked. Well, I saw a procession moving down a street, a bunch of flowers exploding into colour, smoke belching out of a factory, and a child looking on. Bring them out, bring them out into life, urged Irena, show them to me. And I did and behold, I was starting to paint. I nearly became a painter and might become so yet if I have enough time and the courage to face failure. Metaphysically, her lesson was important. Failure in painting and in life wasn't the end but the necessary precursor to achievement. It was very close to what I had learnt at the Quaker meeting.

Harry and Irena didn't mind my becoming a rabbi but, like my mother, they took exception to my Christian leanings. They had never believed in Christianity but after the Nazi time they didn't even respect it.

Sometimes I sat back and tried to piece together all the truths that were coming to me – Quakers, Colin, the lady in the threesome, Leslie, analysis and Wittgenstein, the Venerable Bede and Hampstead, Fred, rabbis and the Church of South India, Vinvoo Street, Balliol and building societies. I couldn't put the jigsaw puzzle together. I still had a lot of experiencing to do before my debut.

29

The Weimar Republic in the Cafe Cosmo

Through Irena and Leslie, I received a parallel education while I was at Oxford and of a very different type from my studies there. I was educated in London during the vacations by these remnants of the Weimar Republic who had fled just in time and settled in north-west London. My 'tutorials' took place in the Cafe Cosmo in Swiss Cottage, and I was tolerated by the intellectuals there because I was worshipful. I was allowed to supply my teachers with coffee and *guegelhupf* and to listen in, translating their German into broken Yiddish and then into English.

Both systems of education took place in the same years and I became frantic trying to put together the lessons I learnt in both. It wasn't the question of truth and lies. It was the profounder question of truth and truth as Boethius had said in the sixth century: 'Why is there such a division in the nature of reality, an everlasting struggle between truth and truth?' How true! Truth and lies is simple. Truth and truth is a great problem. And there was me trying to bring all these together into coherence. No wonder I found the daring Oxford Marxists as dated as the Zionists and Colin's Anglo-Cat pious platitudes.

Leslie said (most of my thoughts around that time begin with this formula – part of it was genuine admiration and part transference) that though I now had a body, I didn't know how to use it. So he sent me to the music teacher Alfred Wolfson who could start with my voice. Now Ave (Alfred) was no ordinary music teacher but a disturber, a discoverer and, to his disciples and those he helped, a genius and a saviour. (To those who couldn't take him, he was the devil.) To me he was a saviour. He was a refugee who, for being Jewish, had been thrown off a moving train by a Nazi. In Germany he had been a consultant to singers who had lost or damaged their voices. He had found that if they extended their register to below and above the notes on the piano, their home register improved as well. He also found out that 'home register' was an artificial convention and by this extraordinary extension of their range their personality also moved forward. Breaking through the barriers in the voice broke through the barriers in their mind and spirit.

I wanted to talk to him just as I had wanted to natter platitudes to Leslie, but he wouldn't allow me to talk. I had to sing, to make true notes, high or below my range by making crescendos and diminuendos on them. 'Make this note,' he said. 'Can't,' I replied. 'Nonsense!' he said. 'You can and you will.' Sometimes he got me there by trickery. Occasionally he would throw me against the wall and say, 'Make it!' and I jolly well made it. Sometimes Irena and I crawled about on the floor pretending to rape each other or be beasts. We were both so shaken our voices went down to our boots and sure enough out came sounds like Marlene Dietrich married to Chaliapin. Ave beamed at us as we shook with mixed emotion.

After Ave became ill, his disciple Roy Hart, the actor and director, took over, and transferred me from singing to declaiming and speaking honestly from my own centre. I have never since been able to bear false voices, the castrated high Anglican voice, or the 'higher' prissy 'emotionless' voice of academia (specially awful in synagogues and churches), or the false bonhomie voice of manipulation or the mad voice of Hitler. When I sang or spoke with one of my true voices, emotions and feelings I could hardly bear flooded into me. I was astounded by the choir of voices that lay inside me, which of course included Fred, WW and Old Smokey.

Ave had an inner and outer circle of devotees. I was on the outer. Occasionally at polite formal functions, by chance the name of Ave comes up in conversation. We followers all recognise each other, compelled to speak about his lessons but cautiously. They got too near the bone for us all. I mentioned him on the radio and to my surprise people wrote to me who wanted to research his work. His time had come. I referred them to Leslie and to a long-playing record called *Vox Humana* issued by Folkways which illustrates the extraordinary feats and powers of his pupils.

30

I Make Heaven Happen

Many years later, I was asked about my own student days in Oxford in a Berlin student cafe. I began to describe the post-war scene in Balliol when one of the students, his eyes brimming with tears (alcohol?), clapped me over the shoulder and said, his voice filled with pity, 'You must have been of the pre-pill generation. How hard it must have been. I pity you. Let me get you a schnapps.' I graciously accepted because, put like that, I began to pity myself. I had already had a few schnapps and alcohol always opens my tearducts.

Things really changed after the hippy revolution hit the place. Hip, hip, hippy! Youngsters now began to think for themselves. They no longer tried to be pocket-sized editions of their parents. I remember asking Leslie what sex was. Although it is not the purpose of our life on earth, it can certainly feel like that if you are making do on short rations of the stuff or on a starvation diet. Leslie said it was a device and strategy devised by nature for propagation and group survival. But even I could see that it had become something very different. With birth control, even in my time, sex and procreation were parting company.

Sex is now entwined with romance, Agape as well as Eros, and at-one-ment with God or God in another person or goodness. Today sex serves many needs. People may sleep together because they are frightened of the dark and need to make contact with another human being, because they are lonely or tense, to escape the confines of the ego, because it is a more natural way to relax than taking a tablet or drinking cocoa, because it is fun (a word that Religion finds difficult), because it is a way to keep warm, because it is a way to give and receive pleasure. On the darker side people have always used sex, whether within marriage or not, to gain power over another person, to manipulate them, to get money, status or possessions.

We now understand much more about sublimation and how psychic and physical energy can be converted from one kind of activity to another. Suppressed sexual energy can find its expression in art and in spirituality. Christianity has tried to make general rules about this, applicable to all, but they do not work. Some people can make the switch while others land up in a breakdown or on the bottle. Like many others, I found in those sexless years at Oxford that food, spiritual exercises and cigarettes enabled me to carry on – just.

Christianity helped me, because many Christians also had conversations with God as a matter of course and God also took a human form in their minds. I wondered if I should become Christian. My friend Fred, as I've said, was not that interested. He wasn't into labels or the numbers game – which is another name for the rat-race whether played out in business, bed, in the pews or on the dance floor.

The Judaism I knew during my Oxford years could not help me much, being concerned with family life, claustrophobic community, nationalism (I was a Marxist internationalist though not a Stalinist), Israel (whose creativity awed me but which didn't feel home), and charity committees (the best part of Jewish suburbia, no doubt, but I wanted to get out of suburbia). Christianity seemed to understand my love life though not my sex life and what went on inside me. It was relevant to me just recovering from a breakdown and a feeble attempt at suicide.

Christian friends decided I should read the New Testament and be baptised but I never fell into the font. If I'd been born into it, I would have stuck to it, but I wasn't. So I wavered.

When I decided to read the New Testament, it was a shock. I tried to feel for it as I thought Christians were supposed to do, but eventually gave up. There were too many miracles for a start. I started at the beginning with the Gospel of Mark and it seemed compacted of miracles and miracles were not part of my life experience. I tried to make something of them but didn't succeed. The real world wasn't like that.

The Jesus of the Gospels and my brother–lover in my mind didn't fit either. The former was extremist which the latter was not – 'If your eye offend you, put it out.' Nonsense! I preferred the rabbis' substitute of compensation. It was also elitist ('many are called and few are chosen'). I was more attracted to Buddha coming back to this world to help those still entrapped in its foolishness, and to wisdom and generosity in the profane songs of my student time. 'We'll all go together when we go', 'If you get to heaven before I do, just bore a hole and pull me through'. There was also so much anger in the New Testament – the cursing of the fig tree, the poor porkers hurling themselves down the slope to be drowned, and not casting 'pearls before swine', i.e. non-Jews. There was a fair amount of anti-Judaism too in the New Testament, some of it dangerous.

There was much that drew me too. The topsy-turvy logic of the parables of the Kingdom of Heaven. The beginnings of a wider vision of God beyond law and covenants, which reminded me of the solicitor's office. The intensity of the love between Jesus and his disciples. It left so many questions unanswered. Jesus was a single man in his thirties with only male disciples, though with a feeling for women. All this was very strange in his days. Was he a homo like me? The Anglican bishop Hugh Montefiore speculated about this too.

So I sat in the church next to Balliol reading, meditating, just being, talking silently to my Friend, and something began to happen. Not startling like his appearance out of nowhere. The atmosphere of these places stole into me, the vision in those angels and saints reached out to me. And I reached out to them in the friendly gloom and found myself in heaven. And I knew heaven was my home. Another great reality of my life had fallen into place. 'My soul there was indeed a country far beyond the stars.' That was the country I had been hitching to years before. Knowing Heaven was my home saved me from a lot of earthly mistakes and follies. During the Blitz I had learnt that earthly homes are not substantial and the dreams of a lifetime can easily be blown to bits by a very small bomb. Now I was no longer so terrified by thoughts of dry rot, wet rot, woodworm and all the ills brought by mortality which afflict our bodies, minds or possessions.

But it was not enough to receive heaven. Outside body experiences were easy. At Oxford parties my centre of gravity shifted and I was looking down on myself and the world about me with compassion and amusement.

My sad Slav family:
(anticlockwise) Grandpa, Grandma, Hilda, Abie, Ma and Lil.

Blue at sea.

Kim looks younger, I look older.

I also had to make heaven happen and it happened whenever I did something for heaven's sake. Heaven also happened when I took courage and crossed some barrier inside myself which had been blocking me because of fear or meanness.

I also found out that my heavenly 'progress' would seem both jerky and inconsistent. That was because a part of me had gained a foothold in heaven but it could take me a long time – a lifetime – before the rest of me caught up.

I had discovered my soul among the Quakers and was about to discover my body, but I had no idea how to integrate the two.

31

Why Not Become a Rabbi?

My last year at Oxford was make or break. My tutors tut-tutted and said I should get a First, but they knew and I knew I'd spent more time on my breakdown than my studies. I could fail.

But I no longer thought about grades or even passing. I just thought about sitting the exams and not walking out of them or running away from them or making excuses or being conveniently ill. My triumph was to take them fairly and honestly. I could then bring things to a tidy end and pick up the pieces. I'd at least come out with my own self-respect. Sitting exams you know you might fail, especially if you were a bright boy like me, requires courage.

What would I do with a mere pass degree or a fail? I wondered. I probably couldn't continue academically to higher degrees and didn't want to. I prayed to WW in the cold bleak Balliol chapel, but got no answer. But the answer came, though delayed a few days. At breakfast I idly leafed through the pages of the eminently respectable *Jewish Chronicle* and my eyes were riveted on an advert. It requested well-educated Anglo-Jewish young men to apply for scholarships which would lead them to a rewarding career in the Anglo-Jewish ministry. Now I was more Anglican than Anglo, but I thought I must be Jewish enough, since I wasn't Christian enough to become a monk. The request came from the Liberal wing of the Jewish establishment of which I had little knowledge and no experience. I was certainly liberal, anarchic even, though that had better be suppressed. I excitedly told Robin about my 'call'. Why not? he thought, though I would have to become a lot more respectable than I was. 'Keep quiet about your Yiddish,' he said, 'they don't like that sort of thing.'

A correspondence then began, and it seemed like a love match.

We got more and more interested in each other. During the vacation on Robin's advice I dropped in to one of their synagogues in which I would fulfil my rewarding ministry. I knew at once it wouldn't do. It was too far from the Judaism of my childhood, the East End, and my Yiddish roots. I wrote them a letter explaining, hoping they would convert me to their way of thinking, but they didn't, though politely, and that was that. Janny told me I was right in being honest. I wasn't so sure. Did religious 'style' matter so much?

Then another 'call' sidled towards me. Old WW wasn't letting up! My mother told all this to her old friend, who was married to a rabbi manqué who was attached to a rival group to the Liberal Jews, who called themselves Reform Jews. He wanted to steal me for his own lot and I was very willing to be stolen. This time, before I committed myself by correspondence, I cautiously dropped in to some Reform services and found I liked them and so did WW. It was all low key but the prayers were more recognisable, and there were Quaker-style short silences (too short) and Anglican-style decorum. I found it very restful, and liked the rabbi. He was Dr Katz and he shook hands with me pleasantly after the service. He asked about my studies and to my surprise we talked about Horace, his quotes being in better Latin than mine.

I wrote a letter, received an untidy letter back from another rabbi who really wanted to interview me. His name was van der Zyl and I knew my mother would go dotty on him because I was told he was blond, clean-shaven and bluff. When I met him I went dotty on him too because he actually seemed to like me as I was.

'By the way, Mr Blue,' he said 'there's another student application from Oxford for rabbinical study. His name is Michael Leigh.'

'I'm afraid I haven't heard of him,' I said.

'Well,' replied Rabbi D. Wernher van der Zyl, 'he's certainly heard of you.' Well, that ends that, I suppose, I said to myself. My jaw dropped as I looked at him. He wasn't just smiling, he was laughing his head off.

He then endeared himself to me by getting down to money. 'I'll get you interviewed by the committee and until you get your scholarship I'll arrange some private tuition for you to live on. In the meantime here's a cheque.' I told all this to Ma, but she couldn't believe anyone would pay me to instruct them in God. I thought it a bloody marvel myself.

I corrected myself and deleted 'bloody' even in thought. The Reformers were a respectable lot, a mixture of Jewish families who'd been allowed back to England by Cromwell, learned, well-educated, German high bourgeoisie immigrants, and an increasing number of East Europeans (like me) who preferred Judaism Anglican style to Russian Orthodox style.

The services were mercifully short (Jewish services can extend themselves like the Russian Steppes or American chewing gum with mind-numbing repetitions) – half an hour for Sabbath evening and an hour for Sabbath morning. They were quiet and decent and I was touched by their lack of pretension. It wasn't exactly love at first sight but I felt this small organisation on the fringes of Anglo-Jewry could become my home. And so it has proved. Being English, they didn't make windows into people's souls. I would have room to move and flex my spiritual muscles. They were friends of Israel but not Zionists. The new Jewish state was not messianic for them. I was told that a traditional sage had been asked for his view of the Jewish State. He had replied in Yiddish, '*A ge'ulah es ist nicht ober a refu'ah es ist ja*': a redemption it isn't but an alleviation, a healing, it is. I agreed.

I formally applied for a scholarship and was formally interviewed by a committee. It was all very civilised, almost unJewish in its English politeness. No one asked me about my beliefs and when I tried to state them the subject changed rapidly. Instead I was fed small cakes, asked about Balliol's chances on the river, the answer to which I made up. But I liked them, they were nice, and niceness can be a rare quality in religion. (Lots of religion can be quite nasty.) They obviously relied on Dr van der Zyl's judgement and so I was in!

Why had I really become a rabbi? I asked myself in an empty Room of Prayer in a silent synagogue. There were two very valid reasons. I had fallen in love with what seemed to be God and I didn't want to live my life without him. I didn't know what to call him but it was enough that he called me and answered me, to my surprise, whenever I called him. What was God? My home – I called it/him heaven.

The other main reason was my heritage from my East End and

Zionist years. I felt a duty laid on me by the Holocaust. I was no longer certain about Israel after its refusal to face the problem of the Arab refugees, but I still had to do something, say something. That something would reveal itself in the course of time.

There were other reasons too, and because of the honesty I had learnt in analysis, I was also able to face up to them, though I wasn't strong enough to tell anyone about them except Robin. I needed status and a pulpit (not a soapbox) that I could mount and speak from. I wasn't capable of the cut and thrust of business life, I was still too fragile. I needed to study more, to learn more to recoup my forces, i.e. a scholarship. I needed an ecclesiastical bolt-hole.

I eventually did manage to tell God in prayer my very mixed motives. He calmed me down and told me that I was only at the beginning of a religious life and I should leave the worrying to him. He would worry for both of us. I had never before realised how helpful it was to have a God. I blessed him.

32

A Good Job for a Jewish Boy?

My mother was even more muddled than me about my choice of profession – she could never work it out. When some of her friends congratulated her on my piety, she was sure they were taking the mickey out of her. Confused, she rang up her father, because it was all beyond her. He said he would consult his boon drinking companion, the broken-down traditional cantor, who must surely know about such things. The cantor said, 'A Reform rabbi! Mr Goldstein, your grandson is on to a good thing. Don't interfere with him. I have to sing my guts out the whole week and what do I get for it? Not even a bottle of good whisky! But your grandson will only have to tell people to be good in English, and he'll make a fortune.' My grandpa conveyed this message joyously to my mother, who smiled falsely to all her friends, telling them it fulfilled her mother's dream – which it probably did, but not hers.

Now if my ma was in a muddle and I was in a muddle, the community I was going to be trained to serve was in an even bigger muddle. The problem was that the Jewish world had changed so radically in the twentieth century – the years and events had been so catastrophic and apocalyptic that no one was clear what a modern rabbi should learn and what problems he should address. It was no use appealing to tradition because these were new problems and new situations and the past was of little help or even irrelevant.

Traditionally, rabbis were trained as canon lawyers. In the past they were legal experts and researchers, and in practice they acted as mayors and judges of Jewish communities. Old-time rabbis did not 'drop in' on households in the congregations, beam at babies and act as untrained social workers. Traditionally, their congregants did not 'drop in' on their rabbis either, they requested appointments. From my Anglican experience, as a student rabbi I did 'drop in', but speedily dropped out when such visits were perceived as embarrassments rather than misplaced chumminess.

I think my fellow student Michael Leigh and I in the early days of our rabbinic studies devoted three-quarters of our time and effort to Jewish law, and deciphering the strange Aramaic in which the Talmud, the great repository of rabbinic law and lore, was written. On the other hand, after I qualified, I doubt if I was asked to untie such legal knots more than a dozen times through my entire career. To unknot them I referred to the Talmud only out of curiosity – the real tools of my job were common sense and pastoral psychology.

Practically speaking, my main task was to form a religious family, a community, out of a collection of refugees and children of refugees, with different memories and traditions. But above all I had to relate the chaotic past to their present and not merely make it relevant but helpful. I could tweak the ceremonies and formulas into place, but what could I say about the questions rituals covered?

These were some of those questions:

- Since so many prayers had been said in vain in the cattle trucks to the concentration camps, why pray?
- Where was God in Auschwitz? (Many members of my congregations had lost parents, partners, children and family. Some had even been imprisoned there.)
- Was there life beyond death?
- Was it right for members of the congregation to make their own 'pick and mix' assortment of rituals and precepts from the Jewish past?
- What about the nice Jewish boy who wanted to marry the nice non-Jewish girl who lived next door or whom he had met at university?
- Was the State of Israel a Messianic event or a mistake? Should members of my congregation settle in it or, if not them, their children?
- What food laws should we as a synagogue keep officially? What food laws need we keep privately? Was the latter my concern?
- Do Jews have spiritual experiences, Christian style? Should a

Jewish community, used to cut-and-thrust committee meetings and prayers that stretch like chewing gum, have a shot at meditative silence?

- Had God revealed himself to us in our valour and vulgarity, our sacrifice, loyalty and laughter? What was his message?
- Did God only give messages in the past? Were we a Jewish Confucianism, a Jewish ancestor worship?
- Do Jews struggle on or just put out the lights and get out? Become Buddhists or Quakers or Catholics and make a fast exit? Was Jewish life really possible under the shadow of its far greater daughter religions, Christianity and Islam?

These problems came to a head for me in the late fifties or early sixties. It was in the sixties that *Fiddler on the Roof* (also known in some countries as *Anatevka*) was shown in a West End theatre. Jews fell over themselves to get seats for it. It showed the Old Country, the '*Haym*' that all my grandparents came from, seen through the sentiment and feeling of Chagall and the idealisation of memory. You couldn't get a seat! I managed to squeeze in because I was becoming a rabbi and had pull. The song that hit us in our innermost parts was called – you can guess it – 'Tradition', and my eyes wept like the rest of the audience as the stage was lit up by the light of Sabbath candles.

While *Fiddler on the Roof* was playing to full houses, another play, *The Bar Mitzvah Boy*, i.e. 'the confirmation boy', was playing nearby. I went to see it three times. There was no difficulty in getting seats. It gave a pretty accurate picture of religious life in a Jewish suburb, but Jewish suburban people didn't want to see themselves and their troubled faith as it was in the muddled post-Holocaust present. They preferred ancestor worship and a world that might be imitated but not re-created. As an old cynical rabbi said to me, while he was surveying the packed congregation at the Memorial Service on the Day of Atonement, the holiest day of the Jewish year (standing room only), after I had remarked on the congregation's piety, 'Do you think so, Lionel? I think they have come to say memorial prayers for the religion of their forefathers which died.' I shivered.

I must mention 'Old Smokey' again and the role he played in my rabbinical life. He wasn't just an ornament or a private indulgence but a necessity. It was only through appealing to him and then listening that I began to find out what my role was, what was the message of my rabbinate.

The Holocaust had left European Judaism like a hard nut. The outer shell of communalism and nationalism and memory had never been stronger. But deeper inside that nut, the questioning of Jewish existence and Jewish purpose had seldom been stronger too. Only Old Smokey could give my ministry meaning. Only he could turn it away from becoming an Auld Lang Syne society to our task in the post-Holocaust world. Religion has always been real for me when it is at work in my life. Often I frequented empty synagogues and churches, not just saunas, during the fifties and sixties, and paid flying visits to unlikely monasteries and friaries. It was not just to sort out my muddled love life, but the muddle of religious love life and that of my battered people. The problems enriched each other.

33

What Had I Signed up to?

The Association of Synagogues in Great Britain (Reform) was not used to training its own rabbis. In the past it had imported them from Germany or America. But the Berlin seminary had been finally shut down in 1942. (The Nazis had kept it going as a showpiece until the final extermination of Jews.) It was feared that if I went to America, where Reform Judaism was very strong, and salaries very high, I might never come back. So rabbinic education in London was important for them as well as for me.

But Dr van der Zyl and a few sympathisers had a different perspective and agenda. For him this small very English organisation had to take on the mantle of European progressive Jewry. It was now its turn to provide the European leadership in the post-Holocaust years. British Jewry was the only substantial part of European Jewry spared the Occupation. So he had already summoned the remaining seminary teachers of Berlin and Breslau to London. He could barely pay them a pittance (he had to go around begging) but he could provide two students, Michael Leigh and me – 'Oxford men,' he said proudly. Mr Leonard Montefiore, a scholar himself as well as a philanthropist, funded us.

Michael and I didn't dare get ill at the same time. If we couldn't come, the sages couldn't teach (they were paid by the hour) and presumably didn't eat. So we were raised urgently from our beds of sickness, despite the flu, bronchitis, broken bones or pneumonia, and brought to our lecture room (there was only one) by taxi, limousine or ambulance. I wouldn't have put it past them to have hired a hearse. We were also sent to University College to take a degree in Hebrew and Aramaic. There we learnt irregular verbs and how to deprecate modern historical criticism.

I did learn theology of a sort from the lives of my university teachers. All had been badly wounded by the Nazi horrors. Dr Stein knew intellectually with his mind that modern criticism might be correct scientifically, but his emotions led him in the contrary direction – so he was sad. Rabbi Dr Wiesenberg conscientiously taught us biblical criticism (higher and lower) but made it clear he didn't go along with it unless it went along with tradition. Dr Weiss from Hungary and Israel brought modern and traditional knowledge together but in a paradoxical relationship, on the basis that the more absurd it was, the more belief and faith were needed. They made me dizzy, but they were so nice! What I did learn from all the rabbis and teachers was how to be a refugee in your old age with dignity and without hatred.

Our course of studies was jerky, some far above our heads and some from another world – Kaiser Wilhelm's Germany – but it was never slick or silly.

About 1956, Dr van der Zyl revealed his hand. His teacher Leo Baeck had died and he wanted the seminary (even if it only had two and then four pupils, when another two joined us) to be a memorial to his name. Now Rabbi Dr Leo Baeck was a scholar, but then all our teachers were scholars. He was in addition a saint – though Judaism doesn't really recognise saints – just people more faithful to their duty, that's all. He became Chief Rabbi just as Hitler became Führer of Germany in 1933, and had the most heartrending and tragic duty any rabbi has had to perform. In 1939 he was in England trying to arrange for more children to come over from his doomed community. Then he smelt war and rushed back from London to Berlin before the borders were closed. The young rabbis should leave but the greatest duty of the old was with the sick and those who couldn't escape. In 1942, he was arrested and sent to Theresienstadt Camp. But another Baeck in some bureaucratic confusion was sent to Auschwitz in his place. Leo Baeck continued to survive as a non-person in the deportation camp, giving lectures late at night on such matters as the Greek influence on Judaism. Like earlier rabbis, he was determined that even if the whole world was becoming barbarian, Jews would be the exception.

When the Russians liberated Theresienstadt and handed over the guards to the prisoners, I was told that it was he who prevented their summary death. They deserved fair trial too.

Many didn't like it, but he was one of the first rabbis to return to Germany, an 'accursed' land. He hated Nazi barbarism – but he never denied German culture, of which he was part.

He died in 1956, just as the college that was to bear his name started. I had a few lessons, conversations really, with him. There are things he said which I shall remember.

'It was easy to be liberal,' he said, 'when I was a student at the beginning of this century, i.e. the twentieth. Liberalism was in the air, it was the Zeitgeist. But it was not easy to remain liberal and believe in human goodness during the Third Reich. That's when liberalism came of age. It was no longer a social convenience, it had to be religious.'

It was during a talk with both Baeck and van der Zyl that they asked where I was taking my holiday. 'I'm not sure,' I answered. 'I might visit some ultra-Orthodox friends in their Yeshiva, their academy. Or I might go to a monastery to see friends from Oxford, who are taking their vows.' Suddenly I realised they were both liberal, reform rabbis, and what I said may have hurt them. It might have sounded disloyal. They both noticed my discomfort. They said, 'Mr Blue, our Judaism is your religious home, it is not your religious prison.' Since then that is how I have always thought of it. That sentence has meant a lot to me. I could now be an honest Reform Jew.

34

My Curious Chaos of Instruction

One of the problems surrounding the birth of the Leo Baeck College is the paucity of Dr van der Zyl's writings. The vision of the college was in his head and heart but not on paper. This occasionally disturbed both Michael Leigh and myself when we were his first and only students. When Dr van der Zyl triumph-antly told us the constitution of the college was now on paper, this turned out to be some scribbled notes on a scrap of newspaper.

Both Michael Leigh and I got to know his thinking well. He trained us personally even before the college started, as acting director of our studies. As I have already mentioned, he was convinced that a new birth of forward-looking Judaism would happen in Europe because, unlike many others, he thought new life would come, indeed was coming, to what some regarded as a European cemetery. In this new post-Holocaust Europe, Britain would have to take the lead as the only large community which had not been decimated by the Nazis.

He also thought Britain should finance it until such time as Continental Europe could begin to pay for it too. To exist on American or Israeli charity would be easy in the beginning, but weakening in the end. Europe had to begin to believe in itself for its own college to make sense and, though working closely with the American centres, do so as equals not just as recipients of transatlantic handouts. This reliance on America turned out to be the weakness of the Paris college which started out at the same time.

Dr van der Zyl did not think of the London College in a committed ideological way. His model was the Berlin Hochschule and the more conservative school at Breslau. Therefore it would turn out rabbis for all sections of Jewry. This was a daydream, because of the increasingly bad-tempered polarisation of Jewish religious life which was taking place in Britain. But I remember him being pleased when a Leo Baeck student decided to transfer to the orthodox college.

Nearly all our lecturers were German-speaking and German-thinking, which required a different mindset for English students. Our teachers' level of systematic scholarship was high, which ours was not, and I remember being in a daze during seminars in which vast folios were passed from one to another for judicious textual examination while Michael and I were struggling with the most basic of verbs in the Hebrew language. Thou kildest – he killed, she killed, they killed, we killed. ('To kill' is the grammatically regular verb that is declined in Semitic languages.)

Looking back on my confused education, I think what I learnt best was what a rabbi scholar should be. In the long run, this meant even more than what a rabbi scholar should know. The ones who taught me law and lore and theology and codes taught me above all about themselves. They were Jews of a completely different type from the East European ones I remembered from my childhood in London's Yiddish East End. ('Yiddish, Mr Blue! *Gott in himmel!*') It was like learning to be a gentleman at Oxford but another type of gentleman.

Apart from their scholarship, they tried to teach me rabbinic propriety. I have never forgotten their concept of practical rabbinics. When visiting a congregation, I should always travel first-class rail, and if I couldn't afford a first-class ticket I should arrange to leave the train at least from a first-class door. This was one piece of advice. Another was to wear black silk socks as in the Kaiser's day – though I privately thought them kinky.

But what I respected about them was their high view of the rabbinate. They were not populist nor politicians nor entertainers, and some delivered theses instead of sermons, which were way over their Yiddisher congregations' heads. Some remained perpetually bewildered by Britain and never knew why they were not appreciated. One, I think, committed suicide, because the tragedy of European Jewry was too much for him.

Without regular funding in those first years or a regular intake of students, Dr van der Zyl had to be pragmatic in the English manner and this in fact suited him well. He got handouts from

Leonard Montefiore and support from some other continental rabbis, refugees themselves, who espoused his cause. He also managed to rustle up enough additional students to keep the college structure going. Some were brilliant, like Dow Marmur from Sweden. Some were too deeply wounded and flawed by their sufferings to survive as English rabbis. One nice quiet chap had an even worse breakdown than me. He also had experienced too much.

I personally didn't mind being a guinea pig for future generations. It suited my temperament. So I picked up whatever I could from wherever it came – Jewish mysticism from Dr Joseph Weiss, and deep Jewish traditional piety from Dr Wiesenberg at University College, prayer from a variety of East European-type house synagogues near my home, and the theology of the 'third Talmud' from Rabbi Dr Maybaum, though I couldn't yet read the first one. My spirituality and cosmic views came from the Sri Ramakrishna Vedanta Mission at Muswell Hill, and the intellectualism of the Weimar Republic from my friends Irena and Harry. And I learnt dollops of Aramaic grammar from everybody. Though it was of course the language spoken by Jesus, it was rather like chewing gum because it didn't have a firm grammar or syntax. As I didn't have a firm centre either, it suited me very well.

Looking back to my first years of rabbinic education, I realised that I had learnt far more than I thought. The confusion of it had deceived me. I studied the following questions:

- If you laid the Passover table and a fire worshipper came in and turned it over, what did you do?
- If you wrote the divorce document for your wife on a leaf and then transferred to her the ownership of the entire tree, was this a valid 'delivery'?
- Should we pray or davven (i.e. chant)? Was the feeling or the meaning more important?
- Did a package holiday to Israel constitute the 'Return' spoken of by the prophets?
- Could you wear a self-winding watch on the Sabbath?
- Was biblical criticism basically anti-Semitic?
- Since God was the source of everything, was he the source of evil too? If he wasn't, who was?

- Was it good that humankind had to leave the Garden of Eden?
- Were Jewish sufferings in our time the 'birth pangs of the Messiah'?
- If you were pursued by a snake in the desert, and the only places of refuge were a church and a mosque, which should you choose?
- How Jewish was the European 'Enlightenment'?

There were many, many more subjects and questions I touched or delved into. These few give the taste of my erratic, extra-ordinary education. At the time its lack of order, like the Talmud, maddened me. Later on, I rejoiced in it.

To my surprise, all this rich rather chaotic instruction seemed to gel. The congregations I preached to as a student rabbi enjoyed my sermons and I enjoyed them and their enjoyment, but I hadn't yet come to terms with being spiritual adviser to the bourgeoisie, whose silent leafy suburbs I'd been plotting to leave for years.

35

Question Marks

Harry: 'Why don't you ask me about my business?'
Sam: 'Sorry, Harry, so how is your business?'
Harry (wringing his hands): 'Don't ask!'
(Traditional Jewish joke)

My training didn't answer many of my Jewish religious questions; rather, it increased them. When I complained about this to one of my teachers, he said that was indeed what the Talmud, the great repository of rabbinic law and lore, was like: unending argument and few decisions. While studying rabbinic Judaism, I became two people – one immersed in the cut and thrust of dialectic and exegesis, like my East European ancestors in fact, and the other a product of the Enlightenment for whom so much of all this seemed nonsense. I was uncomfortable with this and asked about this separation – I did not like being two people. I felt as if I had fallen down a (rabbinic) rabbit hole like Alice. Part of the problem was the course itself, being made up of bits imported from Berlin, Breslau and Jerusalem. But part was more deep-seated.

I went to a seminar of Professor Sholem, the greatest modern scholar of Cabbalah, and seemingly an Enlightenment critical chap like me. I asked him straightforwardly, because I genuinely wanted guidance, why he devoted his life to the intricacies of such a subject. Was it interesting as an aberration of the human mind or was it a key to the cosmos? He was so annoyed and upset by my question that my elders and betters told me to shut up or leave the room.

In a similar manner, when I asked in another seminar about the motives of the teachers who considered the legalities of situations which could never occur or were too bizarre to occur,

I was again told to shut up. I did shut up but I wondered what life was like in Babylon of the third, fourth, fifth and sixth centuries AD/CE (Anno Domini or Christian Era). Perhaps they were bored out of their minds in provincial Babylon between the Tigris and Euphrates and without power could only play legal acrostics.

And yet I knew there was something more, something I had not sussed out. Sometimes the most profound and courageous (and outrageous) stories and insights lay embedded in this scholastic, legal rabbit warren. But a chasm, or rather two chasms, separated me from the flow of it. The scriptural texts were only understood in a pre-critical manner, and the logic used was a curious form of early medieval scholasticism. Only a few voices in the corpus realised that history (my subject) was moving and that present, past and future could not be simplified into a world in which time stood still. As children, we used old tattered copies of the Passover service in which the Jews on the exodus from Egypt were dressed like medieval men and women leaving a medieval walled city. But it could not have looked like that. The new Science of History told me so!

Gradually my understanding increased. The Talmud and the rabbinic writings were not the tidy blueprint of modern Judaism, but the untidy workshop in which 'a' not 'the' blueprint might be worked out. Like all workshops or studios or ateliers, it was untidy, messy and curious – a mixture of junk and jewels, and you had to find the latter for yourself in the chaos. About three thousand people left their mark on the Talmud between the time of Jesus and the sixth century when the meandering arguments had to come to a hurried close because of external persecution. If it hadn't, I suppose further volumes and compilations of the Talmud could have gone on for ever.

It is not possible to count the commentators, codifiers, legalists, mystics and unnamed anonymous ordinary folk who together made a religion, rabbinic Judaism, one of whose results was the goodness and piety of my own granny.

Sometimes I felt a part of this tradition, and sometimes a half-outsider who had to transmit whatever was relevant in that closed ordered rabbinic world to another world which was pluralist, permissive and open. We now needed to start a new Talmud and bring together religion and reality for our own time.

It is the openness of the modern world that I appreciate most.

Sometimes I feel nostalgic for the old Jewish world I lived in until the war and the evacuation – for the world of My Yiddishe Momma and Yiddish jokes and the warmth and kindness that went with it. But truth has come to me from too many directions to be simple. I cannot wear my grandparents' clothes, I cannot believe their faith. I have grown out of both.

I think in my lifetime the authority of that old rabbinic world gradually died for the majority of Jews. (Neither rabbis nor synagogues are mentioned in the Hebrew Scripture, the Old Testament.)

The questions which came to me in the synagogues I serve belonged to a new Jewish world being born, which we couldn't as yet grasp. That world depended on so many external events over which Jews have no control – such as a possible return of political anti-Semitism, the future of Israel (did it have one?), the recovery or dwindling away of the Diaspora.

I remember discussing these matters years later with my friend, fellow student and colleague Dow Marmur. We were both Reform rabbis, enlightened and liberal   what did we learn from this rabbinic confusion? It would affect the way we thought, even if not what we thought, till our dying day.

I no longer felt any need for a great man or godman religion. The Talmud was the work of a whole class of people, sometimes of a whole people. Though they were not exactly aware of it, a new revelation had come democratically through them. It had not come from the top of a mountain accompanied by unearthly sound and light effects but from the lecture rooms of provincial colleges and the suburban centres of Babylon.

A new Talmud was now being built in the same piecemeal fashion after the Second World War. My discussion with Dow in his office was part of it. Jewish holy history was working through us. It did not proceed by certainties our generation did not possess but by honest argument. We were two small pieces in the great jigsaw whose picture would emerge as one little piece was fitted to another and another to yet another.

From the Talmud I learnt you could build a religion on small things. What it lacked in pomp and in grandiose theology it made up in flexibility. It could also laugh at itself.

So the Talmud also taught me self-laughter and self-caricature. Most religious preachers seem to inflate as they talk. Laughter, small observances, acceptance of my own smallness – one small voice among so many, the holiness of argument, being true to the present not just to an over-dominant past or future, being practical and pragmatic for God's sake – these are what I learnt from Talmud and rabbinic Judaism. I also learnt to accept the cul-de-sacs, the mistakes of tradition, and its dottiness. You can learn from mistakes.

By trial and error, I learnt how to conduct the committees which took up most of my time, rule 'points of order' out of order and defuse potential sources of trouble by kicking them upstairs, i.e. referring them to a Constitution Committee where they could do no harm but help the members feel important.

I wish I had been taught how to keep and not lose diaries, and how to introduce members of my congregation to each other, when I had forgotten both of their names.

By sitting and listening to my superiors (even in German, which I empathised with bits of Dutch and Yiddish), I sort of knew what to do when my formal education ended and when I was let loose on real congregations in 1958. I was regarded as odd, startling, and idiosyncratic, but 'class' – that was my Oxford accent. In a class-ridden country, it was the most precious gift I got from Balliol.

36

Go East, Young Man, Go East!

After I decided to become a rabbi in 1953, I began to dither. I had resumed relations with the Jewish community to reacquaint myself with my base, but the legal forms of spirituality and the plethora of committees I was invited to sit on already began to dry me up. Without my inner life, I felt spiritually starved. Part of the trouble was that I didn't know what was where in Judaism, in the vast collection of codices on codices and commentaries on commentaries. There were fewer miracles, thank God, than in Christianity, and Judaism was certainly the religion God had put me in, but I wanted something more open, wider and cosmic rather than communal. I had also read Isherwood's translation of the Gita, and I liked the way Vedanta included all my life experience and didn't say God was in this bit but not in the other bit, when life didn't feel like that at all. I knew in Judaism there were vast areas I knew nothing about, like its mysticism in the Cabbalist Zohar, but when I asked about it, I was told to concentrate on Hebrew irregular verbs and the cycle of festivals. When I was forty and clean-living and of good reputation and a pure scholar I might make an attempt, but not now. It was a case of jam yesterday and jam tomorrow but never jam today!

The papers and news at the time were full of the brain drain of British intellectuals to America. Everything was bigger and better there, especially opportunities and salaries. British establishments were frightened that we rabbinic students would all Go West.

But I didn't think such materialist thoughts. If I was going anywhere I was going East – not even to the Middle East and Israel but to the Far East where terms such as Jew and Gentile had little meaning. My motive was spiritual. While my elders had been worrying about brain drains I had become aware of a soul drain. The best and holiest of my generation were moving east, far east on pilgrimage. Like the wandering scholars of the Middle Ages, they were looking for a teacher at whose dusty feet they could sit, and an ashram where they could hole up, and a Himalayan cave which they could retire into. Public school boys and Beatles all felt the urge and so did I.

I nearly went, hesitated, nearly went again and then found they'd all gone without me. Never mind, I consoled myself, the East was coming to me. I could read Kerouac hitchhiking from Oxford to London, and I sat with groups of saffron-robed disciples on street corners. I wasn't prepared to sing out Hare Krishna Hare Krishna along Bond Street, but I was willing to gingerly hold the baby of a dreamy couple that had no such inhibitions. While holding the baby, curiously peaceful like its dreamy parents, not at all like bawling materialist suburban babies (was it doped too?), I tried to work out the attraction of the East.

Spiritually speaking, western religion was tired and really rather clapped out. The Romans, the RCs, were snooty about Anglicans and so authoritarian they reminded me of my childhood Marxists. Like the latter, they had the answer to every question but after the first hundred wrong answers I had my doubts. I didn't like the gold and glitter of their churches either. I wasn't interested in hierarchies and establishments and buildings. Judaism was also declining into a Country Club-ism, cosy ghettos but platinum-plated for an upwardly mobile middle class. If you wanted spirituality they stuck you on committees. I just wanted to get to another dimension fast because I couldn't sublimate sex enough in this one and was liable to explode, and because I was convinced of that dimension's existence from my own experience, but I didn't know how to break into it.

Even Leslie Shepard, my analyst, to my surprise caught the bug. He went far east too and ended up in an ashram, and he attained enlightenment through an exploding tooth abscess. He then told me that the greatest guru he had discovered was life itself. This thought lodged in me and became part of my thinking, subsequently confirmed by the BBC and by my own common sense. Life was my great guru and I could learn from my guru any place, any time, anywhere. The journey outside was just a metaphor of my journey to enlightenment inside. This made sense. In my Marxist days I had met so many people trying to get to Moscow, and what they had found there it was best not to think about. Enlightenment could be found in Balliol and Basingstoke as well as Benares – so was my journey far east really necessary? Not really, it was just another romanticism and I did not want to use holy things as escapisms – that was a real blasphemy. If I used them in that way I would never respect them. The realisation of this was another nugget of wisdom.

Leslie also pointed out a few other truths which I pondered and tried to absorb, though this took me some time. He pointed out how bored those babies would become on such a bare diet as chanting Hare Krishna over and over again, rather like repeating a word over and over again as a child, when the result was not enlightenment but reducing the word to nonsense. Even a miserable Sunday School lesson would be exotic compared to the economy of the HK diet.

I also asked how he liked being back in the comforts of England after sleeping rough on the pavements of Bombay. I then tried to sort out in my mind the distinction between comfort and happiness. It took me a long time to understand that comfort was things outside me and happiness a state of mind inside me. I had been brainwashed by adverts. There's a lady with the beatific smile on her face and her arm is resting on a fridge freezer. It is a materialist sermon. If you buy that make of freezer the beatific vision will come along with it as a freebie like trading stamps or points. It doesn't happen. Or a young man lies on a palm-fringed beach. The sun is shining, the sea is blue and a girl is lying at his feet. The moral isn't hard to work out. If you take a holiday like that the sun will shine for you and a girl will lie at your feet and you will both find true love, hey presto! It is all a confusion of internal and external worlds. Looking back on my own holiday experiences, I realised that I had been both happy and unhappy in grotty boarding houses and in five-star hotels. Yes, I would far prefer to be unhappy in a five-star hotel than in a boarding house, but that isn't the point, is it? Another very basic point to learn!

Unlike many of my teachers, my mother, who knew me better, took my far eastern hankerings seriously and my hankerings to set up as the local guru. So she now encouraged me fervently to continue my rabbinical studies which was by far the least worst option.

She even joined a synagogue and dropped in unannounced when I was giving one of my first trial sermons. Unfortunately for her it was about God visiting the sins of the parents upon the children to the third generation. She took umbrage and left hurriedly before I had time to notice her presence or absence. She couldn't read Hebrew, of course, but made up noises which sounded like it, and these convulsed or awed the whispering congregants around her.

On the other hand she had a natural goodness unfettered by dogma. She noticed other 'outsiders' in the synagogue who sat at the back or at the sides. One was a German woman who had never converted to Judaism but who left her own country with her husband in the Nazi time. She had no children and her Jewish husband had died. She was alone. It was Ma who put her arm round her and listened to all she had endured in her own homeland. Dad presented her with flowers from his garden. It took me some time to realise what kind people my parents were. Being dysfunctional wasn't their fault. Painfully, I was growing up. I could no longer say gravely, 'My parents didn't understand me, you know. They were bourgeois.' Perhaps they understood me only too well.

To my surprise I found that I wasn't the only one looking to the East. A fellow rabbinical student was also the disciple of a swami, and a traditional Jewish minister was contributing to a Vedanta journal. One of the greatest holy teachers in India itself, I was told, even the great Ram Das, had once studied for his Bar Mitzvah – confirmation in a synagogue or temple in success-hypnotised America.

The writings of Swami Vivekananda had a profound influence on my thinking. Even the gods were the creation of our imagination. Behind them and us and in them and us was a cosmic power, not a national or institutional one of which we were all manifestations. I saw that most religious disputes were the results of different paths to that undifferentiated core. Christianity looked at in this way was Bhakti Yoga – the way to that core through the path of love and the feelings. And Judaism was a western path of Karma Yoga, the way to self-realisation through the performance of duty and obligation and keeping the world going round. Most of the disputes in the synagogues I knew were about different paths of Yoga. I kept away however from Tantric Yoga, an approach to the divine using sexual energy. Prudently, I realised I wasn't up to that one yet.

I tried to worship and meditate in Vedanta style but found I needed mythology for practical purposes. Whosoever Whatsoever (Fred) was the fruit of my imagination in part but my soul, my better self, and my heavenly home were real. It was the closest I could get and the best I could do.

I asked a holy man where the universe was heading. 'To lift matter into spirit,' he said. It is better than most answers.

37

Debut in the Near, Near East

Instead of entering an ashram in the Far East, I journeyed to the very near Near East indeed by crossing the North Sea to Amsterdam a few years later in 1956. I had broken out spiritually and now I needed to break out sexually. If I tried to stay in a closet all my life I'd go pop. I was sorry to do it but I wrote a letter of resignation to Dr van der Zyl, which I found out later he sensibly didn't pass on. (I owe him yet another thanks.) I didn't want to disappoint him but needs must.

Actually it was a member (in good standing) of a proper and fashionable London synagogue who chanced to introduce me to the gay world of Amsterdam and I was enthralled. For the first time I would be free, and 'normal', not carrying on my back a crippling rucksack of inhibitions. It would be like being reborn. I promptly shed my Harris tweeds and M & S underwear together with my scholarship to the Leo Baeck College. I was at boiling-over point.

With great daring, I bought a pair of light blue jeans and a closely fitted shirt that opened all the way to my navel but which even when closed allowed tendrils of fur to curl out. (If you didn't have enough you could then even buy hairy chest pieces in both London and Amsterdam.) I was still 'young and gay' and going to make up for lost time. I would never say no again, or not for the next six months. I didn't realise I was the enemy of my own content!

The homo hotel I nervously signed in to was basic (bed, basin and breakfast) but not basic enough because it had a mirror, and the mirror reflected not only my fur but also my mortality. I watched in horror as my head hair fell off in a gentle shower of dandruff loosened by my comb. I panicked. I would soon be bald and who would want me then? That old 78 record of Bessie Smith turned round and round in my mind: 'No man can use you when you're down and out'. This was before baldness became fashionable and I felt like crying. By the time I was thirty, only God would want me and I had said goodbye to him in Harwich as I took the ferry across the North Sea. (Perhaps three years of hairy success would be enough, but it wasn't enough for me and wouldn't have been for most of you either.) I wanted love and passion: 'You've got moonlight in your hair, babe, and starlight in your eyes' – I was a child of fleapit cinemas.

I pulled myself together. Like Mimi in *Bohème* and Violetta in *Traviata* I would be gay on borrowed time and then a bullet. My first feeble silly thought of suicide would be a practice run for the real thing. It never occurred to me that I knew nothing about what love meant.

Actually my future was not so dramatic or melodramatic as all that. Returning to London on a short visit, I was recommended to an austere specialist in hair who asked me why I was so concerned. I hummed and hawed but decided that honesty was the best policy (it wasn't) and that I would tell him I was a hairless homo just about to join the gay action.

He didn't seem to like this one bit but his lips smiled thinly. The female hormones he prescribed for me, he said, would very possibly nudge my hair away from falling out entirely (it did) but 'ha ha there would be two drawbacks'.

Sweetly he told me that as long as I took my ha ha hormones, they would neutralise all my sexual desires – ha ha! He admitted under pressure I need only take this vulgar-sounding drug (Stilbesterol) for a few weeks. You will know yourself when you have to stop it – ha ha – he repeated. When your breasts begin to rise, he thought, ha ha! I should desist. I went white and answered him pronto that when they did, I would desist very pronto, no ha ha about it. The effects of the hormones would disappear as soon as I stopped them, which was a relief.

He had a wicked satisfied look on his face as I gave him his cheque, and he courteously showed me the door. I did take the hormones and discontinued them pronto at the appropriate time.

But I must return to the mirror. The point I am making is that I was a heavy, humourless youngster who was a worrying oldie long before I became young. Only as I became older in years did

I become fresh and free and frolicsome and fit for petting, let alone loving.

And another surprise. Religion, which I thought I would discard because it made me too wise and woeful, has done nothing of the sort. I have remarked how light and soufflé-ish I felt tripping away from the Quaker meeting. As I trusted more and clutched Whomsoever Whatsoever even closer, I became gayer and more amused by life. Once I knew there was a God, you see, I no longer felt I had to be his stand-in. I'd do my bit but he'd have to solve the problems of his own world. He had the master plan. I didn't! To my annoyance, I felt I amused him.

It took me decades to learn the divine lessons of love – how to pleasure two of us and not just one, to sleep, really sleep, after sex with my partner and not to flee over the far horizon, not to regard the whole exercise as an exam or as part of the numbers game, but to laugh at a climax and be amused by the physical tangles two bodies could tie themselves into. I enjoyed sharing slices of Black Forest gateau with my bed partner (in bed, where else?), or giggle sympathetically when an erection inconveniently collapsed (it's not concrete), etc., etc., etc. Humour had helped me to have fun, a rare word for religious people, and religion had guided me to humour. It was an astonishing, unexpected blessing and I was grateful.

I was so grateful for the divine humour and the realisation that I was a joke too that I started to tell jokes to ease other people's path through life. Pious people were surprised at them as I told them. When they thought they knew all the answers, a subversive joke could unobtrusively remove the platform they didn't realise they were standing on and, if they didn't resist it, they had a moment of enlightenment, a Zen experience in traditions where no Zen should lurk.

38

Dutch Courage

'Who is wise?'
'One who learns from all.'
(The Talmud)

We learn from both the official and unofficial colleges in our lives. In the former I learnt Aramaic verbs, Anglo-Saxon charters, the Wars of the Roses and which rose was which, how to pass exams and 'get on'. In the latter I learnt life studies. The most important of my official colleges were Balliol in Oxford and the Leo Baeck in London; the most important of my unofficial ones, a back street in London's East End, our Blitz shelter, contemplative monasteries and a Dutch 'mature men only' sauna in a backstreet in Holland. It is the last that I shall tell you about now. I 'studied' there intermittently from 1957 onwards, often during vacations (in which I spent the daytime studying at the great Jewish Library, the Rosenthaliana at the University of Amsterdam).

I first saw its advert in a sauna listing in a newspaper in the early fifties just after I got my degree from Oxford and I hadn't started at the Leo Baeck College. I rang up and a pleasant lady's voice assured me it was only for men. She wanted to say more and I wanted to ask more but bad English on her part and English inhibitions on my part prevented us from going any further. But some years later after I thought I had resigned from rabbinical training, I met a gay guy in a bar who again mentioned the sauna.

It wouldn't interest me, he said, because I was too young and it served the needs of mature Dutch men. 'Even pastors, priests and dominies,' he added too innocently. He looked at me meaningfully and giggled.

This time I made it. I was trembling as I took a clanging tram, for something in me was singing a spontaneous psalm of my own composition – 'A Song of Ascents' like David in the Bible. As he danced naked before the ark and preferred handsome Jonathan's love to the love of women, he might have felt at home there too. I stumbled over it in a side street, though only a plain sign and a discreetly curtained window indicated its presence. Hesitantly I entered and was about to rush out when suddenly I recognised from the next room the same pleasant voice I had heard on the telephone a few years before.

She was an older middle-aged woman in a spotless pinny with a comfortable bosom and her gold hair was turning silver. She soothed me, called me 'Mijnheer' politely, checked my passport to make sure I was over twenty-one, and chatted with me, putting me at my ease, clucking over me, telling me in motherly fashion always to be careful with my money and valuables and to leave them in a little bag she would keep for me in her cupboard. She also kept one shoe so that I couldn't leave without paying, either. This set off my paranoia again and made me want to rush out once more, but I was already half naked and wearing only one shoe and she was just being pragmatic in the Dutch manner. After I undressed, she issued me with a little bar of soap, and a towel that wouldn't quite meet around my middle, told me that tea would be served in an hour's time, led me to the door to the sauna and gently pushed me through. When my session was over, she said, I could come to her and tell her all about it. Her English clients liked that, she said, and I didn't wonder. At home we couldn't talk about IT to anybody without risking blackmail or prosecution.

It was heaven – at first. I was at last among men like me who were politely doing what men like me needed to do. Being young (comparatively), I had scarcity value here and another piece of self-knowledge fell into place. I preferred mature men to young ones. Another piece was that I didn't enjoy sex without a relationship or romance, whether the relationship was real or fantasy. I wanted my sex life cocooned in bits of Mills and Boon. No, I underrate myself. I wanted affection and trust as well, in a gay version of a Jewish home just like that of my grandparents. It was a tall order at that time when so much had to be hidden in a closet.

I wasn't for example getting as much pleasure out of the sexual rugger in the steam room as the others did. Once again I felt an outsider. An exasperated outsider too! Here I had everything I had ever wanted, but I didn't enjoy it. I then remembered Abelard's definition of heaven in the Middle Age. 'Heaven is where you get what you've always wanted and when you've got it, it will be as lovely as when you still wanted it.' I later learnt that this impediment to gay bliss also applied to straight bliss too. This knowledge stood me in good stead years later when I administered an ecclesiastical divorce court for my small section of the Jewish world.

My dissatisfaction came to a head when I cried out in desperation to old Whomsoever Whatsoever, never believing that he had crossed the North Sea with me. His answer astonished me by its sharpness and clarity. 'You don't get much, Lionel, because you don't give much.' That said it all. It wasn't a block in my penis but in my soul. As I mulled this over in the steam, I also realised that in sexual matters, I was crippled by fear. Though of what I didn't know. Even after analysis I was overpowered by anxiety. I thought I had left the days behind when I was sure I had caught a dreadful disease or fertilised a girl from a lavatory seat. Obviously not!

I learnt a lot about psyches and souls in the sauna, my own and others. I was not being fanciful when I said this was also my college. Heaven and hell were laid out in front of me. These were some of the lessons I learnt.

The most important lesson was that God has no prejudices. He speaks in a sauna as well as in a chapel and his advice gets to the heart of the matter.

I experienced hell there. An embittered ugly old man, annoyed that I had declined his rough advances, whispered it around that I had got a terrible illness and the others should keep clear of me. Nasty but for a while an effective spoiler.

I met heaven too. A handsome young Frenchman pleasured the oldest and most decrepit clients there. 'Are you attracted to such people?' I asked. 'Not particularly,' he replied. 'I feel I must do that for them.'

I was forced to face my own cowardice. Mevrouw, Madame, I'll call her Tina, told me that a young Jewish chap was in trouble. His parents were trying to force him into marriage. Would I meet him and them and advise them. I declined. I was frightened of mixing my two worlds. Old WW (Whomsoever Whatsoever) was not very pleased and we didn't speak for a while. I reminded him rather pointedly, as the rabbis in the Talmud had done centuries before, that I had to survive in his creation. He didn't! 'I wonder who dealt me such a peculiar hand?' I asked nastily. He shut up. It was one of the few times I scored.

I was forced to face my cowardice again when a 'romantic' situation did happen. I paired off with a nice chap who one night in his flat told me he was suffering from an incurable illness. I couldn't catch it, he said, and his doctor said so too. But I wasn't so sure. To get out of a difficult situation, I issued blank cheques of affection I knew I couldn't cash, promises of love I couldn't live up to. I wasn't ready to be anyone's saviour. I still didn't know what love meant. I would do less damage if I recognised my selfishness and limitations. 'About time too!' said WW.

In the sauna I learnt the ten commandments of gay life. Here are some of them. Keep your word! If you've made an appointment, then turn up, even if you've met someone nicer in between. If you've got to say 'no', then say it nicely, especially if the person you're saying 'no' to is older then you. Thinking back to those early sauna years, I learnt more than ten commandments – more like twenty. Learning to keep them was my problem. As usual I had gone ahead of myself.

If the sauna was my college, then Tina was my teacher. She was a kind woman and also a practical one, who had survived the occupation with a Jewish husband. Through cowardice I let her down too but that comes later in my story.

The side effect of all this sauna visiting was that I rejected my body much less. I was no Apollo but I wouldn't have kicked myself out of bed either. I was now less smelly and much cleaner. I even got interested in men's toiletries and have given myself a scrub daily ever since. My Dutch friends publicly congratulated me and presented me with little bottles of gel and aftershave. My English friends never of course referred to my new cleansed state. That's the difference between England and Holland.

39

Old Smokey Follows Me into the Sauna

A ghost but a holy one. I never expected him to stay around after I made my debut in bars and saunas but he didn't dwindle or fade away on me. I began to realise that he wasn't just sexual sublimation and he was going to have a more permanent place in my life than I expected. I found out that I needed Old Smokey more in those places than in respectable ones, because very little has been written about how you keep your soul while cruising in a bar or how you finish a one-night stand with kindness and satisfying memories for both of you, and Old Smokey always responds to need. When I ask him or invoke him or just say, 'Help!' he's there somewhere around me, though I might not locate him for a while. Like most spiritual people (whether religious or not), I needed him when I felt unsupported and out of my depth and he was the only one I could cling to. I was more out of my depth than ever after I discarded bars and saunas and tried instead to set up a traditional-style Jewish homo home, because there was no social support or pattern for such domesticities. Religion didn't help. It preferred to undermine them, not make a place for them.

That was the strength of my spirituality, my need for him. At first I thought of him as my lover but after I had enough of the solid variety, he became my true friend. God was 'the friend of Abraham', Old Smokey was mine.

Now you may ask, 'Does he exist?' Well, I've asked myself that question too. Now some people come to him through their reason or through tradition – I came to him through my need, as I've said, and my imagination. 'Yes, you heard! My imagination! And don't be an intellectual snob.' You need a lot of imagination to speak to someone who isn't there, and imagination is the basis of all art, a lot of science too, and wherever we try to get into a dimension beyond our senses.

I don't think you can speak of the Beyond Life except imaginatively or mythically. Mythically doesn't mean unrealistically. If it did mean that, I wouldn't have bothered with my see-through friend in high places. I'd have ditched him long ago.

Here's how we, Old Smokey and I, come together. It's early evening and I'm walking back home, my mind infiltrated with bits of anger, worry and discontent. I rehearse conversations that should have gone like so, but didn't, because I was too cowardly to say what I wanted, and there's a lot of self-hatred in me too. And suddenly it's 'as if' he puts his 'as if' arm around me and tells me to give him all my inner garbage, make him a present of it. That's what he wants, he says. He's as bored as me by all those prayers going on and on and on like 'Old Smokey, you're great, you're wise, you're wonderful, you're the tops, you're transparent, you're super-duper divine etc. and usw/etc.' Wouldn't you be bored listening to that parrot prayer three times a day if you're Jewish and even more in other religions?

But what I like about him is that he's very practical. Under his guidance I make a mental ball of all my inner garbage and hurl it up to heaven and say, 'Catch!' And he or somebody must catch it because I don't worry about it much any more that evening. I sit in a pub instead and wonder what can I do for him. One good turn deserves another. I used to puzzle over what that good turn could be. I didn't need to. All I had to do was wait and something would come along. My problem was in spotting the passing opportunity. It often seemed too small to bother about. But I gradually discovered size wasn't that important to him.

He helped me in other ways too. I'm not good with blood. The sight of it makes me feel nauseous, which I suppose is why I ended up training to be a rabbi not a doctor. Souls are bloodless. But what we avoid has a nasty habit of stealing up on us, so I ended up visiting the sick in hospitals where I had to see a lot of blood.

When I did one of my visits and smelt that hospital smell even at Reception, I just used to invoke Old Smokey and say, 'Help!' and he came. I got enough strength from him to do what I had to do and only after I left the hospital did the nausea return. Then I treated myself to a custard pie and strong cappuccino. That problem incidentally cured itself in the end. I even enjoyed watching the blood flow into me and then out of me when tied to a drip. But I don't know if he was responsible for that.

He also helped me think of people's real needs, not the needs I foisted on them. At a dinner party when one chap wouldn't make conversational chit-chat but burst into tears over my famous treacle tart, I swallowed my anger and resentment because that's what Smokey would have wanted of me. I gave the chap a comfortable chair in the corner of the room and put a table beside him with toothsome canapés and beer and left him to it, visiting him occasionally to cosset him and check up that he still wanted space and to be on his own.

I also invoked my Smokey Ghost not just at dinner parties but at formal committee meetings. I was Chair while waves of distorting ego and ambition slurped through our proceedings. My ego and ambition were about to join the fray and indulge when I resorted to this device. I asked him to sit in a chair – not my Chair, not on my lap! – at the other end of the room, and when my own passions were getting out of control, I looked at his chair and got my balance back again. That kept me out of political games that are so tempting for religious people. God is difficult – or they think he is – and the games serve as a substitute.

But here's a tip if you are a bit neurotic and meeting up with a holy ghost. Don't get your ghost mixed up with your compulsive behaviour patterns. No hammer of God fell on me as I munched a sausage (don't ask!), and in a wobbly way I felt Old Smokey was proud of me when I didn't go out of my way compulsively to pray in some distant chapel. The public bench in the main road served just as well. God is there whenever a human heart welcomes him in. All the best traditional authorities say so.

40

Courage to Cross a Frontier

My flight to Amsterdam, lovewise, had been a puzzling failure. I had learnt a lot about other people and even a bit about myself – my soul as well as my body, which was unexpected. But I still didn't know how to find love or how to give it. So one morning I decided to travel on because the cosy world of Holland was giving me claustrophobia and I was being drawn into the sex numbers game, which was as pointless in its own way as repetitive piety and prayers, though more banal.

On impulse one morning I went to the Central Station, bought a ticket and crossed the frontier into Germany for a muddle of motives just as I had done ten years before. I was curious. Two of my 'lovers' were pursuing me. I wanted to learn about Germany to know myself and I had learnt from experience that I had to make a physical journey outside of me to make a spiritual journey inside of me. It's only when you're out of your depth and can't keep your balance that His hand becomes real enough to support you, so that you begin to believe.

I had twice before tried to cross that awful frontier, but each time had turned back at the border. Even this time when I did cross I wondered what human cargo had travelled on these rails to the camps and murder and nearly turned back once again. Why was I able to carry on now when I hadn't been able to before? Because of a confusion of motives which I shall set down in a confused way. The Holy Spirit isn't choosy about what material it works through.

In the few years since knowing Leslie, Germany had came to me from many directions. From Irene and Harry, whom Leslie had introduced me to, I had discovered the Weimar Germany of the twenties and early thirties. Its caustic writers had sliced through the smugness of my English suburbia. I sang the 'Dreigroschenoper' of Brecht and Weil in the early fifties before the raw violence of 'Mac the Knife' become high fashion. These lines from it gave me some hope in the clumsy encounters that were all that was available to me: Irena and I sang them together in Hampstead: 'Don't stare at the dirty plate on which love is served but throw it away for love lasts here just as well as anywhere.'

Germany also came to me from my new teachers I had just got acquainted with before my flight to Amsterdam – the German rabbis and scholars at the Leo Baeck College, from their formidable scholarship, their mixture of high Kultur (e.g. Kant and Kafka) married to my granny's wayward Cabbalistic piety. I was awed by the dignity of their lives. Their lives were all they had left. Their libraries, their eminence, their language were lost in their emigration. One, I think, a great man in his own country (Germany) couldn't carry on – though this was hushed up. Jews didn't do this sort of thing – but some did!

By them I was introduced to Buber and Rosenzweig and – surprise! – Franz Kafka. They weren't sure what to make of me. I was too disordered, too East European, not Jewish enough but far too Yiddish, not German but English eccentric, which they couldn't file away in orderly fashion, which either amused them or shocked and bewildered them.

Germany also came to me from young students I had met at Oxford and in London. They had problems with the older generation – but then so had I. They began to teach me the complexity of Germany and its history. It was another world, with a dynamic so different from that of England and the France I had hitchhiked through years earlier. I am still ignorant of its moods and violence. Like many Englishmen I know no Goethe, I have never read Schiller or Lessing and I only knew Hegel because Marx had philosophically turned him upside-down!

It was not only Aryan youngsters who initiated me into the strangeness of the Fatherland but Jewish ones too. I realised that our Zionist youth movements were not *sui generis* as I had believed in my first ecstasy. They were not only the beginning of something never before attempted, they were also the last flicker of the *Wandervogel.* Our shorts, open-necked Aertex shirts, pooled pocket money, back to nature, and judgement on our bourgeois parents were the signs I couldn't miss.

I was astonished as I realised that I had made more good friends from Germany than from any country, except Holland.

Germany came to me in another way through its revolutionaries, its renegades and reformers – wonderful people! There was Dr Magnus Hirschfeld (1863–1935), an MP in the German parliament, who dared to speak up openly for gays and lesbians when rabbis and other clergy didn't want to know. When I saw *Madchen in Uniform* at the cinema and the repression it pictured, I began to realise his courage and was abashed. 'Tante Magnolia', as he was known, was a great guy. It's a pity that religious leaders only jumped on the bandwagon after the battle for sexual minority rights was almost won by the Quakers and a few enlightened politicians.

But there were non-Jews too who threw in their lot with the poor, the gays and the excluded. They were few in number but they redeemed Germany. There was of course Friedrich Engels, an upper-middle-class scholar and businessman, who threw in his lot with Karl Marx, and conducted his businesses to confirm and illustrate the teachings of his friend, associate, comrade and more flamboyant teacher.

I have a devotion to an odd pair, who could never have known each other, and would never have understood each other, coming as they did from the opposite poles of belief. But they are united in my mind by the integrity of their beliefs, and their pure practical expression of them.

The first in time and sympathy is the anarchist Rudolph Rocker (1873–1958), of solid Aryan bourgeois stock who went to New York and stood up for the poor Jewish garment workers there, helping them to unionise against brutal bosses, insanitary working conditions, sweat shops and labouring for peanuts. He identified himself so strongly with them that he taught himself their Yiddish and became a fluent speaker and 'rabble rouser' in it.

After I returned to the Leo Baeck College, I attended a memorial meeting for him in the late fifties in a Soho cellar frequented by anarchists, and I was reluctantly allowed to honour him by saying quietly – even if only to myself – the Kaddish, the traditional Jewish memorial prayer, in his memory. The idealist anarchists were no friends of established religion or any religion and, being a member of that establishment, I understood their opposition very well.

The second object of my devotion was an established member of the Catholic Church, very reliable and very pious. Franz Jaegerstaedter was a quiet, conservative civil servant who refused to send in his Nazi German call-up papers because it was obvious to him that Germany's war was not defensive and therefore he could take no part in it. His wife, his bishop begged him to compromise – they would find him a non-combatant posting. He considered but regretfully decided he would not accept this cosy compact with the devil. He was 'officially' murdered by the state.

His crime was that he had seen the obvious. It is strange that the official State Lutheran Church didn't see it, nor Pius XII, nor Opus Dei, nor some 'saints', whom Pope John Paul has canonised. Perhaps they did, but didn't like it or found it inconvenient to speak out or just couldn't cope. Jews who have been refugees don't see Palestinian refugees either.

Anyway, one of the most straightforward 'saints' against evil in our time has been passed over in favour of some semi-collaborators. It's one way of throwing the entire class of 'saints' into disrepute.

I also got to know Germany in another way. A Hamburg artist picked me up in Amsterdam harbour. He thought I was 'rough trade' and was amused to find he had caught a student rabbi instead. We were curious about each other, and liked each other, though the loving was indifferent. Through him I met other men in bars in Bremen and Hamburg. Some told me their life stories in the bar and some in bed. They were still chilled by what might have been done to them in concentration camps – pink badges attracted more sadism than Jewish yellow ones.

Those encounters forced me to reflect on myself in a fund-amental way and not just on myself but all rabbis, my future colleagues and present teachers. While listening to their instruc-tion, I couldn't help wondering what would they have done if the Nazis had left Jews alone and only shot gypsies, beheaded homos, and tortured socialists and liberals? Would they have passed by on the other side, or rushed to the rescue? Would they have distanced themselves from such human 'rubbish' or remembered that religion means more than respectability? Who knows?

But even that question is too easy. The hard one is what would I have done if I'd been a German rabbi at that time? Would I have been a hero, a conformist, a mild Nazi even?

I don't know.

41

Why the Holocaust?

The black hole of the Holocaust wouldn't disappear. It pulled me towards Germany just as Germans were pulled towards me. It bonded us together, though it wasn't easy to puzzle out our roles. This I had not expected.

In Germany I was bewildered by the power I exercised. Though I had lost no one from my immediate family, only distant cousins, I could forgive crimes I had never experienced at first hand, never even heard about or known.

A German chap in Amsterdam, older than me, had ended up in my arms. We held each other and contentedly smoked in the darkening room. He asked me what I did and I told him I was a rabbinical student on the run. (A familiar question and a familiar answer!) He didn't tell me what he was but what he had been, a Nazi soldier on the Eastern Front. He started to tell me what that meant but he couldn't bear it and neither could I. He held me tightly, tossing and turning as the tears trickled down.

In Germany another man asked me to intervene with his daughter. He had delayed joining the Party till the last moment and got reprimanded and warned for trying to put out the flames of a burning synagogue on Crystal Night when they were all torched. The Nazi regime seemed impregnable, so to save his family and himself (in that order) he had joined it. Did his daughter, he asked bitterly, not understand what life was like in those times? I got to know her and she said she would think about it.

An old man in an old age home told me he would never vote again. He had voted the wrong way once and look what had happened! Voting and democracy were not meant for gullible people like him.

There were many other people like him. I began to realise that in the years after the war, in the fifties and sixties, I was standing on an enormous pulpit formed from the six million dead Jews. That was why much later, when I was a European Director of the World Union for Progressive Judaism and a rabbi, I was invited to lunch with the German President. I felt inadequate but so would anybody else perched on such a strange eminence.

Hitchhiking around the country, I felt the human tragedy and grotesque comedy. Being British, fortunately a bit of me could keep my balance.

Some drivers who gave me lifts lectured me almost hysterically about the DDR, insisting it was Central Germany not East Germany. They were still entrapped by that nationalist dream that wouldn't stop. I had lockjaw. I could say nothing until they had gone, waving back at me on an approach road to another Autobahn.

As to my love life in the Fatherland, like Amsterdam nothing quite went right. One chap who fell for me was married, a complication I couldn't cope with. I was coming out of one closet and I wasn't going back into another one. A pity because I liked him a lot too, being slender, sweet and ten years older than me.

My real success was with one German woman. We became the closest of friends. It was like love. I shall call her Rita. I met her in a working-class sailors' cafe and bar in a north German port. She was the only elegant woman there and I asked her to dance. We danced as lovingly and physically as I had ever experienced and at first I didn't hear the catcalls directed at us. Rita was a woman who had been born into a man's body, and after work this downmarket cafe was the only one that would accept her as a woman. By day she worked in her wealthy family business as a man.

She became my girlfriend and I took her formally and she took me financially to the opera, to ballrooms, to chic restaurants. Men looked at her because she was so elegant, so Paris. I was the lucky guy who had got her. We acted sex but we never had any, just affection. But all the sadness came out as we parted and I returned to Amsterdam and then in 1957 to northern England – out of bohemia and back into suburban reality.

And she?

She never went for her operation in Copenhagen as she

planned. She had had enough and committed suicide instead. This I learnt later, but I guessed something had gone wrong because her scrawled postcards had stopped. She was German but a more hurt human being than me. I felt for her deeply.

Some women like her in desperation go to lesbian pubs. Some of the lesbians are kind but some can only be ideological. One of them told me she must have been a secret spy from the men's world – paranoia in spades!

42

Another Might-Have-Been

It was like repeating the journeys of my adolescent years. Holland, then Germany, then Holland again and then back to England. And again I hadn't found what I was looking for. So the train journey from Germany to Amsterdam Central Station was a sombre one. The remains of the Holocaust had not yet been buried under the new affluence of the *Wirtschaftswunde*. I had liked Germany, so what had gone so dreadfully wrong there less than twenty years ago and why?

Mentally I listed all the reasons for the Holocaust that I had heard. I knew the Marxist reason, of course. I knew a mystical reason too – why for some crazed mystics it was 'the birth pangs of the Messiah' and they danced into the camps and gas chambers. Some believed that God had taken away our six million dead but the rebirth of Israel was his glorious compensation prize. One rabbi told me he had only really believed again when he saw the first Israeli army marching into Jerusalem. But an intelligent modern professor had also assured me that the Holocaust was the punishment for our apostasy and running after the ways of the Gentiles. It had been proved to him. On a Saturday in Berlin he had seen all the Jewish shops pillaged except those that had been locked up for the Sabbath. He had had a vision of the angel of death passing over the ones that had kept God's law. I didn't think much of any of these reasons either. To a few liberal rabbis, it had happened because we had not understood the non-Jews we lived among well enough. We had not brought enough blessing to the peoples around us. But I thought we had and more.

For me, the Holocaust was the release of the irrational into political life which had been going on steadily since the

160

Enlightenment and has not finished yet. The diabolisation of the Jews was not a Jewish problem at all. We were merely the victims of it. I swallowed a glass of schnapps on the train and shivered.

My private life seemed pretty hopeless too, and as we passed over the Dutch frontier again, I realised how close I had come to being sucked into the numbers game once more. It was becoming a form of obsession, for 'love' can be an addiction as much as booze or cigarettes. You pass from one person or body to another because you can't cope with real intimacy. I was also becoming hard – not in my penis, where it is normal, but in my soul, where it is not. Soon I would only know sex and no longer know love. I prayed to God in the train. 'Why didn't I meet Mr Right?' I asked. 'I only wanted someone to love who would love me and together we would build a homo home close to the Jewish ideal.'

I was silent and let my thoughts wander. As usual my prayer and question boomeranged back on me. Perhaps I didn't know what love meant, what it involved. Perhaps an affair was as much as I could handle. Perhaps I couldn't see the reality of life, only the cinema fantasy of it – another shadow moving across the screen of my mind. Perhaps I had been left so solipsist by my years of withdrawal that I couldn't really see another person at all, only my own reflection, only what I intended to make out of that other person. No wonder my lovers didn't stay long. The price of a climax was taking on the burden of my life. Who wanted that? The price was too high to be worth it. Then another thought and one which floored me. Perhaps I had bumped into many 'Mr Rights', perhaps the Almighty had put them in my path. Perhaps they had been staring me in the face but I hadn't seen them because I was so self-centred I could still only see myself and my needs. Perhaps I was just a piece of sounding brass, a tinkling cymbal.

My self-questioning went deeper than I can indicate on these pages and I arrived in Amsterdam in the late evening, shaken to the core. I didn't ring up friends to put me up with a place on the floor because I was too muddled and unfit for society. Instead I pushed my way through the crowds surrounding the station to a hotel where I had once stayed, which would accept anybody not a nuisance – straights and bents, s/ms and t/vs, all anonymous, all welcome, if you didn't wake up the others and behaved in moderation. There was a friendly manageress there too, who would listen like Tina if that's what you wanted. She knitted behind a little bar that had a cuckoo clock.

But she was away and the deskman said they were decorating and the place was full. No room at the inn. It had happened before. While I was pondering whether to cut my losses, make my way back to the station and find out if there was a night train to London, a voice interrupted my bleak thoughts, an English voice, and a northern one. 'He can share mine,' it said. 'Then I don't have to pay double for a grotty old attic.' The manager confirmed this was so and I confirmed I would pay my half with a bit more for double usage.

The voice was that of a big man, a hard man and an ugly one, and I shall call him Eric. But after seeing me strain with my cases up the lethal Dutch stairs he was decent enough to swing up the biggest one like a toy. A little kindness and heaven can happen. A little of it happened for me in the form of gratitude and I began to make contact with a real person in a real world. I was curious about him. Not many people knew about my refuge.

We marched up steps and through long attic corridors. Then he threw open a door and I realised why they were decorating. It could not have changed since the Germans marched out and the Allies marched in. And then he swooped on me and groped me and it hurt. Perhaps he didn't know his own strength but I think he did. I headbutted him and wondered what else could happen on this terrible day.

He sulked but I brought out my bottle of schnapps and some sandwiches and we ate silently together. I eyed the bed. It would be difficult. There was only one, big but with a sagging mattress. If you let go of your edge you would slide into a clinch with your bed partner whether you wanted to or not. I need not have worried. When I climbed in, he was clutching his side ferociously, dressed in the thickest flannel pyjamas ever. He had even screwed up his eyes so as not to see me starkers and I didn't dare laugh because I didn't have the strength to take on Tarzan again. I courteously wished him a good night's sleep but there was no answer, not even a shake from the tufts of his hair above the sheet. Silently I prayed 'Help!' and then added 'Tarzan too!' and fell asleep exhausted.

When I woke up breakfast time had gone and so had he, but he had left me a cup of coffee by my side of the bed and a jam buttie which was nice of him. Before I left on my way to the great Hebrew library of the Rosenthaliana, I left a note for him telling him the rough places in the city he might like and how to get to them. He was obviously a fish out of water in this busy, busy place – I could tell that by his ironclad pyjamas. I'd never met another gay there who wore such garments. They suited the style of our undecorated attic.

During the day I saw him occasionally from afar, drinking at a bar alone and a long way from the places I'd mentioned. His loneliness and singularity touched me. Packing up at the library in the late afternoon, I saw him again. 'I know a cheap Indonesian restaurant,' I said. If he wanted to, he could come along. I also told him that after that I was going to an organ concert in the Oude Kerk. I didn't think he'd want that one. He gave me a withering look.

He did come along to the concert and we sat side by side among the darkening pillars as the glory of Sweelinck and Dutch baroque boomed around us. (I later found out that at his orphanage he had been forced to listen to organ music at the compulsory services. He had not taken against the instrument.) While the organ was playing, he put his open hand beside me and I put mine in his – two sex waifs, strangers in the night before Frankie Sinatra, two people seeking an antidote to the solitude of a big city. On the way back to our hotel, I kissed him in the lamplight, which was daringly public then, even for Amsterdam. Before he went to sleep, I risked another assault and kissed him decorously again. He was still in ironclads but didn't resist. I then scuttled back to my own edge and fell asleep.

The next morning I missed breakfast again and he was no longer there. But he had left a mug of coffee beside me and a cheese sandwich. I packed up, for I was leaving for London. I telephoned London and they confirmed that my rabbi had never sent my resignation to the college and had booked me in for services in the north of England. I had caused him much merriment, he said. This was kind and I vowed never to let him down.

Again I left in the attic a list of places Tarzan might like. I was just about to add my London address and number when I remembered the advice of a good friend who warned me against being so open with people I didn't know, me being a minister and all that, and London not being free like Amsterdam. So I was a coward and anxious and didn't, and never heard from him again.

God had given me my chance but Mr Right didn't look right in my fantasy and I had in any case been too cowardly to follow it up.

Many years later, lying in a hospital ward during the dead hours, when it was anti-social to disturb the snores all around me by putting on a light or a radio, I started thinking morbidly about the might-have-beens of my life. He was one. What would have happened if I had given him my telephone number? More than I bargained for, I think, because I was just beginning to feel for him when I left. Perhaps it was better so. He could have hurt me physically but I could have hurt him more deeply because I was still pretty neurotic. Perhaps I should write a novel about it, that was safe, and I could put in all the body bits too and bring together the many faces of love. But that is something *autre chose, n'est-ce pas?*

43

Pick up!

I came back to England from Amsterdam, and took sedate services in the provinces which my rabbi had arranged for me. I was complimented on my sermons for their maturity. I then returned to London to complete my studies at the Leo Baeck College. There I tried to set up as normal a life as I could. Though my rabbi was understanding, the police were not, and unlike Holland all gay relationships were still surrounded by fear of blackmail, prosecution and precautions which wrecked any real contact, like never risking your right name or address. But I had to risk it because I wanted to find a partner and set up and settle down in a real home and live a Darby and Darby life together till death did us part.

I met JB wandering dejected in theatreland. I was wandering around aimlessly too. He was returning home to Canada from Scotland, a defeated PhD student, just out of hospital with a breakdown and with his high hopes brought low. A year over here and he had withdrawn inwards, making no real contact with students or professors. I had known such a withdrawal and I warmed to him. He was a fair handsome man with a cold look, which I was sure I could warm into love. I took him to my parents' home in the early hours. He was a neat person, and later on he told me he had nearly walked out on me when he saw the confusion of my bedroom.

I promptly set the pace to implement my dream. I could develop enormous horsepower. I bought a small terraced house cheap because the front wall was falling down, and proceeded to fabricate heaven on earth as I had imagined it. He would have nothing to do with buying the house, but then he became more attached to the house than to me. I never knew whether I loved him or only a romance in my mind in which he was a character. I certainly suffered for love of him. This was my condition when I was met outside the British Museum one day by my astonished conventional kind-hearted colleague Dow, just as I was sobbing my heart out after a row.

We had been together for over three years when I escaped from him. I gave him the house (mortgaged), and I got back my self-esteem.

What went wrong?

Many, so many things. Sexually we did not fit. Both of us were 'active' types, but I played the 'passive' role and he walked out on me when I wanted to try reciprocity. Just before I escaped, he offered it and said he would like to try with me again. I think this was just a delaying tactic. In any case, it was too late, I was already on my way out.

He met people and went to parties and to meetings which lasted all night. I half knew and then knew he had many loves, mainly male, probably some female. One of the male loves was so deep he nearly left me. It was a pity he didn't, because when he didn't I had decided to leave him. I found other partners too but I was too guilt-ridden to enjoy, being basically a monogamous type. I really never knew him very well. He could be a closed person. I was frightened of him. There had to be a release of aggression before we came together and we easily became competitive and locked horns. For me, homosexual relationships were not wrong but more difficult, or with a set of difficulties different from the hetero sort. They were a more difficult fit, physically, psychologically and socially, though the results of both the homo and the hetero kind were in the end the same – commitment, fidelity, companionship and trust.

JB gave me many things. He taught me to look after myself, and how to dress myself. He taught me order and rational living, how to make my first cake (pineapple upside-down), how to soften bath water, the conventions of bridge – which I didn't use, preferring psychics and often winning, which exasperated him – about launderettes and how to clean lavatories, about all the bread and butter things my odd family had forgotten to show me. (They were only concerned with school marks – except my father who had more sense but I had rejected him.)

On another level he introduced me to Richard Strauss and

tried to teach me Wagner and Mahler. But all this 'Spaetromantik' seemed 'schmaltz' to me, like the mummy and daddy of film music. (I had just returned from Holland and the paeans of Sweelinck and Buxtehude on baroque organs.) I snored during *Tristan and Isolde* at Covent Garden after an exhausting day and he was white-faced with anger and shock.

We fought meanly on many occasions. It certainly wasn't easy explaining a black eye to my curious congregation.

He could be very tender after a row – we both could. A release of aggression was necessary to release his tenderness. When it was released it was wonderful, even though being incompatible physically. I sometimes thought of Amsterdam and other people while he was in full passion.

He had not intended to have a real relationship with a homo lover and a house, but my driving fantasy was stronger than his breakdown. And there were moments, and sometimes hours, and one or two days, when it all seemed worth it. Looking back on it, I think I repeated the dysfunctional parts of my parents' marriage.

I was of course impossible for a person like him. I was chaotic within and without as I have said, very demanding though I didn't realise how much, and replaying all the inner fears and dramas of my evacuation years. Would he leave me? Wouldn't he? Would he? It was I of course who left him. I was terrified my – our – his house would fall down. But the house was me. Was I falling back into a black hole?

I do not have anything for JB to forgive me for nor he for me. We didn't fit. Too much worked against us. Good 'well-intentioned' friends invited us round for dinner (I refused to go alone unless it was work), sitting me next to nubile vivacious Jewish marriage prospects, who would lure me back to the ways of righteousness and respectability. They never thought of the tension it caused between me and JB. (They hardly talked to him during the entire evening – poor chap!) With friends like these, who needed enemies? Later on, when he had friends too, the same domestic drama was replayed with me piggy in the middle. Most gays and lesbians have had to endure these attempts to subvert their striving for fidelity and union. Most people (though not most ecclesiastics) are more sensitive these days about the treatment of minorities.

The truth came out curiously enough in a 'game' of Tarot cards which were given me as a present at my birthday party. Knowing nothing about them, I dealt hands and with the aid of a book interpreted the hands in a clumsy fashion. A tangled love affair emerged, and signs of doom, death and a falling tower. It brought out what was in our unconscious knowledge. I have never 'played' with them again.

Towards the end all lines of communication dropped between us. We took no holidays together, and celebrated no birthdays. I was more alone than I had ever been, he less. I was also convinced I was ignorant and a fool, which I am not.

'Get out,' said my friend and former analyst Leslie, 'get away from him!' JB hated him. But with whom or to whom should I escape? I could not go from something into nothing. I panicked. I should have gone with Janny . . . perhaps. I went with a charming chap called Kim instead, who offered me a chicken sandwich in a West End bar, but this is later in my story.

I only ever saw JB again, fleetingly, twice – by chance, not intention. Once in a crowd he brushed my arm and once in a bus when he didn't see me, thank God. I would have been putty in his hands. I have never forgotten him, or my early belief that all marriages should be for ever whatever the circumstances. As I have said, there were a few occasions when everything seemed right. It was first love. Years later I was browsing in a charity shop near our old home. I suddenly saw a well-worn leather set of the Shakespeare Temple Classics. I had given him such a set once to buy his love. Yes, I was right, in them were his copious notes. I wavered. Should I buy them back? Seeing those books in that shop, I knew that he was dead. (I was later told that he didn't have an easy time of it.) I returned to the charity shop twice. But one cannot buy back the past. One can only learn from it.

44

Re'ach Turns My House into a Home

Love did come but under a different guise during my time with JB. I did not know how to love a human being (nor did he) so I loved a dog instead. I bought her from a pet shop hoping she might bring JB and me closer together. Many people have a child for the same reason. Having Re'ach did help us linger together longer than we should have. An honest divorce would have been better for all of us – a sort of gay 'Get', to use the Hebrew term. Later we bought another dog, Djilas, to be her companion, in the way that marriages on the rock have more children. But such strategies, in my experience, do not keep shaky marriages together.

Re'ach's name meant 'odour' in Hebrew and 'royal' in Gaelic, said JB. She was a big black dog, a cross between a Labrador and an alsatian. She wanted to be treated as a lapdog, though she was anything but. She was a coward, an opportunist and more paranoid than me. If a car exhaust went off, she dived under my bed, got stuck and it took two of us to loosen her out. She was also frightened by mice, which I was not. If she suspected the presence of one, she buried her head in the corner for if she couldn't see the mouse then the mouse wouldn't see her. Sometimes she turned her head round, heaving her great back, for a courageous peek to see if the monster mouse had gone. But with all her faults she transformed the desert of my domestic life and I loved her.

On Friday evening after the Sabbath came in, because in theory I was a bachelor and the families of my congregation sensed that I was in no hurry to return to my empty house, they actually vied for the pleasure of my company. They were pleased to have me not just in their homes but as part of their families. I was not only invited into their dining rooms but their kitchens. Their hospitality went deeper than I expected. And I had to review all my disdain for the bourgeoisie I had once wanted to blow up. But I could not be a perpetual guest, however welcome. My pride said so! So did synagogue politics! So did the dignity of my profession! And I finally began to say 'no' with genuine regret and gratitude. I used to return to my empty house to light the Sabbath candles but now, with my dog Re'ach for family, company and congregation. It worked in its limited way, but after the candle-lighting Re'ach was no dinner companion. She was as restive as me.

So after the prayers and the hallowing of wine and bread (and dog chocs because it was Re'ach's Sabbath too), I packed up my washing and went with her to the friendly launderette near the bottom of the road which served the students and bachelor boys and girls from bedsitter country. Together we sent out for fish and chips from the frying shop nearby and for flagons of beer and cider, because as I had a regular job, I was considered flush and could pay for it.

Re'ach was ecstatic. She was petted and made much of, and fed bits of batter, and barked when the bubbles of beer got up her nose, and chased the white detergent suds, and yelped when she got trodden under foot, and licked my face and anybody else's she classed as friendly. This was a Sabbath indeed. I began to realise that in the loneliness of a big city your true family need not be your blood relations but your friends.

Sometimes I held forth on the problems of my job. How it irked me that I couldn't bury spouses or partners of different faiths in the same cemetery, however long they had lived with each other and however deep their love and care. To the students and 'love on the dole' partners, this was living anthropology. Once again I could see the ecclesiastical world I now inhabited both as an insider and an outsider. They used to egg me on to tell them more bizarreries of my religion of which indeed there are many.

Now, was Re'ach religious because she accompanied me not just to fish and chip shops but into my religious life? She certainly sat obediently in the Church of the Tyburn Martyrs where on my way to work I used to meditate while the enclosed Sisters prayed behind their grille. When they stood, she stood and when they sat, she sat. Conformity is easily confused with piety in both dogs and human beings, and the congregation whispered what a devout pet she was. But I knew her better, or thought I did. Miss R. was wondering what was in it for her – more dog chocs maybe! I wondered if the Sisters would take fright from her snuffling behind their backs. But they sent me a message via their confessor that she was very welcome.

I did in fact learn some very important spiritual lessons from her and through her. Strange as it may seem, she was as much a messenger to me, and messenger means 'angel' in Hebrew, as with Balaam's ass or Dante's Virgil. This is not whimsical but fact and here are examples of the spiritual messages she brought me. People trying to journey from the world of things and appearances to the dimension of the spirit usually require help. Dante had Virgil, as I have said, Bunyan his angel guide, the rabbis had the spirit of the prophet Elijah. And now I had Pooch. A guide is necessary when you journey into unexplored territory, and this is where the spirit was taking me.

The difficulties of my own spiritual journey only hit me when I contemplated my dog's strange behaviour some years after I bought her. She had started by refusing to eat her dog food unless some human food was added to it, i.e. food we were eating at table. Then I began to notice her dog bowl moving – she was steadily pushing it with her nose through the kitchen door towards the dining room table. I was intrigued rather than annoyed. Then, having to leave London, I left her and the house in charge of two dog-loving friends from America.

When I returned, her plan was laid bare. Now she sat on a dining-room chair, and her bowl was placed on the table. I had not the slightest doubt that if I had come a few weeks later, it would have been replaced by a plate.

I took her bowl back to the kitchen and ordered her back there. She bared her teeth at me for the first time ever, and I hit her over the nose with a rolled newspaper. She slunk back to the kitchen thinking murderous thoughts about me. (I later found out at the pub that she had also subdued the barman to her will, and lapped up a saucer of watered-down Dubonnet at his bar.)

Her game, though it was no game, was obvious. She was no longer prepared to accept second-class pet status. She wanted to cross the line which separates animal kind from human kind. She wanted to better herself. I sympathised with her and admired her. But she had no idea what being human was about – no idea of its heights, and its depths, its inconceivable (to her) responsibilities.

Suddenly I made the connection between her situation and mine. I also wanted to rise in the cosmic order of things and get above myself. I wanted to rise from being a little higher than the animals to a little lower than the angels, as the psalmist said. But I had no idea of what being a spiritual being or angelic meant. I could not conceive of such a displacement of my ego. From the Gospels and the Buddhist scriptures and the mystical rabbis it didn't sound like a hedonistic joy ride. I'd have to change an awful lot to fit into a spiritual world. Would I like it if I ever got there? God knows, and I mean that literally.

I also learnt a lot from Re'ach about possessions. I had given her a squeaking plastic chop which she was quite content with until my American dog-lover friends added to her possessions by buying her a rubber bone that growled when bitten. Re'ach was nearly insane with delight over the quality and quantity of her possessions and she tried to hold both chop and bone in her mouth. But even her mouth was not large enough and she was forced to choose. She could either have the chop or the bone but not both together so she sat back on her haunches and howled with frustration.

God in the Book of Deuteronomy tells us, 'See I have set before you good and evil, life and death. Choose that you may live.' But like Re'ach we do not want to choose. We want to have everything and its opposite. But our mouths, like hers, cannot hold both at the same time. Sooner or later we have to choose between this life and the beyond life. And many of us feel that this is hard. But it is one of the most important lessons in life and I learnt this through Pooch.

45

Checking Religion Against Reality

Heaven (and hell) fine (or not so fine)! Little chats with Fred, Jesus – Whomsoever Whatsoever – very cosy and also fine. Mystical feelings blooming in my present Jewish or my past Anglo-Catholic kitsch – mmmm – a bit sticky but I'm more sold on sentiment than I thought. (Irena and Harry never approved, which gave me pause. Nor would Irene, my psychotherapist, have approved later on.) It was all very fine but did it work?

I gave little talks on spirituality at synagogues and retreats and looked around on my way to them at the people crushed against me on the Underground, almost sitting on my knees. Being Londoners they didn't speak to each other, but read from papers and booklets inserted as with a knife in the tiny space between their bodies. Were they reading the Talmud that my teacher had told me to talk to them about? No! Were they fingering a rosary? No! Were they sobbing about the Jewish problem? Couldn't care less! They were trying to turn the pages of holiday brochures.

Either my mysticism helped them with their holidays in the brochures or it was just my private self-indulgence – like the sentimental B-movies running round in my mind, hotted up with sex and gender change. 'He rained passionate kisses on his upturned breast!' Part of me was still Marxist Jew and this part insisted on what worked in real material worldly reality. If my metaphysics and voices couldn't help people (and me) begin to have a happy holiday and come back still speaking to the people we went out with, then it was alas another excursion into Cloud-cuckoo-land fantasy like the kind I had known in the East End as a child.

So in my talks, sermons and writings I tried to marry real problems with my see-through insights and encounters. Looking at my own life, I went to religion out of need, and it proved itself if it worked. Crude but simple! Most of the listeners shared this Reduced Theology though they were shy of admitting it.

The see-through stuff for example did prove itself by improving my holidays and other people's too. It was obvious that two weeks devoted to happiness was beyond me – I was too neurotic. And metaphysically speaking I didn't just need other people, I needed to be needed by them. Happiness you can't share, for me wasn't on.

Seeing things spiritually gave them meaning and importance. The departure lounge at a holiday airport was my life in miniature. I made myself as comfortable as I could, sharing what I could because WW wanted it. I made pleasant acquaintances, all the time knowing our numbers would be called and we would never see each other again.

Occasionally I managed to see what I had never noticed before, thanks to WW – the tired staff waiting for me to get out and go go go so that they could get back to their homes and families. If WW was with me, I didn't sneer and joke at the students boiled lobster red from sleeping on the beach, but offered them some of my beer to help them cool off.

A girl in a disco heard that I was involved in religion, and came to me to see if I could give her some of its consolations because she had just been stood up by her boy on the dance floor.

To my surprise I could. WW spoke in me because I was wiser with her than I thought I could be. Let's pray together, I said, for you to get some courage to get back on the dance floor, but putting less trust in your boys and more trust in your own inner strength and sense. Remember, I said, rows don't matter that much, especially on holiday, when you're under strange stresses and don't know your boundaries, but making up (don't force it, just let it happen) is divine – in every sense.

She was a shrewd lass and she knew what I meant. When I left the disco she was dancing happily with a boy (I couldn't tell one from another in the ghostly womby gloom).

WW was also important for me, because he told me I didn't have to be superman, and suddenly I wasn't. I didn't have to be a divine doormat or agree with everything or put everything right. I could leave most of that to God. That's what He was for! Phew! A Dominican friend confirmed this years later in a priory.

The incidents above might not seem much to you. They were certainly not miracles and not even wonders for most people but they were a bit wondrous to me, because with WW's help I was beginning to make sense of common reality and cope with it. Lots of you can do this no doubt without WW, but I couldn't.

So, for example, when seven people arrived for dinner I didn't pretend I'd only invited five of them, but sent to the fish and chipper round the corner. The Lord of Creation had created that too. I had plenty of brown vinegar and tomato ketchup at home. It was a cosy evening with the best silver. I would become a recognised eccentric and no Delia Smith but there was no nastiness or lies. Heaven could smile down.

This companionship with On High or Beyond supported me whenever I called upon it. It didn't remove problems. But it did help me face them. And it helped me years later when I hit the difficult part of ageing, which means dependence, loneliness and discomfort.

It helped me continue with my therapist or make it to a monastery, when I didn't want to do either. From outside, both experiences seemed to be painful. When I was inside them, I hesitated for a moment, like a swimmer at the edge of the pool, but when I was falling or diving, I got that extra lift from WW or Old Smokey or Jesus (my own image of him of course).

I have used the word trust, not faith. I don't have much of the latter, if anything. Trust is something different. It is based on experience but it goes beyond experience. Perhaps the two are the same. It is just a matter of which goes first, the cart or the horse. Perhaps trust becomes faith, when it is lightened by love. But trust I do accept, though I do not believe much, partly because I've met too many people who believed too much and took themselves for a ride.

This then is what I can give others. Start from where you are in life! If you're a hypocrite, pimp, prostitute, barrack-room lawyer, sly entrepreneur, or fantasist, or lawyer, or liar, just say it aloud to yourself and to God or your guardian angel in private. He can then show you how to make something good out of it. Apply your mysticism to the little things in life. Your theology too. You can't know what's big or little in your life.

- Be generous (which is not another word for foolish). You can't always love but you can always be generous. Liking, by the way, can be more difficult than loving.
- Look after your own soul and other people's bodies and not vice versa.
- Don't let your religion bully you, manipulate you, or dictate to you. You've got to use discrimination on it as on everything else.
- The truth shall make you free. This also means self-honesty.
- Remember there's always someone worse off than you. Learn to follow the flow of life and to let go. Japanese wisdom says the hardest thing in the world is letting go.

46

Let Loose on Congregations

To become a rabbi, I had to study seven years more after I left Oxford in 1953. Then I was formally ordained by my teachers after being examined in my official subjects, Hebrew, Aramaic, Jewish law and lore, codes and philosophy, and a smidgeon of mysticism. I could not tell my examiners that I had learnt as much from what they were as from what they said. I admired their dignity after a time of disaster. I could also not tell them about my unofficial teachers such as Tina, and the saintly Frenchman in her sauna. Such knowledge would have blown their bourgeois world to bits.

I graduated from the Leo Baeck College in two stages. In 1958 I became a Reverend (which never suited me) and in 1960 a rabbi. Then they took away my nice handwritten Reverend certificate and I was given a printed glossy rabbinical certificate, which I was told to frame and hang over my desk (like a dentist) to show I was legit. It reminded me of the marriage contract which my granddad and granny used to hang over their bed for the same purpose. I thought it vulgar. I at least stopped them antiquing it on false vellum.

I was about this time let loose on congregations. The problems which nearly wrecked them and me together were, you can guess it, gay love (in Britain its expression was still criminal) and the bits of breakdown which were still simmering in me.

I was very naive, despite Amsterdam, Hamburg and the Cities of the Plain. In one congregation the wife of a prominent congregant told her husband she had fallen in love with me (to provoke his passion, I presumed). He made life hell for me. And I thought it was my theology he took exception to!

In another, though I was the minister, there was a prophet on the premises, a really great man, no denying it, whom I liked but he was homophobic. Though he couldn't be quite sure, he was suspicious of something in me and this wrecked our mutual liking. A pity, because he wanted me to be his son, and I needed a father figure. To testify to my 'straightness' I invited my lovely, very English blonde Janny to a service. To my astonishment the roof fell in. How dare I prefer a non-Jewish woman to our local home-grown sort?

I gritted my teeth and sang an English version of a Yiddish song my grandpa sang in his cups:

> Oy oy oy oy oy oy
> Miracles and wonders.
> The rabbi's in the cinema
> Where all the Gentile women are.

My career was also complicated by my desire to become a saint, which normal Jewish congregations don't know how to handle. But of course I could only be a saint in patches, which confused and fascinated everybody. Also bits of Oxford Anglo-Catholic style kept creeping into my rituals. So that a nice boisterous lighting of the Jewish Chanukah candles seemed like a pre-Vatican II prologue to a Mass. It was so religious, it just didn't seem Jewish.

My high view of my calling sat oddly with the low happenings in my love life, such as sporting a black eye imperfectly disguised with talcum powder before a festival. My high view of things ecclesiastic derived from my history studies at Balliol where I had been pro-Pope and anti-monarch about the appointment of prelates.

Nevertheless, I did a lot of good work (in patches) and as was right I learnt a lot from my congregations, formally and inform-ally. The latter was important because I could be an awful prig, saved only by the quirk of self-honesty I had learnt from my mother and also from my assorted analysts, therapists and counsellors.

In my fantasies, I had imagined my first rabbinical office. It would be a long room with two doors and my desk in the middle. Through one door would enter a line of sorrowing congregants. They would sigh and I would sigh as I looked up their problems in my fat folios. Eureka! I had found their answer! All sighs ended as they marched out through the second door, crying out their Hosannas and their gratitude to God and me – in that order because I was humble. I smirked piously over them. Ugh!

Well, I soon wafted down to solid earth, despite the fantasy. I learnt that many problems have no answer – or not in this world anyway. Religion can give us the courage to face them, not to remove them. But when we face them we can learn to live with them, cope with them and see opportunities in them we had never thought of before. I learnt this spiritually at the Quaker meeting. Now I knew it true in fact as well as in faith.

Another lesson from that Quaker meeting proved itself in similar fashion, 'in the field' as the anthropologists say. I was appointed to a new congregation and just as I was closing shop late at night, an aggressive young man muscled in:

'Are you the rabbi?' he said.

'Yes,' I admitted grandly, 'I am he.'

'Well, I'm going to commit suicide,' he said, 'and what are you going to do about it?'

'Let's have a cup of tea,' I said weakly.

None of my Talmud had prepared me for this but my own neuroses had. 'I tried once to commit suicide too,' I confided in him, 'and it's a jolly sight harder than you think.'

We had tea and biscuits and took turns jumping off the sofa, discussing possible painless ways. Then at about 3 a.m. he said that he'd enjoyed himself very much and I told him I had too. He had to clock in now, he said, because he was on early-morning shift. Sorry, I replied, and I meant it because I hadn't discussed the technical side of suicide for years. I never saw him again.

Later on, a therapist told me admiringly I'd done just the right thing and I realised how important my problems and failures were. There's a lot of healing in them, when they are shared. Before I had left the Leo Baeck, my Talmud teacher, who did not take to me – and I don't blame him because I was a chain smoker, and even though I had to sit at the other end of the room by the window, still managed to envelop him in cigarette smoke like Moses in the cloud – said grudgingly but admiringly, after reading my rabbinic thesis, that one day I could do great things with Talmud and Aramaic if I wanted to. But in the field nobody wanted such specialities. They did want to know, though, about my clumsiness, my anxieties, my depressions, my inconsistencies and how I dealt with them. Later on, I found out that there were honest-to-God lewd, laughter-filled, funny, neurotic passages and stories in that mighty work, but of course they were not ones we were taught (Joseph and Potiphar excepted). As a rabbi once said to me, 'Mr Blue, your successes make you clever but only your problems and failures make you wise.' I was quite well provided with the latter.

My next congregation was in the middle of the middle-class suburbia I had been trying to leave for years, so I ministered to it with mixed feelings. It was comfortable and cosy, covered in rose bushes and maintained with mortgages. I was received in front rooms, furnished just like my parents' with a lamp standard, a three-piece suite, a drinks cabinet and a deep Bakelite TV, which the family sat around and which occupied the same place in their lives as the radio during the war.

But because I began to like my new congregants, I graduated (thank God!) from their overstuffed front rooms into their back kitchens. And sipping coffee and munching little Jewish biscuits called 'kichels', I began to listen to them after I'd finished spouting. Some had endured a childhood poorer than mine in the poverty of London's East End. Some had had a childhood of riches but lost everything, barely escaping with their lives from Berlin, Prague, Warsaw . . . Some had arrived on Kinder-Transports, half-knowing they would never see their parents again, waving them off, determinedly cheerful, at a German station. Nearly every family had a dreadful tale to tell about themselves and those dear to them. I could hardly imagine such suffering. I didn't want to imagine such suffering.

I looked at them thereafter and their sane suburban lives with awe. They had come through horror and were still whole. I'd have gone to bits. And yet I was preaching to them about life which in their sense I had hardly experienced. I tried to speak from then on only about what I knew. This seemed only decent. My sermons got much more matter of fact, more real and much better.

I also began to understand their present lives too – not so secure and untroubled as their trim houses suggested. Most were or had become small businessmen, bringing up families on credit from the local banks, their businesses and mortgages shaken by every gust of the changing winds of the British economy and the steady devaluation of the pound. Many I knew didn't sleep at night for worry.

I didn't sleep much either. The chairman of the congregation did not like rabbis, and he was not only vice-chairman and then chairman but co-founder of the congregation. Why he didn't like rabbis I understood very well. His father had been beadle of a large wealthy upper-class congregation and he himself got patronised as a child, pleasantly intended of course, by clergy and congregation. I had been in a similar situation with rich relatives. Now was his chance to turn the tables. I was to be 'his' rabbi and 'his' chaplain. But I wasn't 'his' or anybody's, though I admired his energy and single-minded devotion.

In the end we made our peace after a stormy synagogue meeting. I was at one end of a train coach on the Underground, and he was at the other, both of us staring tight-lipped away from each other. Then my inner Voice and Friend entered into my mind – old Whosoever, Whatsoever. Warily and cautiously I went over to him (he might hit me) and said since I would be leaving, and he would have the congregation to himself, we might as well exit from each other's lives with courtesy. I respected him deeply, though we were on a collision course.

His mouth opened and a surprised look came into his eyes. Old Whosoever Whatsoever had disconcerted him as well as me. That night we went drinking, and told each other in a haze bits of our life stories (mine of course censored. I trusted him but not too far. England wasn't Holland). I told him I would stay with the congregation till it grew too big, which he wanted. I sentimentally wanted to keep it small with services in a hired hall.

For me these were the best times, when the chairman carried in chairs, and the ladies made tea and cakes in our hired church hall, the wardens respectfully covered over the pictures of Jesus, and the harmonium wheezed and our singer Leoni ran through her scales. And a beggar passed by and looked in enviously and was regaled with coffee and cake with no strings, without needing to stay for the service. We became a family on those cold winter evenings and a bit of heaven happened.

When the congregation became bigger the opposite happened. There was a grand service of blessing (we had our own building now – the chairman had worked hard) and the worthies were coming to honour us. A drunk entered the synagogue just before the service, a quiet untroublesome drunk. In fact you wouldn't know he was a drunk, but someone had said that's what he was. A note was passed to me and to the wardens to take him to my office, get the caretaker's wife to serve him tea and cake, give him a pound note and ask him to wait till the service was over when I would see him.

But he didn't stay. He didn't take the pound and only nibbled one biscuit. He hadn't come for handouts, just to experience a bit of religion in the warmth, and we/I had kept him out. How low could you/I get? Putting on the style was leading me astray and old WW didn't like it. He (I) didn't like the fibs I would increasingly have to utter about my private life and partner. The congregation deserved something more normal and I resigned to become a sort of bishop of a bankrupt diocese on the Continent. They gave me, before I left, an electric razor (hint, hint), a smart case, life membership of the congregation and free burial. I would get a hearse, a car, a plot and the customary rabbinic services including prayers in my home. What joy! What bliss! But I was really touched when my chairman and his family came to see me off at the airport. Unfortunately I didn't see him when he was dying only a year or so later.

Another realisation hit me. I had thought so much about the state, the workers' state of course, that I had never bothered to find out who did the work in the state. I just assumed somebody did it or was paid to do it, or more conveniently it just did itself. But it didn't and never had.

Someone had to look after dependent older people and help the parents of autistic children and visit patients in hospitals and make tea for cheery friendship clubs. All this unpoliticised social work, in its true sense, was done by maiden aunts, overburdened housewives, shy retiring daughters and old codgers who gave a hand. A myriad of committees met regularly to provide money for sandwiches, drives for day outings and make sure the lonely had a sort of family life. The people and the committees who did this were an extraordinarily humble lot, much at the mercy of community politicians, but non-complaining. This changed my view of the suburb. I still thought its silent rose-lined streets too quiet compared to the living vaudeville of streets in the slums or bohemia, but I now appreciated the hard work which made the suburbs peaceful and generally speaking contented. (The gay world had a lot to learn from the Jewish world about social responsibility.) The work was given freely, mainly by women who didn't do it to crown themselves with or for their own advantage. Their unconscious goodness showed me another road to heaven.

I grieved when I left them – but I felt I could no longer fib to them about my life. They needed, I thought, a nice rabbi, with a nice wife and nice children. So I said my fond farewells.

47

Go West, Young Man, Go West!

In the early sixties, I was suddenly elevated from Jewish suburban religious politics into the international religious kind. I became one of religion's big boys. I organised conferences, learnt the art of fixing, and how to be a courtier. It was my friend Rabbi Dow Marmur once again who suggested I apply for the post of European Director of the World Union for Progressive Judaism, which was becoming moribund in Europe after the central office moved to New York. No one else wanted the job. It was a high road to nowhere, the salary was low, though the status was high, but, being a bachelor, I could cope with life on the move. (I wanted life on the move because my relationship with JB in London was turning sour, nasty and occasionally violent – though I hung on because I didn't want to go back to bar crawling. JB also frightened me. But we were coming to an end.)

Why to my surprise did I get such a job when I had so little experience? After all, I had only recently been ordained. Elevation to a sort of 'bishop' to a bankrupt diocese seemed premature. I got it because the Americans who really ran the show, and were perplexed by the insane patchwork of petty European Jewish communities and rival organisations, wanted to put the responsibility on any European foolhardy enough to take it on, provided it didn't cost them too much. Europe after all wasn't their priority. Their real interests were in their own backyard of South America or Israel whose wild east frontier atmosphere reminded them so much of their own wild west history, with the Arabs as the Injuns. Also ethnicity, authenticity and nationalism in the new state could serve as a substitute for the spirituality they weren't sure how to deal with.

But I did take Europe seriously! It was my own continent that had astonished me as I hitchhiked across it in my schooldays and which my friends Irena and Harry Landry had helped me understand and love. I made a most moving speech at a conference in Paris about a rebirth of Judaism in Europe. (It certainly moved me!) The head of an American organisation publicly invited me to come over to the USA as their guest lecturer. I shouted out my acceptance, the conference applauded and a few months later, wearing a bowler hat and carrying a tightly rolled umbrella, I boarded a plane to the 'goldene medina', the golden land that my grandparents had tried to get into but had never made it. I dressed up city gent English-style to give the Americans a good show. Corny but effective.

I took to America immediately. Religious America was bigger, better, kinder, nastier, more generous, more manipulative, kitschier, more scholarly, sillier and more sentimental than I imagined and much more fun. Looking back on myself, I wish hadn't been too damned puritan and prissy to appreciate it enough. I disposed of any lingering reservations about the food, which was delicious, satisfying the gourmand as well as the gourmet in me. Real rabbis ordered me lobster and scallops. Once I had got over the shock, I had to admit I liked them and while I was there I never looked back until I returned to more restrictive Europe. Whatever Reform rabbis ate, so did I. 'Away with European inhibitions! Pass me the clam juice, Rabbi!' Old Whosoever Whatsoever said my showy traditionalism was in any case only a kind of defensive snobbery. There wasn't much holiness in it and once again he was right.

Gradually I learnt the way ecclesiastical America operated. Firstly there was a transposition of roles. Ordinary congregants asked me spiritual questions and the clergy (all faiths and denominations) asked me more financial and organisational ones. The former wanted to know what I thought about Khalil Gibran (too smoochy) and the latter about appeals, fund raising, and salary differentials. It was obvious that my understanding of big business and the bigger business that was God's business was too 'hick' to be taken seriously. But I learnt the lessons and ended up appealing for funds myself and collecting a rather tidy sum for my work in Europe rebuilding old congregations, funding youngsters who would train to be their rabbis and me providing new purpose – too tidy for the American establishment's comfort, though it was peanuts by American standards. I shouldn't have been poaching on their preserves. Afterwards I realised how impolite it was (that was Janny in me) but it's so easy to catch financial fever there.

The laymen I loved. Even their manipulation was so blatant. They gave me a laugh in the best sense and just when I needed it. There was a banquet there I've never forgotten at which I spoke completely unheard because too many fascinating things were happening at the same time. The bar had been open for hours and the tables were covered with steak leftovers coated with cigar ash and melba sauce, all the while wandering musicians were playing Liebestraum and a film star was saying grace. Once I got over my pique I had a marvellous time and only wished my friends back home could see me in my glory and that I'd be invited back again. During the later years of trendy, mean, European nouvelle cuisine minceur, I longed for an honest blow-out American style.

There was a generosity about American hospitality that put to shame our meagre European ways. The meal I shall never forget is the Best Dinner I Never Had. I was on my lecture tour through the States which paid for my fare and keep. I had got used to the pattern. An aeroplane, being met at the airport by an excited lady who was going to give me hospitality, the dinner she had planned for me and the town worthies, for Europeans just after the war were rare in those parts, a lecture, a visit to a museum (I'd have preferred a delicatessen or Superduper-market. Culture I could get in Europe but where could I inspect thirty brands of maple syrup?), a thank you, an exchange of addresses which would lie around like reproaches or uncashed cheques because I am a disorganised correspondent, an airport, another aeroplane, another town, another lecture in Europe after the Holocaust.

. This one seemed no different from all the others. The lady who picked me up at the airport told me she had been studying French cooking especially for the dinner that night and all her friends were envious because she had captured so many social lions for it.

She took me to my room at her house, and remarked that I looked a little weary. 'Not at all,' I said politely, 'a few minutes' lie down and I'd be as good as new.' I lay down, dozed and then said, 'Come in!' as I heard a tap on my door. She entered with a tray groaning with sandwiches and cakes together with a bottle of Bourbon and another of Cola – an American combination I had grown to like.

'But I won't have any appetite for your lovely French dinner,' I remarked, bewildered.

'You're not coming to my lovely French dinner,' she said firmly. 'I think you've been pushing yourself around too hard and you need to be alone and take a long sleep.'

'But what about your dinner party?' I said, startled.

'They'll just have to be content with my French cooking and hostess conversation,' she giggled and went out, firmly shutting the door. I was tired, though I didn't think I'd showed it and I was also homesick and after she went out I cried in gratitude.

Well, that was the generosity of Midwest America at its best and I have never forgotten her nor her dinner I never had. I met more pure generosity like that in America than in any other country. It's a great place.

It was also a hard-headed calculating place, not that different from England just more shameless about expressing it. At a well-lubricated ecumenical gathering a minister and his wife told me that their son played in a band and would be delighted to play for us in Europe. He'd be welcome at our new youth gatherings, I told them enthusiastically. 'But our son's mean,' said the wife meaningfully and her husband nodded. In other words he wanted a salary whose size made me laugh. I told them I was here to get funds for my work, not give them away, even if their wonderboy was a new Haifetz or Segovia. They moved off in a huff.

But religiously there was something wrong and I think I spotted the problem while attending a community foundation meeting where I could tell them about European Jewry after the Holocaust. After I finished they thanked me politely, though Europe must have seemed as far away from them as the moon, and asked me if would like to listen in on their business meeting before the barbecue. I did and was fascinated.

The members of the new community consisted mainly of young professional couples with high hopes and mortgages. But with the child worship, noticeable all over America, they only wanted the tip-top best for their kids, be it fashionable kiddie clothes or God. So once again I was surprised by the size of their promises and donations. They were going to get the best rabbi that money could entice to their unbuilt synagogue.

But they were also shrewd business people, who knew the value of money, and the tip-top rabbi would have to keep on his toes with no slacking. He would have to produce results. But they came unstuck when they tried to quantify religious results. How many people does a rabbi or any other minister really influence profoundly during his ministry? A few children, some sick people, some lovers walked out on and therefore vulnerable to the consolations of religion! What price holiness?

Though the young couples were mortgaged to the hilt they were also generous to a fault, shaming the meagre responses of us Europeans. One of them asked me, out of curiosity, what I earned in London. I told him my meagre olde worlde salary and knew at once I wouldn't do – I came too cheap. But, being a canny lot, they would have to goad their new rabbi into constant spiritual action. So they decided to give him a short contract (renewable) with his first-class salary. In that way they could monitor his results and keep him on his toes.

But what are solid religious results when spirituality is see-through? The answer could only be buildings. America was dotted with lovely capacious religious buildings with rooms for classes and lectures and committees to raise funds for the buildings and for work parties to decide on what to do in them. And I am not deriding them, because Judaism is a busy busy communal religion (all American religion seemed to me like that), devoted to good works which need buildings – up to a point. But I also couldn't help noticing how real estate was altering the priorities of a community, subtly changing its agenda and making solid and material what should remain see-through and spiritual.

The religious mistake was a very simple one. They had tried to apply the well-tested ways of business to religion. But religion is not an end product like any other.

When I returned to Europe I realised that this was not only an American phenomenon. In Britain there was the same pull to solid real estate but we managed it less efficiently, that's all. And when I went to Israel it was there but in a different guise. There was a boom in Jewish archaeology and scholars and students digging for God, as we in Britain had once dug for victory.

But too much emphasis on real estate inevitably deflects

religion from its true task. It is bound to influence its priorities and its programme. The danger is that it would relegate inner religion to a second priority or postpone it till the place where it could be taught had been finished and funded.

Now real estate religion appeals to the materialist in all of us, for a building is solid in a way a soul isn't. Too many buildings may not be a sign of faith but of a substitute for it. And this does not only apply to the suburbs of big cities in which most Jews live, it also applies to the Holy Land.

The search for the material roots of Jewish history had led to this boom in archaeology. Affluent Bar Mitzvah parties are flown from Western Jewry to the old Temple Wall or the nearest they could get to it in Jerusalem. Pious tourism is seen as a way to piety, but it can also be a subtle materialist replacement for it. This replacement became politically and spiritually dangerous after 1948 and the declaration of the new state. The problem of Israel and Palestine is the hate and paranoia which are now becoming endemic, not just in the Holy Land but in the refugee camps in Lebanon and in the supporter clubs in the West. They are stoked by secularised political religion and its cult of holy places (buildings again!) which are holiness substitutes.

The former seem so solid, but in Jewish history buildings do not have a good track record. However thick the walls and firm the foundations, they do not last. God does not live in No 1 Jerusalem. He lives as the early rabbis had said, 'Wherever the heart or mind of anyone lets him in.' By the way, I want to make it clear that this danger applies not only to Judaism but to all religions who mix modern ideologies such as nationalism with old faith.

I think this lurch from religion to real estate was partly a result of the Holocaust. So much spirituality was in question, so many questions which were too hot to handle after it. And where was God in it? Was he in it?

I brooded about that meeting to set up a new small American community with a well-paid fresh rabbi for many hours as I criss-crossed the USA on my lecture tour.

I think they knew that material solutions were no answer to spiritual problems, but didn't want to face it. It was too bewildering. This meant that there was a hole where the inner life should be, and I noted that that was already being filled with popular gut and instinct feelings – watered-down Zionism and popular social issues. There was a lot of Almighty God scholarship but less experience of him. As St Rose of Lima said, 'It would be better if they talked about him less and to him more!'

There were other areas where American success did not fit the European situation. Like Israeli Jewry, American Jewry had come out of the war with its pride and self-belief intact, not having to question its own survival. Whereas in Europe after the war, Jews had had to ask themselves if they should be in Europe at all. Perhaps it was an accursed place and it was best to get out of it. Many families who had put down new roots after the Holocaust and had built new homes in Berlin, Prague and Brussels still sheltered behind the fiction that they were only transients on their way to old Jerusalem or new Jerusalem, i.e. New York and California. American Jewry assumed its rightness. It had not had to justify its own existence.

There were two other differences which took me by surprise. All nationalism was suspect in Europe. It was nationalism not communism, the American bogey, which had brought destruction time after time. It was very hard for an American Jew to regard his own nationalisms, i.e. American and Jewish, as being dangerous. All one could say as a European is that he would learn the hard way.

The other difference was the ghetto life of American Jewry. It was of course a platinum-plated ghetto but a ghetto all the same. There were Jewish golf clubs, Jewish country clubs, Jewish businessmen's clubs – you name it and there was an exclusive Jewish version of it. Such a ghettoisation of modern Jewish life had existed in Europe too – but under the Nazis. Some Jewish groups in Europe had even issued 'passports' to Jewish youth clubs, to make sure that they were rabbinically Jewish – very reminiscent of the occupation. But these had been hooted down. I had not expected American Jewish life to give me claustrophobia, but it did. I preferred to risk the occasional anti-Semitic remark and inhabit an open society.

American Jewry therefore did not have the answers to the deeper spiritual problems of Europe, which were not organisational but spiritual. I decided that progressive Judaism there would eventually merge into Jewish communalism and nationalism, and it did. I was frightened that American and Israeli establishment religion might eventually take over in Europe too, and I think this is what has happened in the smaller Jewish community on this side of the Atlantic. I tried to point out the problem and the need for discrimination when dealing with such a powerful and attractive neighbour, but didn't succeed. European leaders were mesmerised by obvious success. Even the Leo Baeck college is being absorbed into the Israeli–America fund-raising network. As a wise rabbi once said to me, 'There are no mergers, Lionel, only takeovers, and the organisation which has the funds calls the tunes.'

Back in New York from my lecture tour, I wanted to taste real America before I returned to London – and not just Jewish ghetto America, which was giving me claustrophobia. Even in the saunas there, I was amused and amazed to see rampant right-wing Jewish traditionalists wearing all the pietistic accessories, skull cap, fringes etc. I kept away from them. I could not mix with them. I would have liked to talk to them, though. They might have had something to tell me about joining the life of the 'two centres', the one which lay above the navel and the other below. I was still not open to human passion and human piety in their many combinations. Perhaps they could have told me something. Priests were there too, I was told, but they did not wear professional regalia, so I could not recognise them. I had not yet stopped being false to myself. I still did not dare to come out of the closet myself and ask. I was too inhibited, too English.

48

Returning Home

I did meet a good-natured Gentile truck driver just before I went back home to London, and sat in his room in Queens drinking tins of beer and munching popcorn, watching basketball games and old gangster movies. American style. He hardly knew of the Jewish Problem, thank God, and never once asked me for a donation to water the Negev or drain the Galilee. He introduced me to a late-night coffee and muffin bar where he exhibited me as a find, and the other clients were indeed fascinated by my accent.

They asked me why I didn't stay over there with them. I munched my American kriller doughnut and thought it over. I was indeed lured by the bigness, the delicatessen, the central heating, the 'yes saying' to new ideas and proposals, the astronomic rabbinical salaries – but decided no. In America it seemed to me you had to be a success or freak out of the entire system. There was no place for respected genteel poverty or tolerated English-style eccentricity that I was used to and found comfortable.

Coming back from America, I also had another ponder. America was not yet a good leader ecclesiastically for the same reasons it wasn't yet a good enough leader politically on the world stage. It was generous, shrewd, energetic and, once it realised that the world was a small place and the price of isolationism was high, it would become interventionist again, doing the unpleasant things leaders have to do, despite the grumbles of the inadequate. But this wasn't enough!

I'm not going to continue about world politics because I am only a sideliner, a kibitzer (i.e. an onlooker). But religious politics I do know. I've not just been a kibitzer, I've paddled in the shallower waters.

I arrived back in London, agreeing with my old mentor Dr van der Zyl. Don't take handouts from anyone, neither from America nor Israel. Keep your independence! Don't give up your own experiences. And with all this, be sympathetic and grateful because America did support what was left of the Jewish world in Europe after the war, as well as underpinning Israel and South America. I must also add that it was America which saved us in two world wars and we should be thankful. If the small European communities became American it wasn't because of American pressure. That's the way they wanted it. They were fascinated by its organisation, its seminaries, its educators, its outward reach (which, being European, they never understood – they were too snobbish) and its success.

When the American Jewish Reform establishment centred itself in Europe, the power and pressure it could exercise were too overwhelming to be located in London or Paris – they were too peripheral. Many European communities regarded it as success to be the junior partners in such an establishment, and were only too willing to trade in their own youth movements, and traditions of organisation and rabbinical training with little analysis of what they were giving up and what they were getting. Realistically, the choice would be New York or Jerusalem.

The Europeans were getting a mixed bag – American know-how, Israeli culture, communalism, rat races for rabbis, real concern for the outsiders in an insiders' religion, a rational approach to ritual problems, small-town Midwest moralism, and a love of the bitch goddess success which vitiated so many of the pluses.

When I came back from America, I looked at my own world with new eyes. It was so small, so formalist, so preoccupied with patronage, so easily bought by 'titles and honours'. But I still decided my job was to help us all to a mutual exchange, not a takeover. I succeeded, sort of, for a while and I think we genuinely helped each other, as far as two such unequal partners could. We kept our prayer books, and our college, for example. But as the Leo Baeck College became steadily more dependent, something was lost. Independence hadn't been forced from us. We had given it up willingly for American funding, Israeli ideology and the promise of playing a role and putting on the style in New York and Jerusalem. This was not what I had learnt from my six years at the Leo Baeck College.

49

'Ascending and Descending' from Israel

(In Hebrew you 'ascend' to Israel and 'descend' from it.)

Returning from New York, I travelled to London via a detour to Nova Scotia to visit the family of my partner JB. JB's family were exceedingly nice to me in the Scottish island manner and I have never drunk so much whisky since. I began to understand him more. But when I arrived back in London JB told me he was going to spend Christmas with another friend, who I knew really loved him. We had half an hour together. You can fake sex but not affection and there wasn't much. I was just afraid of him and loneliness. He didn't love me either, but needed to possess me though why I didn't understand. I was very confused. Passing through one airport after another, I felt as if I was nowhere and relied on my inner voice WW (Fred), the letters of my constant friend Janny who loved me, and thoughts about my animals to keep me going.

I didn't stay in London either. After only two weeks, I was sent to Israel to report on the Jerusalem Zionist Congress to my organisation, though I hadn't been a Zionist since my adolescent youth movement days. The sessions were disjointed, surreal even, because the speeches did not follow on from each other and the speakers did not address each other but the Muse of Jewish History, the Almighty, the Dead of the Holocaust, and their own communities back home who had sent and subsidised them. What with my own problems, I couldn't make much sense of any of it, so I sat instead in the corridors of power outside the big hall, reading a beautiful new Hebrew translation of Dante and overhearing snippets of conversation which were more relevant.

There was one fundamental problem. Zionism was meant to end the Diaspora and I was engaged in rebuilding the European part of it. The two didn't fit.

So when I 'descended' from Israel for the second time I knew I might not 'ascend' again for a long time – perhaps never. Once again I marvelled at the energy and creativity of Israel, at the speed of its murderous cars, its rawness and rudeness. But the same worry returned, the same unease as in my youth movement days. What would be done about the Palestinian refugees in the camps? My questionings startled (unpleasantly) such members of the establishment as I chanced to meet. They didn't know what would happen, if anything. Time would erode the problem, they hoped. They had more urgent and immediate concerns to think about. They lost patience with me and thereafter gave me a wide berth. I was 'unreliable'. But I had a gut feeling that the problem wouldn't go away. The Arabs I met in Israel weren't like that. They weren't cosmopolitan but stubborn and rooted in a Land, not any land, but their Land   just like Jews in fact. And our Lands were the same.

The Israel situation was beginning to unfold. Every war made another war more likely. Israel had won rounds one and two and it would go on winning rounds three, four, five and six. The Arabs could afford it – there were so many of them, they couldn't be defeated. But one defeat would finish the Jewish State forever. Its situation was the same as the crusader states of long ago. Unless of course it could win a peace as well as a war.

Between the wars there was always a possibility of peace. But as the bitterness was deepening, the price of peace was getting ever higher, and one day it might become so high it could never be paid. A scholar in mysticism set out the iron logic for me. Like many mystics, he could see the obvious, which politicians and populist rabbis cannot because they prefer not to. Some of the latter said God would never desert his people. Perhaps not in a mystical sense, but he had done so many times in a political one.

But there were nevertheless some signs of contact, which I cherished because between Jews and Arabs they were not that common. Arab boys were attracted to Jewish girls and occasionally danced with them in discos against the fulminations of their families and all their religious establishments except me. I thought it was nice that human curiosity and bodily attraction should accomplish what our medieval restrictive theologies could not. I also met Zionist and Palestinian Marxists who had kept the faith, were still worried about each other's refugees and sang the universalist Internationale in their hearts. I also joined up with Balkan surrealists, longing to leave the pioneer Holy Land and get to their decadent Unholy Land which was the Paris of André Breton and Max Jacob. They didn't even recognise any identity problem but just gloried in their own impurity and mixed-upness. There were also a few troubled rabbis who met with Muslim scholars but on a level too exalted to have quickie consequences.

When I left Israel for this second time (the first time was with Colin when I was at Oxford), I knew I might not come back. I was tired of all the polyglot backward-looking chatter. But though I was returning to Europe, I could not leave the Israel problem alone because I was connected with that country, though not with the state publicity machine, whether I liked it or not.

My chance came quickly and it came about through the antithesis of Israel – Germany. Some years previously I had helped to arrange an exchange between a German Evangelical congregation near Hamburg and a Reformed Jewish one in London. The members stayed in each other's houses thanks to the example of the courageous rabbi of the Jewish congregation and his wife, one of whom had survived a Russian labour camp and the other the murderous ghetto of Lodz in Poland. They did not lead from behind but from way out front, though the German language must have brought back terrible memories for them. Such contact was necessary, because if Jews were going to remain in Europe they were going to have to work out a modus vivendi at least with the most important chunk of it – Germany. The 'if' was in any case becoming redundant. Jews from the East speaking Yiddish, classed officially as a German dialect – which it is – were regarded and treated as Volksdeutsch and 'repatriated' to their Fatherland where they got jobs and financial help and another dose of alienation. Many said they were on their way to Israel, but the evidence pointed the other way. Their children were going to German schools and even trying to invite their new German friends back home, to the consternation of their 'Volksdeutsch' parents.

Bishop Scharff, the Protestant Bishop of Berlin, was appreciative of my efforts and asked me what he could do in return. I seized the opportunity. Help us to organise a meeting of Jews and Muslims in Europe with Christian facilitators. He was as good as his word, for he had been a disciple of Dietrich Bonhoeffer right through the Nazi years.

Our first meetings were successful in that we agreed each time to meet again. Politics and the Middle East pulled us apart, but some pure religion and our minority status in Europe pulled us together. Our aims were so modest, they disarmed suspicion. We took no money from Israeli or Arab sources. (We weren't offered any.) Christians, wellwishers, many not well off themselves, footed the bill and we made do and mended for the rest. The people who attended represented no organisations, just themselves, and consisted in the main of rabbinical students, Koranic ones and Christian theological ones. There was a sprinkling of nuns, monks and brothers too, and some mystics. Occasionally some members of the German student New Left descended on us and declaimed, but they left (*Gott sei dank!*) after the coffee and cake.

The first meeting was followed by other meetings in about 1965, some in Berlin, some in Bendorf, the home of Anneliese Debray, my Deutsche Yiddishe Momma. Our first meetings were mistrustful, paranoid and precarious, but they continued and eventually these meetings developed, in 1967, into the Standing Conference of Jews, Christians and Muslims in Europe which still exists today, and even in the brutal times during which I am writing the meetings still carry on. It is good to know that sometimes religion is stronger than politics. I want to pay tribute to my dear friend Rabbi Dr Albert Friedlander. Many times things were said about Israel and the Jews, that we were treating the Palestinians as the Nazis had treated us, that we were ordinary capitalist colonialists – which led to a Jewish walkout except for Albert and me, who remained and listened, agreeing and dis-agreeing, trying to counter the rhetoric of passion with under-standing and reason. It was not easy, especially when the student German New Left burst in, very touchy, very disruptive, but they had to be soothed too. Albert had lived through the Nazi times as a youngster, and I honour but scarcely understand the way he has exorcised his anger or learned to live with his own bitterness. He's a great chap! A gent, and I've learnt a lot from him.

The basics of our meetings soon became obvious. The Muslims ran after the Christians, the Christians ran after the Jews and the

Jews ran after the Muslims. Frequently our meetings chased their own tail. We were not balanced dialogue partners either. The Muslims really needed to dialogue with Orthodox Jews, whom they were more like. But at that time the very Orthodox Jews didn't dialogue with each other let alone outsiders, so the Muslims had to make do with us – Progressive Jews of various shades including women rabbinical students and gay ones too. All things considered, they were remarkably tolerant in accepting us, even if it was only as well-meaning ignoramuses. It was also more dangerous for them to come to such meetings than for us. They were sticking their heads out and got a lot of flack for doing so. But when they decided to trust someone, they followed their trust through and I respected them and their Islamic faith more and more. It was not rat-race religion.

There were other fissures too. The Protestants and Catholics sometimes forgot the main purpose of our meetings was to draw Muslims and Jews together. Instead they dominated the meetings with heated discussion on the liturgy to be used and the nuances of Karl Barth – the leading Protestant theologian who refused to swear allegiance to Hitler – whom most Muslims and few Jews had never encountered. One aged Muslim worthy newly arrived in the Fatherland wearily asked a rabbi next to him, 'What are the heretics discussing?' The rabbi had a field day trying to translate the beliefs of Barth into the legal and philosophic language traditionally shared by Jews and Muslims. God really does move in mysterious ways, because these Christian divisions really eased the tensions between Jews and Muslims. As for the arguments about Barth, I thought I understood them at the time, but obviously I didn't, because now I am as confused as the Muslim worthy.

Every so often the situation could get awkward and even dangerous, though we were far from the battle lines in the Middle East. In Berlin after the Six Day War in 1967, a Turk came over to me at a reception and politely handed me a note which informed me that I had been judged and found very wanting and the consequences would follow.

That night I locked the door of my bedroom, had a stiff schnapps and waited for the worst. But it didn't happen. The next day I was politely passed another note. My judges had read a denunciation of me in a prominent Jewish paper because I had opposed all annexations of Arab territory and especially in Jerusalem – both of which I still do. Political problems on their own were bad enough. Mixed with religion, they were the ingredients of a deadly cocktail. And Israel would soon become another intractable problem, like Northern Ireland, Kashmir, Bosnia and Cyprus beyond peaceful solution. This had found favour with my judges who now wished me well and withdrew their 'consequences'. Albert Friedlander comforted me and handed me an even stiffer dose of schnapps.

50

'No Wine, No Swine!'

Sometimes the whole enterprise to foster Jewish–Christian–Muslim understanding nearly foundered, not on political problems but on gastronomic ones. In western religions God comes through the mind and theology. In eastern ones he also comes through the tastebuds and cookery. At the end of an exhausting session the local township decided to encourage our efforts with a party, which we all looked forward to with relief. Later on someone told me that big business usually got asparagus and Sekt, students got coffee and biscuits, and in-betweens like us pickled pork and hock. As the platters and bottles were brought in, panic took hold of our assembly. Muslims grimly said, *'Kein wein, kein Schwein!'* and the Jews did justice to the hock but were equally adamant about the *Schwein*. Paranoia was in the air. It was all the fault of MI5, the CIA, the Israelis, the Stasi, the neo-Nazis and even me, the hapless organiser of it all. All the goodwill we had so painfully achieved in the last few days flew out of the window, and we needed another very solemn and confused session to begin to re-establish it. Nice Christians found it difficult to understand how 'bread and butter' issues in eastern religions could be serious in a way Karl Barth could never be.

Even more horrific were the possible consequences of another well-meant deed of friendship and goodwill. Before another meeting the Muslim representative, an impressive dignified man, and I were met at Tempelhof Airport in Berlin by Pastor Maechler, the President of our organisation and the representative of the bishop. 'We must rush immediately,' he said, 'to the good bishop who had made our meetings possible.' It was his birthday and all the world would be there.

Which we did and at the reception all of us stood in a long line of the bishop's wellwishers each bearing a gift – an old family heirloom for example, bunches of orchids and lilies worthy of a high-class funeral parlour, what looked like a real Rembrandt, home-made wines and precious liqueurs etc., etc. Our presentless state panicked our pastor. Then, noticing how the presents after their presentation were lined up against a wall, he suddenly beamed. He rushed over to them, extracted two lilies from a vase and gave one to me and the other to my dignified Muslim colleague. 'You must present them to him as a Jewish lily and a Muslim lily,' he said. So as well as looking like a Pre-Raphaelite picture we would also be nefarious recyclers of purloined presents. We protested but our pastor was adamant.

The presentation was worse then either of us had expected. Tears filled the good bishop's eyes as he received in turn a Jewish and a Muslim lily. He had never had such fine presents, he said, which was not accurate because he had already received them once before. Reporters crushed round us to photograph us beside the lilies and I wondered when we would be exposed by the neo-Nazi press. Surely the original grower and giver would recognise his own delicately nurtured blossoms and denounce us.

But he didn't, which just shows that God protects fools like us. My Muslim colleague, after ruminating about the incident, finally burst into laughter and couldn't stop. God also moves in mysterious ways and we became good friends.

Many of the Jews, Christians and Muslims became good friends as a result of these meetings, notwithstanding these *faux pas* and *bêtises* – or perhaps because of them. For Jews at any rate they provided a much needed window on to the bigger world outside. All of us, whether Jew, Christian or Muslim, were shut into our own ghettos, though we were so accustomed to the walls we scarcely noticed them. I think we were the only young rabbis with this connection with the Muslim world, and it was only right and fitting that a Muslim woman born in Palestine was later appointed teacher of Islam at the Leo Baeck College.

Though our meetings were small, big issues that could affect Europe and beyond were discussed. Should Muslims as well as Jews set up their own school system? Would the graduates of both become supporters' clubs to their own sides in the Middle East? How far could secular western legal systems integrate or enforce elements of minority religious law? Was it right for them even to try? The results of the separate school system in Northern Ireland were not encouraging. Generally speaking, the practicalities of the European situation drew us together. Could we influence the Middle East? There was no profit in thinking about it. But whatever happened there, hopefully Jews would continue to live alongside Muslims and we might provide some kind of paradigm as to how it could be done.

I believe we all influenced each other more than we realised. Our aim was simple – to proceed from knowledge to the beginnings of affection and trust. I think some of this happened. I hope this policy is continued in the Leo Baeck College. It is not something non-European Jewish communities, either Israelis or American, have explored. Their circumstances propelled them at that time in other ways.

I wandered into a cafe with my friend the pastor to celebrate our success. It was a student New Left cafe. To my surprise, in the alcoholic haze we were greeted as 'the old revolutionaries'. I was gratified. I don't think the young revolutionaries knew what a revolutionary step we oldies had taken in driving windows into our ghetto walls. Someone handed me a banner which read:

Wer iemand mit dem Zweiten pennt,
gehoert schon zum Establishment.

This is too naughty to translate, said my pastor. He was a lovely man, even if he did give information to the Stasi, God bless him! Such muddles ran through German life.

51

My Lady Poverty Enters My Life Again

'Descending' from Israel, I decided on a pastoral inspection of the Jewish communities of my diocese. And I decided to start with Germany, because that is where the Holocaust was born and the leftover problems my small survivor communities inherited. I sometimes studied an old photograph in the Leo Baeck College of the Progressive Jewish worthies meeting with full honours in the German Reichstag, all serious but smiling, only a few years before Hitler came to power. It had not needed a Thousand Year Reich to destroy Jewish life in Europe – only twelve to obliterate the work of centuries.

It wasn't easy to say what Jewish life was about after the war in continental Europe, because few Jews were able to be honest with themselves. They preferred to think of themselves as en route for Israel or as Israelis in exile. It was only when their voluntary exile didn't end that the fiction had to be discarded. It was becoming ridiculous even to them. I don't blame them. For many European Jews, Jews in Germany especially, this continent was a graveyard, an accursed place even. Who wants to rebuild a religion in a charnel house, a cemetery?

But it was because of my lack of means, a gift of My Lady Poverty, that I stumbled on the New Europeans, the Muslim guest workers who were invited to work but not to stay, though of course that is what they did. People settle where they can live a decent life, whatever politicians say. That is why my own grandparents came to London and why I am English. That is why the Saxons and Angles came to Britain, displacing the Celts, and why America was born. I met the Muslims in this way.

My means of transport around my 'diocese' were variable. After a lunch with the German President (I represented few living

Germans Jews but hundreds of thousands of German Jewish ghosts), his sedan put me down near Cologne station. After a decent interval I started hitchhiking and found that as in student days my thumb still kept its cunning. I was on my own. Provided I produced results, methods of transportation didn't matter.

It was on the roads and in cheap night trains that I bumped into Muslims. I began to notice that beside the factories in the Ruhr and in the poor suburbs of Paris, the sky was punctuated by the tin minarets of little makeshift mosques. On those cheap trains I travelled in completely Muslim carriages of 'guest' workers, who were traversing two continents, going to or coming from Morocco or Turkey. 'Who are you?' they asked. They were unused to the company of a 'bourgeois' with a bowler hat, which is what I was wearing, who wanted to share their journey with them squeezed amid their packs and parcels. Now the Middle East was as always exploding and we were all suffering from paranoia, but I was weary of dissimulation whether as a gay or a Jew and I decided to make no bones about my status or affiliation. 'I am a Jewish rabbi,' I told the sage opposite me in loud French that could be heard throughout the carriage. He puckered his face in thought and then brought out a gun-shaped packet. He pointed it towards me and I looked round furtively to locate the alarm bell. 'This is humous,' said the sage seriously. 'It is kasher for you, *cher rabbin!*'

I was touched. As I have said, they were so much like my own grandparents I could have embraced them. They were pious in the same traditional way too. On the long jolting journey they prayed regularly facing Mecca as best they could. They didn't pray like so many western religionists at ecumenical conferences to show the flag, but because God so willed it. Prayer for them was like breathing.

When I returned to London and spoke excitedly about my latest discovery, I was taken aback because no one wanted to know except a few curious young rabbis and students. The others still thought pre-First World War according to which Europe was a Christian continent with a Jewish minority. But post-Second World War fact was quite different. A secular ideology was the established 'faith' in half of Europe, and after Christianity came Islam – now five times larger than the survivor Jewish community and growing year by year. Some Jews and Jewesses were being converted to it – I met them. They were really converted, not just socially converted for marriage purposes. One girl had been received into Islam after she shared incarceration with a Turkish holyman who lifted her among the dirt and degradation into paradise. Faith like that you catch from another person as you catch measles. Judaism was also being overtaken by Hindus, Sikhs and Chinese Buddhists, as well as by Muslims, all making converts while it remained almost closed.

But one thing I was convinced was important. The Jewish–Christian–Muslim dialogue in Europe had to get started immediately, before the same troubles that blighted the Holy Land (for want of a better name) were exported to the capital cities of post-war Europe. Already there had been Muslim–Jewish rioting in Paris, and this could easily spread. Both communities were like football supporters' clubs to their own sides in the Middle East, and separate school systems, which were just starting, would reinforce this separation. Secularised religion can be even more intemperate than the traditional spiritual kind, and inflammatory sermons about Jerusalem, Holy Cities, promised lands were the easy populist way out if the genuine God idea or the God experience was absent. Sentimental too! Almost as moving as a choir singing 'My Yiddishe Momma' but far more dangerous.

My own worry was the triumphalism that swept over Israel and Diaspora Jews after the Six Day War. There was a chance for peace, but it was missed in the euphoria of those days. '*Visitez Israel et ses belles pyramides!*' This was inflammatory, not funny, and could lead to the second (and final?) Jewish disaster of the twentieth century.

A gentle Egyptian said to me, 'When Nasser called for a jihad, this was not accepted by the ordinary Muslim who knew the Israel problem was a political not a religious one. But tell the Jews that they must be careful about Jerusalem. Holy places are important to us Muslims. They should not make talk of a jihad real.' I tried to warn people in an article printed in *Living Judaism*, the organ of Reformed Judaism in Britain. Needless to say, I became a loose cannon in a rabbinate which was committed to Israeli government policy. A silly American rabbi even hissed 'Arab lover' at me during a conference, and the *Jewish Chronicle*, the establishment journal of British Jewry, put me on the front page with a critical disapproving headline. I had merely pointed out the hard truth. Jerusalem had been occupied, not reunited, in 1967 and Israel had taken up a poisoned chalice.

When I had visited Israel earlier on for the World Union, I noticed that the geo-political language in vogue had shifted. It was less pragmatic than before but more fundamentalist and mythical. The occupied West Bank was now called Yehudah v'Shomron, Judah and Samaria – the old biblical names for it – and Israel up to the Jordan (and even a little beyond) was common thinking. Sinai, it is true, was later given up and Gaza not annexed, but then they were never part of the 'Promise'. I had the feeling that the boundaries of David's and perhaps of Solomon's kingdom were not negotiable. I had the foreboding that with the rise of such fundamentalism the past had laid a trap for the present.

A second wise man was even more unexpected – Uri Avneri, the editor of an Israeli *Playboy*-type magazine and maverick politician. His book *Israel without Zionism* was a warning to Israel not to repeat the mistakes of the crusader kingdoms in the Middle Ages, permanently alienated from their surroundings. I invited him over to London to address some rabbis unofficially, which amused him as the religious establishment in Israel preferred not to know him. But what he said was true, and after he spoke he received the accolade of thoughtful silence before the shocked hesitant discussion started.

As I wandered around my European 'diocese' in the sixties, My Lady Poverty also led me to people I would otherwise never have noticed. I think I had a thousand pounds or less to cover all expenses and this of course included my stay on the Continent. Compared to American Jews, European ones were a mean lot. As a result, instead of staying in platinum-plated ghettos, I stayed with anyone who would put me up and travelled with anyone who would give me a lift.

On the road I found myself involved in work I had never expected. It was not enough to knit Jewish communities together. I also had to interpret succeeding German non-Jewish generations to each other. Baeck realised this (but he died in 1956).

I could not afford blank international hotels, and instead I was adopted by families who were aghast at my manifest inability to care for myself. In Brussels a really cultured Jewish chap called Peter, from the pre-war Jewish *haut bourgeoisie* of Nuremberg and educated in an English public school, asked for my help. He wanted me to convert his wife and bar-mitzvah (confirm) his son. He was a considerable musician and agreed to help me out as cantor in the first High Holyday services of my new Liberal Jewish congregation in Brussels. I graciously agreed to do so. Promises, promises!

His wife Liesl had suffered from the autocratic Catholicism of her father, and was both amused and horrified by the small-town politics of my 'liberal' Jewish congregation, the main doers and workers for which were American businessmen stationed in the centre of the new Common Market. Like most international communities, they and their wives were excluded from the Belgian conservative aristocratic upper class, which centred around the King and the Court and which was strictly closed shop unless you were a multi-multi-multi-millionaire – and scarcely even then. Flemish society was also as inward-looking as any Jewish one and equally unwelcoming. Liesl met her future fellow congregants, listened politely to them and their concerns, found that few if any were into horses and declined conversion even by me whom she liked – more than God, she said, whom generally speaking she could do without. I was relieved. I preferred her as a friend rather than as a congregant, as the antidote to my ghetto rather than an extension of it.

She put me up, arranged holidays for me with her family, provided meals at all times and was uncritical, even when I fell asleep still smoking Belgian lorry drivers' cigarettes, to which I was partial, and leaving burnt bullet-like holes in her linen sheets. I used to recline on the fur coverlets in her home while she described life in Austria during the Nazi time to me, and how undignified and vulgar the regime was. Her friend, a Hapsburg princess, raised her hands in horror over its philistinism – a gesture I had read about but never before witnessed.

Liesl and Peter also taught me the art of conducting a row affectionately, especially at breakfast, when she and Peter had their regular set-to. They fenced with each other and modulated their voices according to the cut and thrust. Sometimes their arguments rose to classical heights, worthy of Racine tragedies and even Corneille, sometimes it was reminiscent of the Algonquin in New York in the Dorothy Parker and Robert Benchley days. I listened open-mouthed because they slid from one language into another, and each asked me for support, which made me choke just as I was consuming a slice of delicious dried beef or wurst. Then we went and ate steaks '*au bleu*' which I thought daring though cannibal. It certainly whetted my carnivorous tastes. The children, all of former marriages, who dearly loved them both, used to do a bit of prodding to keep the home fires burning.

I had never before had a row without feeling remorseful, guilty and screwed up. I realised then how many of my values had come from the world of Dagwood Bumpstead. If I had the sophistication earlier which I later acquired from them, I would not have made such a 'booboo' in forcing people like my mother – and perhaps my father too – into playing Happy Families.

Needless to say, Tommy, Peter's son, did not want my ministrations either. He was not a believer but a doubter and very politely asked me to lay off this bar-mitzvah business, which I did. Both he and Liesl became my great friends. Peter, because of his memories of the great synagogue in Nuremberg, did his stuff on the High Holydays. He was so anxious about his cantoral performance that he lost his voice but the strange counter tenor he produced in its place was weird and awesome. Our organist was American (she was heroic too), our prayer books came from France and our music from London – so our texts didn't fit the music and we were all used to different rituals. The result was odd but moving.

It was Peter who introduced me to a circle of administrators, artists and thinkers all involved with some aspect of the new Common Market which had made Brussels its home in 1957. They were not acting from their ego centres but for the common good, which awed me – this was real religion. For once I sat listening not talking, trying to understand and evaluate rationally and reasonably like them, not working on a basis of raw, unrefined emotion. It was Baron von Uxkuel who made the most impression on me – not because of his clarity (he was one of the woolliest exponents of ideas that I have ever met) but because of his charity, his limpid and otherworldly goodness. He was an Austrian aristocrat who had before the Anschluss taken Jews to dine with him into his reserved officers' mess. In 1944 he went into hiding because he was linked with the plot against Hitler. When I met him he was working for refugees in the United

Nations and the Common Market. He was as poor as a church mouse, for his family's estates had long ago been expropriated. This he scarcely bothered to mention. Again and again in the late fifties he helped refugees from Hungary after the uprising against the Stalinists to get work permits. He showed me that in much maligned Belgium you often need only assure an official that someone was genuine and had a good heart and this dispensed with files of bureaucracy. I began to see why so many more Jews had survived in Belgium than in Holland.

Another family which adopted me was in Holland. I came to them, as always, by a peculiar route. In London the poet Mike Horowitz had showed me a poem written to him and about him that had been published in a literary journal. He handed it to me to translate. I was startled. One four-letter word followed another and I dreaded having to give my opinion. But I was not asked. 'It is an Ode,' Mike said with consideration and I promised him I would look up the author when next in Amsterdam.

When I did call upon the author of the Ode, I got a cool reception. I had gone along with a friend, a German literary student whom JB had brought back home from his evening classes. The writer of the Ode shut the door and raved. My friend bowed slightly and formally, being polite, and Rob the author shouted he would have no more homos in his home and especially not Prussian ones. Well, I was homo certainly but my poor friend wasn't and he was anti-Nazi into the bargain. We all shouted at the same time in a goulash of languages, including me in jukebox Dutch. The row brought up Hedda, Rob's wife, from the basement and in straightforward Dutch fashion put us all in our place, giggled over the Ode, and asked admiringly who on earth had taught me such Dutch. She was Jewish herself, had known Anne Frank and liked having a rabbi around.

Whenever I dropped into Amsterdam, I stayed with Hedda and Rob who educated me in arcane New Left lore and the facts of life. Rob was a revolutionary publisher, and I persuaded him to publish the new magazine I had conceived and set my heart on – *European Judaism*, bourgeois though it was. He also published a prayer book for the British Reformed Synagogues, but without enthusiasm, at the same time as a cookbook for anarchists. He was more interested in the latter. It was as if I was putting pieces of a complex jigsaw puzzle together.

Both Rob and Hedda thought I should have a go at heterosex and it nearly worked out, but a miss – though a narrow one – led to a sorry mess. It may have been my lack of courage. They liked Janny, my 'girlfriend', from Oxford, and she came to stay with me in Amsterdam. But that didn't work – it was my fault.

In Geneva, where I had gone to preach, my 'friend in need' Robin introduced me to some of his friends, who were German, American, English and Dutch. We came together because you can feel very alone in a polite but closed Calvinist society. We jokingly called ourselves 'The Family' and have, over the years, become one. After thirty-five years we still meet together with our spouses and partners at birthdays, Christmas, in trouble and in success. I realised that families of friends could be as real as families of flesh and blood.

There were other families, societies and individuals that took me in as I circled around Europe trying to visit my scattered congregation. I learnt these things from them:

More fundamental than being Jewish was being a human being.

Seeing the obvious.

Letting all the ghettos I lived in cancel each other out so that I was free.

Behind these discoveries was my low salary and lower expense account, and My Lady Poverty who blessed me as she had St Francis of Assisi, despite our differences, so many centuries ago. Atta girl!

52

Our Guru Hunt

Hitchhiking, rushing to catch second-class trains, and bussing (even cheaper) around Europe in the fifties and sixties, I dropped in on committee after committee, chairing ecumenical ones, servicing new congregations, drawing up minutes with my colleagues – an important busy, busy rabbi of confused communities who, like him, had not quite got back to normalcy. I got only limited help from Israeli sources, who saw me as a small rival. The purpose of Zionism, they told me, is immigration to the Promised Land. Many Jews did emigrate, but many came back and many also compromised by staying where they were and taking package tours to Jerusalem as a sop to their conscience. This was not the Return the prophets had promised, but it was better than nothing.

I had my own personal agenda wandering through Europe. I not only wanted to find families who would cherish me as I cherished them, but also to discover teachers who didn't just teach about religion but religion itself because of what they were. I was only repeating what the medieval scholars sought as they wandered along the robber-infested roads of France, Germany and Italy. I needed gurus, enlightened gurus, saints, half saints, very human beings, provided they were outside the rat-race and the success struggle, and who were in the service of Heaven whether they realised it or not – they usually didn't.

In this guru hunt I had a companion, Dr Jonathan Magonet, who was a medic turning to religion. We told each other about the teachers we found and occasionally we learned from them together, though our needs were very different. I personally wasn't very interested in clever people. I had known too many at Oxford. I wanted wise people who could point the way to heaven.

This is how I met Jonathan. It is a circuitous tale but, since our teachers played such an important role in our loves, it is necessary to tell it.

When I took on the World Union job for Europe, I was also made World Union Youth Director. This inflated title in effect meant youth affairs in Europe. Once again it was a case of a long title, not much money, substance whatever you made of it. That is how I came to meet Jonathan Magonet, a very recently qualified medical doctor who though untried in the field was on the way to becoming a Harley Street specialist. He was good looking and *comme il faut*, a sought-after *parti* in Jewish north-west London. He knew it, of course, which riled me, but I needed him or someone like him for my work.

We were very unalike. He was organised, tidy, establishment and good-mannered, and could accomplish through his fine intellect what others accomplished through their feelings. This is of course my view of him, not him in himself. To my surprise he had became conscious of the same spiritual realities as me though by a different route. I therefore introduced him to Leslie Shepard, my Reichian analyst and Vedantist whose quality impressed him immediately as it had done me. For many years Jonathan and I worked together on the God business. He has been successively my pupil, colleague, co-editor, co-author and employer. He is a true friend, though what we make of each other I don't know.

What united us at the beginning of our friendship was the desire for 'true religion', not the rat-race variety, nor the populist variety, nor the schmaltz variety to which modern post-Holocaust suburban Judaism is attracted. To this was added the fascination of a post-war revival of Judaism in Europe. As is natural, we belong to different generations and now go our different ways. He is the venerable Director of the Leo Baeck College and I remain what I am – well, not very sure . . . which is exactly what I have always been.

In his student days he used to wander round the jazz clubs and folk lore cafes of Europe with a guitar, strumming and singing songs he had written himself. Some of them were kitsch and some fun, and some summarised that time in the fifties and sixties when Judaism in Europe had not quite gelled again after the disaster, if it ever would, and all sorts of futures were still possible.

Jim and I getting to know each other.

A right mixture! (Clockwise from top left) Kim's Jim, my Jim,
Kim, Pauline, Sister Mary, Ma and Dr Charlotte.

Twenty-three years and it don't seem a day too long!
Henry is where the party is (2nd from left).

With Japp – Darby
and Darby…

Jim and me –
grey and gay!

The American and Israeli models had not yet taken over. It was one of the great times in my life, though I was kippered in cigarette smoke and on my way to a heart attack. It was one of his great times too.

One of his songs which was not just catchy but pointed to a deep truth was about a Cavalcade which included all the people and guides Jonathan had bumped into or discovered in his search for enlightenment. I knew a few of the guides mentioned in his list because they were my guides and gurus too.

Here is the key to some of his verses about the spiritually powerful people we met, encountered or stumbled over in the confusion:

> *Leslie*
> The teacher's tenderness, as strong as it is clear,
> Using his glasses you can see beyond your fear
> And watch with wonder as he'll slowly disappear
> And you may never see his like again . . .

Leslie now lives in Dublin and looks as he has always done, an unobtrusive tidy poor elderly man whom your eye scarcely registers. He does not stand out because he has no axe to grind, and he sees the obvious.

He takes a pessimistic view of the prospects for western politics and culture. So pessimistic that I smiled indulgently with others a few years ago over his strictures. But after the first few years of the new millennium I consider them with more respect. The old trite phrase is true. We know the price of everything and the value of nothing. This will be our downfall.

> *Anneliese*
> The grey-haired mother who likes her whisky neat,
> Without intending she's adopted half the street.
> Though she has nothing she always makes ends meet
> And you may never see her like again . . .

If I gave Jonathan Leslie, he and Jeffrey Newman, another rabbinical student and then colleague, together gave me Anneliese Debray, whom they had met at her Home for Mistreated Women and her Ecumenical Centre in Bendorf near

Koblenz. For many years I pilgrimaged to her regularly. Almost as often as she pilgrimaged to me. *Notre sublime s'amalgama!*

She had been the secretary for Catholic Youth under the Nazis and then secretary for Catholic Women. She had taken part in underground resistance discussion groups, but felt it keenly that she had never ended up in a Gestapo prison or concentration camp. When the war ended she was at a spiritual loss, going through a crisis of faith, and wanted to learn at the feet of young Jews. Perhaps they could bring God back to her.

Like many truly godly people, she did not see that God was at work in what she was doing. She was among those who collected parcels of food and clothing for the Germans expelled from the eastern territories in the years before the Wirtschaftswunde when such things were in short supply in the West. But like all truly godly people she did more. She sent parcels also to the war-weary, tired and hungry Polish peasants who were occupying the vacated farms and lands of the German refugees. An unpopular move – but then, her religion was not populist.

With no money she adopted about a dozen children. How she was allowed to, I don't know. But her practical goodness convinced bureaucrats and bishops – and also Mrs Adenauer, who trusted her and never ceased to support her. When she died I found out that she had given up all her pension rights to fund Jewish–Christian–Muslim meetings. Not many clerics would do that, myself included.

Anneliese gave hospitality to anyone who could bring her back to God. She could be both very practical and very naive, like my own grannies. One lady turned up in Bendorf who insisted that she was God. Anneliese listened to her with concentration. But got annoyed when the God-lady demanded a double portion of the chocolate dessert. 'This was greedy,' muttered Anneliese indignantly. I tried to point out to her that rank has its privileges but she remained scandalised.

She worked for 'guest' worker Turks, rootless Jews, battered wives, gays as well (after I got at her), jobless Germans, forlorn Moroccans – she was a sucker for anybody in distress. She never realised that the God she was looking for was safe and secure within her and always would be. She was my *Deutsche* Yiddishe Momma – a great gal! She was also great fun unless you tried to pin her down with appointments. Whenever she caught a whiff of the Spirit (WW or Fred) from anywhere, she was away on its track.

She was a wonderful carousing companion, generous, impulsive and willing to take a chance. We were good shoppers together, plundering charity shops, fascinated by kitsch, and she didn't become mean even while drinking. She flowered! You don't see the likes of her very often in this life. I feel guilty that I didn't appreciate her enough while she was around, but then I feel guilty about nearly everybody – just as she did about God, in fact.

Winfried
The clown is innocent, the clown is very nice
And just enough a clown to have to pay the price
He's strangely wise but always takes the wrong advice
And you may never see his like again . . .

This is White Rabbit (the Rev. Pastor Winfried Maechler) who like his namesake is always late for the Duchess's party. I first met him in London when he was the incumbent of the German Dietrich Bonhoefferkirche. He walked into my office in London and asked me if I would join the Prague peace movement. I told him politely that I did not join 'Stalinist front organisations'. He gave me a tired knowing look but did not insist. I learnt from others that he had been the pastor of a semi-underground church in Nazi Berlin, and with Pastor Grueber, one of his heroes, had desperately worked to get the remaining Jews visas to North America, South America, Holland, Shanghai – anywhere!

He came from a line of clerics, ethical, educated and cultured, and he was all these too. Christianity was part of the air he breathed. But though he never talked about it, I felt that the official forms of it had let him down during the Nazi time and the years leading up to it. A parody of it reigned in the seats of power. He once told me how he and other pastors who followed Bonhoeffer and Barth had been summoned to an interview with the 'official' Nazi-acceptable Bishop of Berlin. The bishop had not called them to tell them off but to instruct them. 'What was the greatest of Christ's teaching and the most important of Christian commandments, the essence of Jesus's teaching?' asked the bishop. This bishop answered his own question as they hesitated between love and faith. 'Obedience!' he said triumphantly.

Winfried Maechler did his best during those Nazi years. When he was called up he worked in hospitals for the war wounded. His faith was firmed up by a Russian prisoner who looked after his wounded and suffering enemies with selfless love and compassion. Winfried never told me his name and it doesn't matter, but I have often thought about that prisoner of war.

After the war, when there was a general share-out of posts and honours from the newly vacated bishoprics in Germany, Winfried asked for nothing and got nothing. Like Anneliese, he couldn't decide where truth lay and did his best to reconcile East and West, the DDR and the Federal Republic. He introduced me to religionists on both sides of the Berlin Wall, never taking up a fixed position, just wanting me to see. I was not surprised when I heard after the DDR secret Stasi files had been made public that dear White Rabbit stood quite high in its hierarchy of collaborators and informers. Anybody who tried to reconcile was on their lists. It also did not surprise me that the information he turned in on me, and other rabbis and our work for Jewish–Christian–Muslim understanding, was harmless. It merely told what was already public knowledge or no great secret. We were all too powerless to have any great secrets in any case. He was a good man in a terrible time. His vocation was dialogue, and few appreciate its importance and difficulties when the battle and propaganda lines are drawn up.

Fortunately his practical loyal wife supported him. He needed it, because there must have been a lot of anger in him. He had seen and endured so much darkness, senseless cruelty, and misery without glib reassurance or sentimental belief and still hung on trying to do his best in a mad world. Only very occasionally did it appear for a fleeting moment in a cynical look, a tightening of the lips, an unnatural detachment. Then I realised what a fool I must have seemed to him – an interesting fool, a worthy fool probably, but a fool who didn't know the half of it. He was right and I thank God I didn't. I would have probably committed suicide like Primo Levi or Zweig.

Rudi
The dancer waltzing through the nightmares of the past
Working with parables and dreams that have to last
Knowing the dangers when the music plays too fast
And you may never see his like again . . .

This is our friend Rudi, a dancer before he became an Evangelical minister. As a boy, he told me, he gave his all to Hitler. Then, enlightened, he transferred it to Christ. He is atoning for more than a human being can bear. I haven't seen him for many years. He is '*treu*'. I hope he allows himself a measure of ordinary human happiness.

Lionel
It isn't nice to see the way the prophet eats,
He tends to dribble and he's far too fond of sweets,
But when it matters he's the one who never cheats
And you may never see his like again . . .

This is me as Jonathan saw me. My table manners are now tidier because my partners have retrained me and the families, who adopted me, civilised me.

The cast assembles, the overture begins
Parading angels in their badly fitting skins.
Off-stage the invisible director slowly grins
And you may never see his like again . . .
So hang on, don't be afraid
You too can join the cavalcade . . .

I sometimes click my Arab worry beads, or a battered rosary. The beads are remembrancers of the very human and heavenly teachers I bumped into or stumbled across as I rushed around Europe, advancing from one committee meeting to another.

53

Visited by the Angel of Death

About 1964 and 1965 the angel of death became a constant visitor in my life. My home was dying because JB and I were finishing and a house always reflects the death of love between the people in it. But there were also two or three people – and then a dog – who died about that time, who were among the finest I'd ever met. I was so involved in Religion I didn't notice Goodness when it was staring me in the face.

One was a Polish chap who felt at home among Jews and might have wanted to join us on his deathbed. It was JB who told me that he was in hospital, but I didn't visit in time because I was too busy extricating myself from JB and didn't want another violent row. Also my second love hadn't gelled yet, and another friend and teacher was committing suicide at the same time and I was near breaking point because it was all too much and so my Polish friend died before I could visit him. It was JB who had brought me the news about Stanislaw and I was suspicious in case it was another device of JB's to get me back under his power. I realised too late how much I honoured Stan. Another casualty of the paranoia brought about by too much tension. Still, one of the great things about believing in God is that he can complete what his creatures leave undone. There is such a lot of unfinished business in our earthly life, but in my prayers I can at least say sorry!

But all these events were overshadowed by the death of my own father. I was only beginning to realise what a good man he was when he died about the same time as my Polish friend Stan. (Both men liked each other and lived near each other.) How he supported living with two such characters as my mother and me I don't know. But he was a provider who was always under the domination of somebody – his own strong mother, his even stronger wife, and me. He couldn't stand up to my mother when I needed his support as a youngster and I hadn't forgiven him. I shouldn't have expected it. Unpretentious service and self-sacrifice were his satisfaction and Ma and I, though generous, were not built to appreciate or even notice such virtues.

I felt puzzled rather than bereft when Dad died. I suppose that's why Dad got the biggest and best tombstone in our family, no expense spared. It made up for the tears we didn't shed at the time. But over the years I have come to think more and more about him and his inarticulate concern for me and to understand his goodness. The real mourning, when it came, came slowly but it went very deep. I think my mother had the same problem. Though I thought that because I had an analysis that I knew it all, I began to realise I didn't know half of it. I didn't begin to know what my parents really felt for each other. I had been misled by their constant rows and bickering.

Now I'm pleased they stuck together, because to my surprise and confusion they did come together again but after I left home for Oxford. A week before he died my mother told me he had had cancer for two years. She had kept the truth from him and from me and shouldered the worry alone. When I visited him, she made me promise to talk to him only about his 'ulcers' and our first planned continental holiday to Ostend.

In my naivety I had thought I had kept them together because they both loved me inordinately. I just couldn't support the weight of so much love. So when he wanted me to become an athlete and she wanted me to become a lawyer, I did the dirty on both of them and became a rabbi, which gobsmacked them both. To my surprise, my traditional father on this occasion stood up for me. He saved his pocket money to buy me candlesticks and an Aramaic dictionary and made me special bookcases to put them in. When Ma criticised my piety, Dad actually told her to shut her mouth. She was so surprised that she did.

My father was a careful tidy man (utterly unlike me) with a drawer of significant mementoes, medals, silver cigarette box, hairbrushes, wallets with precious photos and letters. After his death my mother handed them over to me. She had no feel for such things. I didn't either because they soon disappeared. At that time I couldn't care for things. I could scarcely care for myself.

It took a further ten years of therapy before I began to understand what an example he was! He had never commented on my homosexuality but had been generous, kind and helpful to all the friends and acquaintances I had brought home whether macho, lisping, city gent or drop-out. He was an inarticulate man, and I could never have reminded him of my physical puberty love for him which he had rejected and which had left me seared with embarrassment for so many years. What a mess! You didn't have to go to the southern states of America in the company of Tennessee Williams and Truman Capote to discover such tangles. Golders Green, London, NW11 could be just as haunted.

My mother and father were a generous pair. Some hitchhiking students arrived on a lorry at their home in the early hours of the morning. I had given them our address. My mother set to and made them pre-dawn kippers, and Jewish potato pancakes. My father brought in blankets and my mother told them to sort themselves out on the floor whichever way they wished. My father, noticing one kid had a cold, gave him his coat (for keeps). That was better than the respectable tight-arsed ritualism and exclusive nationalism I was expected to preach.

Then another brush with death! After my final fight with JB in which my glasses got smashed, I suddenly learnt that my former teacher in theology and mysticism had committed suicide. I owed him a great debt because he had tried to save me from the treacly religious kitsch which had attracted me. I tried to help him but it was not enough – or useless. He had retreated into a locked world of chessmen, with which he played games for his own sanity. He was from central Europe and had died from alienation, killed by the Holocaust.

> The moving finger writes; and, having writ,
> Moves on: nor all thy piety nor wit
> Shall lure it back to cancel half a line,
> Nor all thy tears wash out one word of it.
> *(The Rubáiyát)*

It took some time before I felt the full force of all these deaths, but I felt the death of my second dog, Djilas, immediately.

> Who is thy servant but a dog?
> (From ancient
> Semitic inscriptions)

The story of my second dog, Djilas, did not have a happy ending. I have told it to my former therapist, who told me I was taking unnecessary blame on myself (as usual). But I do.

This is what happened. When JB and I broke up, my new friend could take only one dog, not two. Djilas was supposed to be JB's dog (though in fact she was mine), so when I moved I had to leave her behind. But I heard she was unhappy and I went back to get her, met JB and nearly lost an eye. In the fight my spectacles were shattered (again). But I left the home with Djilas.

A lady who liked dogs took her in, and I watched Djilas trot away proudly with her new mistress. I didn't ring so as not to interfere with the new relationship. I learnt on a visit three weeks later that Djilas had had a phantom pregnancy, defended the lady against all comers, including the lady's husband, and got put down. The subject was taboo in the English manner.

It cast a shadow over my new relationship that never dispersed. I have never had a dog since, though for a while I supported a three-legged one in Malta until he was properly adopted. (For a while he must have been the only dog in Malta with his own bank account.)

54

Kim and Sailing

Kim was my second partner. I met him accidentally when the love between JB and me – apart from a few unexpected, moving moments – had died or turned sour. Janny finally wanted us to get married now, and said she would convert to Judaism. And looking back, I think I should have gone ahead with this, but I hesitated to try it. I was too neurotic and inexperienced for such unknown territory. I could wreck two lives, not just one. I was also distrustful of our fantasy. Kim was my third way, my escape. We met in the sauna of the old Imperial Hotel. He invited me to a chicken sandwich at a place nearby.

Me: I'm a rabbi and [proudly] my hobby is sailing.

He: I sail too.

Me: But I've been on a diploma course in sailing on a lake in Holland. [I didn't tell him that I had not passed my diploma!]

He seemed impressed. We may have things in common, he said. Later on I learnt he was one of Britain's greatest yacht designers – world class.

Of course we had things in common and more than we knew how to acknowledge in words. We were both hidden homosexuals in a time of repression, persecution and blackmail, and our eyes and knees soon sussed this out. I was between breakdowns and he was on the edge of a massive one. His doctor had advised him to 'find his way to a solution'. He had – he found me, and we spent the night together in his blank smart businessman's pad near Hyde Park. Sex adequate rather than satisfactory. Affection and kindness and comradeship tremendous. Physically we each knew our place and we fitted. Not knowing such basic things had helped destroy my life with JB. It was a holiday for me from the anger and violence of my own 'home' and I clutched at it. He took me to a smart restaurant and my depression began to lift. He thought I was the best thing since sliced bread and I blossomed.

He wondered if we could be each other's solution, he said, though he was rich and of a different class. (What sauce! thinks me.) Well, I had culture and education, I told him, and he apologised, which mollified me. He was a gentleman. But being rich, he added, he had the means for both of us to escape from our present and past. (Now he's talking! I was physically and mentally exhausted from trying to put together some remnants from the Holocaust in Europe as well as the remnants of myself from a dying household.) Let's make a bonfire of our present lives, he said, and sail through the West Indies where he had a boat. I could scarcely imagine it. As the sun sank slowly in the west we could drink rum on deck at anchor off a desert island. He loved the West Indies, the blue seas alive with fish, golden suns, glittering stars and black beauties.

I resigned from my job, we went to the West Indies, came back, his breakdown broke, and for the next twelve years we were carers not lovers to each other, living by a yacht club with blazers and club buttons and pink gins in the Home Counties, or in London's West End. Instead of tangles with Talmud, I tangled with ropes and knots, and practised injecting sausages with water on our doctor's advice as prudent preparation in case Kim got so crippled by a migraine in a gale over the North Sea that I had to take over (God help us!) and also give him an injection. Little did he know that I was showing my first symptoms of epilepsy. He seemed to take my possible captaincy for granted. My jaw dropped but I persevered. In our own ways we were quite brave.

The yacht club folk were kinder than I expected to this Jew who popped up at the same time as their hero's breakdown. The only one who wanted to run me off their island was a pathetic chap who also didn't fit – but in a different way from me.

In the first years of caring for each other, sex was out (and I nearly climbed the walls) but love of a different sort drifted in and lit up our lives. On Friday nights after the gins at the club, Kim, dog and I closed the doors against the world, lit candles and gave each other records, Roget Gallet soaps, and kisses. When I came back from the Continent from a Jewish–Christian–Muslim meeting, he would drive at night to a distant airport to meet me. I hadn't expected it. He had missed me, he said. Our meeting was so blessed it felt painful. He also drove me to synagogues where I took services to make a living.

I admired him enormously. He did have class. He wasn't just cafe society. He was '*treu*', a gentleman, the real thing, and also I think the brother I never had. He had been the youngest naval officer in charge of a minesweeper. I was proud to be with him because he accepted responsibility, never tried to pass the buck, and always appeared sure of himself even when a clash of feelings raged deep inside him, or a gale at sea raged around him.

At midnight, walking home from an 'extended' boozy lunch, a young constable addressed him.

'And where are you going, sir?'

'None of your business, Constable,' said Kim sharply.

'I was only doing my duty,' answered the constable aggrievedly.

'Well, go and do it somewhere else!' said Kim brusquely.

Being from the East End of London, I would never have dared speak to the police like that. I never had such a sense of my own worth and standing. Neither did Kim himself during these illness years, but he never allowed this to show. I think that is why his breakdown was so massive and seemed such a surprise.

We gave our life experience to each other.

He gave me the sea and brought out the fortitude in me to cope with it because he believed in me. I was overwhelmed by its power and its beauty. I was exhilarated diving under the boat freeing ropes trapped around the propeller, and relying on him not to press the wrong knob and reduce me to rabbinical hamburger. With our two sailing friends, Harold and Noel, I enjoyed the perfection of four chums bobbing together across the North Sea, even when we found we'd forgotten the box with all our cigarettes and baccy on the pier.

But all this came to an end when Harold and Noel died one after the other, being older than Kim and me. Harold was one of the most courteous people I've ever known. Noel was a gem, a diamond of the purest water, straightforward, honest, a gentle Nimrod, a mighty hunter, who was incapable of any meanness or malice. He was a living example that Jews had no monopoly of rectitude. Vestiges of that cosy claustrophobic belief still lurked in my mind. The presence of Noel dispelled them.

And then one day – jumping ahead in our story – Kim came back from his new doctor. The old pills and tablets which had reduced his inner fires were suddenly taken away. Within days a new Kim emerged who no longer needed a carer, who resented a carer, who no longer needed me in his bedroom to assuage his nightmares.

We decided to go on another honeymoon together to re-find each other, but I was scared of his mercurial moods and irritation with all he thought held him back. Just when I made my mind up to go along and face the music, he went on our honeymoon without me but with a girl we both knew, a refugee, who had gone through a tough time herself. I stayed behind in London, touched bottom and had my first full epileptic fit though I had had half ones before.

When he returned, we made another try to re-find each other, and we were blessed in a private ceremony by a well-meaning Anglican clergyman. But ritual is not magic. It is not a mystic fixative to keep couples together who have grown away from each other. Kim had found a pleasant Jamaican with whom he had a lot in common. They enjoyed restoring antiques, gardening, dancing and property renovation. I was no good at any of them. The end was no longer in doubt but we still had to divide a house and a home. Second time for me – I had transferred my first house to JB. But now I knew there was a life beyond divorce, and the world went on however much it felt like death and the end. I was older and wiser. The old black hole had again opened up in front of me.

55

'And His Mother Came Too'

After Dad's death and I'd gone off to live with Kim, Ma also had to find another life. She certainly didn't intend to vegetate sweetly and gracefully in her old house. She had really little feeling for places or for death or for the dead. She just wanted to be where the action was, where it was all happening. That was of course with me and Kim, whom she cared for because he appreciated her loyalty and treated her like a lady. So she moved into our guest room, and if that was occupied by a guest she slept on the sofa or the floor. She distributed her clothes wherever. It didn't really matter. A house guest one night said he had had a most extraordinary dream in which a naked woman materialised out of the wardrobe in his room. I told him he must have drunk too much the night before. But that was no dream. It must have been Ma!

Nothing was too much for her. She would take down dictation at dead of night or buy hamburgers for us at dawn among the drug pushers in Queensway, or comfort Kim or me when the other wasn't there or take us to a pub or walk the dog or do our accounts. She was on our side and nothing we did could possibly be wrong.

In return Kim chose her to launch his new boat with a bottle of champagne. She partied through the night with yachtsmen, attended Christmas Mass with my favourite Catholic Sisters and ran a kind of confessional in the local pub. She flowered, becoming more herself, more generous, more gypsyish, wearing more makeup, more self-sacrificing and kinder than ever. There was actually a lot more Yiddishe Momma and her mother in her than I had given her credit for, but it was mixed with a lot of flapper and a buoyant energy that kept our problem household afloat. In her own peculiar way she was pious. Because she was good-natured everyone liked her, even the Mormon missionaries she made sheep's eyes at while stuffing them with so much cake they couldn't talk. She just liked looking at them.

All this was of course beside her job at an office. She never told her age to her employers. She just lied about it, she confessed to Kim and me, so she stayed on long after she should have retired. It was the puzzled tax authorities who eventually became curious about her because of some bureaucratic point about what oldies masquerading as youngies should pay in tax. That's how her horrified office tumbled to her years. Pity! Otherwise she would have gone on forever.

Recently a lady from Ma's former office wrote to me about Ma, recalling what she looked like. The lady is now Dr Amanda J. Turner but was then a photocopier. Here is an extract from her letter. I can vouch for every word.

She was a real character and had a fantastic sense of humour. My other friends and I in the office used to go out with her for lunch and she loved to party, so often came out with us on social occasions, even disco dancing! (She must have been well in her sixties then, if not seventy?) In return, she invited us to tea and proudly showed you off. She never stopped talking about 'my son Lionel' and his friend Kim (as it was then), although in keeping with the times she resolutely chose to ignore the subject of homosexuality, although we all knew you were gay of course.

However, the things I remember about her most were her 'eccentricities'. She was still firmly dressed in the 1920s with drop-waisted dresses and shoes with a bar strap and buckle at the side. She was often to be found sitting at her desk with her mirror propped up against her typewriter, resisting the marching on of time by touching up her dyed black hair with a mascara brush! Her nails were always painted and she appeared never to remove it, daily adding further layers so that they appeared about an inch thick. She called everyone 'dolly' and swore in Yiddish, happily translating for those who didn't understand.

I was extremely fond of her and she made a big impression on me, even though we lost touch as I moved on. I have often enjoyed remembering her.

Ma savoured every moment of life like a connoisseur rolling wine around his mouth. That was why she left the house in the morning as if shot from a gun, banging on her hairpiece back to front or any which way provided it was quick. She loved sitting by the window in a lorry drivers' cafe, hoping to see two zimmers clashing, or lovemaking by the lamppost, or a traffic warden getting heated over a parked car. She enjoyed giving, and one Chinese waiter used to run after me telling me that she had left him a £5 note as a tip. It was too much and I should put it back in her purse.

When in hospital with a dodgy heart she didn't want flowers, which were a nuisance, but a big bottle of Charlie perfume instead so she that she smelt nice for the specialist. She certainly didn't want my aunt Lil around, whose conservatism cramped her style. 'I wouldn't bring her along, Lionel,' she said, 'she's too old. Just give her best wishes from me. Tell her there's no need to reply, she can say it with some of her fried fish balls. Tell her to make them sweet and add plenty of almonds!' she wheezed as I was going out of the door.

My aunt was equally dry-eyed about Ma's condition. I told her I'd take her along to see her. My aunt considered this but rejected it. 'I'll send her a postcard instead along with the fish balls. And Lionel, don't make us get sentimental over each other,' she added shrewdly. 'Your ma and I have gone through too much together to play games. If she really wants me I'll come but not till then. It's nice to potter round without her and I expect she feels on holiday without me.' She did.

Once a letter arrived at my home addressed to M. Bellew. I assumed it was for me and opened it. It contained a membership card and programme of a cinema club which showed blue films to adults. Ma snatched it from me, admitting it was for her. A girl she had met in a pub had introduced her to it. She used to buy a steak and kidney pie and, with the agreement of the manageress, who liked her, munched it in the back row at lunch time. The cinema was warm, said Ma, and educational. She only wished she had known once what she knew now, she said knowingly. I told her I often felt the same. We were both late starters and I opened a bottle of Advokaat, her favourite tipple, to brood over this truth, serving it with a dash of cherry brandy and a dollop of cream in the way she liked. I warned her not to get herself into trouble but of course she did – not because of promiscuity but generosity, which I should have expected. She was strangely innocent about sex and never could understand why men thought so much of it and about it.

But back to the blue film club! During the darkness Ma felt the pressure of a friendly knee. She pressed back and the two knees canoodled together. But the light went on as it always does and the young man beside her saw her, shrieked and bolted. He worked at a nearby office, and was very upright and proper. Ma promptly gave chase, tottering after him on high Louis heels. He looked back in panic and shrieked again. 'Why were you frightening the poor lad?' I said sternly. 'I wasn't,' replied Ma indignantly. 'I just wanted to tell him how happy he'd made an old lady and I wouldn't say a word about it to anybody.' The next day Ma told me he had reported sick. Should she find out his address and visit him with grapes? 'Leave well alone,' I told her sternly. 'I know you mean it for the best' – did I? – 'but the best is getting off his back and letting him have his little breakdown in peace.' Ma sighed but accepted this philosophically. She wasn't a harpy, just a good-natured, curious gal, a graduate of the old La Bohème dancing rooms in London's East End.

She got other propositions too. One of Ma's old boyfriends had died, and some years later she started to go out with his staid, successful, but much duller friend. One morning she asked me if I would marry her. It took me a few minutes to realise that she was talking about respectability, not incest. 'Sure!' I told her and Ma said she thought he would propose to her today. I wished her good luck because she was as nervous as a kitten and Kim gave her a pink gin to steady her. She would now soar up to dizzy, fizzy, social heights, leaving Kim as well as me applauding from our lower homo depths. She promised not to cut us and we all burst into peals of raucous laughter.

Ma returned home in the early hours of the morning, tired and cross and banging on the door which made the dog bark. We had to pacify her before we got a coherent idea of what happened. Yes, the old boy had proposed to Ma, and Ma with qualms said yes because she was still in love with his dead best friend. Ma then suggested why wait for nuptials. There was no time like the present and with quavering arms he began to disrobe her. He was unfortunately too taken with her, got over-excited and had a heart attack. Ma with great presence of mind half dressed him and then called the hospital. She then stayed beside his bed till after he had recovered. She decided she never wanted an old lover again but a young, healthy and lusty one, which obviously she couldn't get. So that was the end of the affair because she wasn't a hypocrite.

A handsome elderly lady pointed out to me that men were scarce commodities when you were eighty. Unlike women, who were hardier, they mostly died off in their seventies. She told Ma to become a lesbian like her. The sex wasn't up to much but young girls, i.e. in their forties and fifties, often took a shine to hardy specimens like her and Ma. I enjoyed the rare opportunity of seeing Ma shocked. Anyway, Kim and I comforted her and told her she always had us and Ma asked us if we had any letters we wanted her to bang out on her old, crash, bang-bang, wallop, ting-a-ling typewriter. We always did and she quickly recovered and they all made a fuss over her at the pub and at the nearby convent where the Sisters really enjoyed her.

Ma could never understand why people made such a fuss over such a silly thing as sex. My next partner Jim, who succeeded Kim (who later on met a very nice Jim himself), came down one morning some years later and discovered my mother starkers behind the living-room door.

'Hetty,' he said sternly, 'Lionel's told you you must only dress and undress in your bedroom, not the living room.'

'Yes,' said my mother, placating him as one does a precocious infant. 'I'll remember that for next time' – which of course she would never do. Jim went to look for her staid, elder sister Lil, who was in the kitchen searching the rubbish bin to find her false teeth. 'Lil,' he said, 'you had better go and see to Hetty. She's in the living room without a stitch on.' My aunt took the news philosophically. Peering up from the rubbish bin, she said to him speculatively, 'You know, Jim, some men would pay good money to see that. She hasn't got any shame, never did have.'

But my mother had another quality apart from generosity, and it was vitality. There is so much religion that is mealy-mouthed and debilitated that my mother's racy approach to life was a treat after the half truths, evasions and avoidances of ecumenical meetings. Ecclesiastical dignitaries and their wives could look so grey and sexless that a little bit of life with my mother would have freshened them up, so that they could give thanks to their Creator with conviction, realistically as well as ritualistically. Her sins were very little ones. She was just a modern Magdalen, that's all.

She meant well, but she had a genius for treading on people's toes or saying the wrong thing especially when she was trying to be helpful. I do not say this in any spirit of criticism, because I began to like my ma more and more as she matured into her pure, unadulterated self, her essence.

She was hilarious at religious celebrations. At a traditional wedding, Ma tried to help out an old rabbi who was giving a speech in Yinglish (Yiddish–English). Now Ma used to translate for the Jewish women who used to steal along furtively to the Marie Stopes clinic in fear of their husbands, so she added her own widow's mite to be helpful.

'In our time ve arc fighting ze-ze battle of . . .' 'Britain!' interposed my mother helpfully. The sage gave her a withering look. 'Of Chewdaism,' he shouted back at her. After the meal it was announced that there would be no ballroom dancing with men and women, so as not to offend the aged sages present. Only holy dances for men alone were permitted. Now Ma had been looking forward to her chassés and black-bottoms, for which she had been famous, and was put out. But she brightened up when some godly mystical rabbis did a ring-a-ring of roses on the dance floor while the women looked on.

'Hetty,' said two bookmakers (our family was a mixed lot), 'what sort of dance is this?'

'Oh, I know,' said Ma in a flash of inspiration, 'it's a knees up.' And all three burst into the Cabbalistic circle, singing 'Knees up Mother Brown . . .' and putting the pious to flight, drastically changing its character. I was politely told by our host sotto voce to please restrain my mother. My host and I looked at each other and burst into laughter, knowing that to be quite impossible because she was on a high. She'd get down in her own time. To my surprise the ultras were quite nice about it. They had to look disapproving but they were giggling too. I had misjudged them quite unfairly – which was an important lesson for me.

Ma was addicted to the nature films on TV and the four of us (Ma, me, Kim and pooch) used to watch them companionably. We were fascinated by one in which a female octopus ate her male partner alive after impregnation. 'Surely,' said Ma, 'it could have been organised better? What do they say about it in your seminary?'

'They don't,' I answered laconically. 'It's another subject too hot to handle.'

Ma sniffed.

Being a naturally generous, kind woman, Ma didn't need much Religion of the formal supernatural type, the kind spelt with a capital R. But I was not so generous and did. That's the difference between us.

56

Praying Again after a Holocaust

In 1967 I needed a job. Kim was recovering from a stroke and we didn't know what form our life would take. So a normal congregational job wasn't possible. It was also just before 1968 and the liberation of the most cautious private gay sex from criminality. I did take Kim with me to a conference but, though he was ill, he had to stay in a separate hotel and get smuggled in to me, poor chap. I discussed it all with Ma, who was becoming a thoughtful listener, because she loved me and was beginning to love Kim too.

I wanted a job in which the work could travel with Kim and me together whether in London, Amsterdam, by the North Sea, Malta or the West Indies. Would, could, the macho world of yacht clubs really accept an open gay relationship? Actually I found some of my best friends in life from that world. Would it be better to start a new life again in London, where everything went but not much mattered, or in Malta which was quiet and gentle and off the edge of the world, or the West Indies where the rum was cheap and we could join the well-off American drop-outs and work hard at having a good time – though I knew the good life was not good living. Kim had his boats. I needed something I was passionate about too.

Once again it was my teacher and mentor Rabbi Dr van der Zyl who turned up trumps and pointed me towards work on the new Reform prayer books and liturgy. Liturgy was alive for me at that time because I relied on its regularity and strength in an irregular world. I held on by praying regularly in any chapel or synagogue I could find, and this kept me together, protecting me from the confusion around me. I didn't need the approval of people and I could cope with being a member of two ghettos, a gay one and a Jewish one, as long as the Inner Voice was behind me or in me. On Friday evenings the liturgy worked its weekly wonder. Kim and I blessed the bread and the wine and all three of us (the dog was there too, keeping an eye on us for any deviation from regularity which she detested) were melded into a family and love was born again between us. The house became home. They were shining times in my life, and Kim felt it too.

Now Dr van der Zyl had come to me out of desperation. English was not his native language but he liked it enough to lose his German accent except when excited. He also knew English well enough to realise that the previous attempts at reforming our Reform liturgy hadn't worked. The Three Festivals Prayer Book produced by the Assembly of Rabbis was an erudite, interesting non-starter. It had some very new and good things in it indeed but the congregations couldn't see them because they were foxed by the layout. The influence of Form Criticism was so strong that the liturgy couldn't work, however academically correct. The excess of clever, very blank verse confused reader and congregation. Both text and translation made pretty patterns on the page.

The English was a twentieth-century attempt to reproduce a nineteenth-century imitation of the seventeenth-century English that pious people then assumed God spoke. The basic problem, though, was not one of style but one of generations. Apart from an occasional formal prayer, the old liturgy barely recognised the shattering changes in European Jewry. The bulk of it could have served synagogues just as well in 1860 or 1960 – Hitler, Auschwitz, Israel notwithstanding.

I had once shown Dr van der Zyl the Canadian writer Mordechai Richler's modern English version of a rabbinic prayer, and Dr van der Zyl had not forgotten. So I got appointed to have another go, because – as so often in my life – there was no one else who had the time. My colleagues were pleased that someone else would take on the responsibility and I was pleased to have a job that was central to my life and kept me out of the limelight. The work occupied most of my time for several years and restored my self-respect. I barely got paid expenses for it. So, once again, I went to Dr van der Zyl and started to teach at the Leo Baeck College. He believed in me.

That's how things happen in the real world, though they don't

234

appear in the minutes. Both jobs fitted in with sailing and then moving back to London's West End.

I asked permission from the Rabbinic Assembly to co-opt Jonathan Magonet, metamorphosing at that time from doctor to rabbi, to assist me with liturgy and revision, and Rabbi Hugo Gryn replaced Dr van der Zyl (who retired to Majorca) as Chairman of the Prayer Book Committee.

Let battle commence! The first skirmish was over language – bluntly stated: 'thee-thou' or 'you-you' English, which? Hugo wanted 'thee-thou' and so did a lot of just over middle-aged congregants, and I said if 'thee-thou' was in, they should include me out. Instead of composing prayers and editing services, I had to cajole. I now had trouble on both fronts: the home front and the work front. This actually was very good for my spirituality. It's only when your feet are slipping that you really pray, and that you experience a hand holding you up above the murky waters.

A word about my relations with Hugo. I admired him, and liked him, and I think he felt the same for me though we were both strong characters who could get exasperated by each other. If I had gone through his experiences under the Nazis and in Auschwitz I would probably have become very bitter indeed, not the force for dialogue, ecumenism and understanding that Hugo became. In later years we began to become close to each other. From his background he was naturally more communalist, nationalist and ethnically Jewish than me. We were also both insecure but in different ways. Hugo was wonderful if you were below him and needed him – and I did many times, but I wasn't the assistant type and frequently we were working over the same ground in different ways for different ends. This brought on Hugo's refugee insecurity and my paranoia and we both had to swallow hard.

Hugo was in favour of 'thee-thou' and read out plangent letters from upper-class schoolkids, reproaching Jonathan and me for depriving them of their tradition. Many sounded as if they had been put up to these by their parents. I was getting paranoid. The strain of life was beginning to tell.

Jonathan and I had to win in the long run because there was nobody else who would do the job. I strongly objected to antiquing modern English thoughts and feelings because I felt the result would be false, and I preferred our old 1920 prayer book, which was thin but honest, to a phoney 'antique' translation. Where would the antiquing stop? After antiquing our prayers, would we antique the book itself and in the end antique our faith? Hugo had been educated in America. I had been educated at Oxford. I loved the English language I had learnt there – and insisted our translation be real just as Bunyan's and Blake's English were real in their time.

After some rows Jewish style, the result was a draw. Because so much time had been spent on style, hardly anyone noticed how the traditional format diverted attention from the entry into a conservative prayer book of such dissenters as Freud, Marx, Walter Benjamin, Kafka, Emma Goldman and their like. There were also phrases from Nicholas of Cusa and Colette. Jonathan Magonet was a brilliant anthologist, and because of my dis-ordered life I could write prayers and pleas to God with conviction.

Jonathan and Hugo each had their own vision of the new liturgy. Mine was as follows.

I had seen how religion was suppressed in the Stalinist East, where only formal services were permitted as an expression of a living faith. I had also seen how religion was so eroded in the West that the Talmud, the codes and the commentaries, were sinking below the horizon together, and for most, the mystical texts in their contorted Aramaic were an unsolved mystery. The result was that the only holy book from the past which was not a museum piece for most Jews was the prayer book, which at least came into their hands as a matter of course several times a year. The prayer book also had one great advantage over all other holy books – it had never been finished. It was still open to change – just! – provided the change was carefully inserted and wrapped up in traditional blessings. It would now have to extend enough to include the emancipation, the open society which came with it, the horrors of the Holocaust, the rise of Israel, the golden age of Jewish intellect, and then the revolution in women's rights and status, and the liberation of sexual minorities from the closet. Since the post-Holocaust communities that it served were insecure, it was not a case of change or tradition but something more complex. The more traditional our prayer books felt, the more modern matter could be absorbed into them.

Prayer books ask, 'Why?' Modern science asks, 'How?' The

former communicated through tradition and mythologised history, the latter through the logic of maths, quantity and quantum. I felt that only in individual lives did they come together so the new prayer books were rich in human experience of all ages and from all conditions of people.

Looking at the post-war Jewish experience in eastern and western Europe, this prayer book might be the only carrier of the wisdom and virtue of European Judaism into future years, decades and centuries. So the new prayer books had pictures of living and dead European synagogues and, what is more important, an inclusive anthology and selection of the wisdom that European Jewry produced. It had to be more than a straightforward prayer or ritual book. It had to be a home companion for life, to rest by a bedside, or packed for a holiday, hospital, concentration camp or gulag. It had to be used for life as well as in synagogues. So wherever truth came – from America, or Israel or the USSR – it had to be recognised and honoured too.

My own Judaism had hung by a thread during the war years on a little book given to evacuated children and Jewish soldiers – the Chief Rabbi's pocket-sized *Book of Jewish Thoughts*. Later on, religion flowered for me in another spiritual anthology – Victor Gollancz's *Year of Grace*. Was spirituality a waste of time? Because of these two anthologies, my answer was a resounding 'No!' I didn't know what to make of such spirituality, but it contained common and uncommon sense and it exalted me and lifted me into another dimension.

More riskily, to satisfy traditionalists, old doctrines were not censored. It was part of the deal that kept Hugo, Jonathan and me and all the Reform synagogues together. These doctrines stayed as a monument to past belief, though this contained a hidden danger. They might of course be taken to apply to the present and future and not just the past, and so fuel nationalism, obscurantism and bigotry with disastrous political consequences. (In the event, some of this happened.) The Torah of God, for example, remained 'perfect' though it was obvious that in the way we had it, it wasn't. It too had evolved, and there were some gruesome primitive passages in it. Readers would have to work out for themselves the scope of Torah, the five books of Moses, the Bible, the Talmud too, all the truths of Jewish tradition, all the truths of Jewish experience – who can know all truth?

We all had our personal likes and dislikes. I disliked the passages from Rav Kook lauding Jerusalem. Jonathan was moved by them, though to me they were dangerous sentimental kitsch. Also Hugo preferred God to pay us for 'our good deeds' in this life. I preferred him 'to pay us for our labour', the labour of our living. Hugo's version was accepted, not mine. Fair enough! But I pointed out that God Save the Queen had been left out after Hatikvah. This was significant, I protested, and it went in.

Eventually, Rabbi Dow Marmur, by now the rabbi of a prestigious suburban synagogue and I manoeuvred the Funeral and Sabbath Day Prayer Books through the Rabbinic Assembly. Some colleagues still considered the latter too revolutionary despite its conservative look. Jonathan was in Israel at that time and the manuscript was prepared in haste in Rabbi Marmur's synagogue, in a room he allotted to me. The people who did this preparation were a typist studying for conversion; Kim, my partner (C. R. Holman in the book); Mary Kelly (a Sister of Sion); Teresa Gribbon (another Sister of Sion); and some others that I've lost contact with. They got no payment for it, and Kim often used to take us out to lunch. They are mentioned in small letters at the end of Jonathan's and my introduction. They should remain in the succeeding editions. They deserved it.

The major theological problems were the interpretation of the Holocaust and Israel. Jonathan helped to point our prayers in the right direction by including the words of the Israel Constitution itself about the hand of friendship to be extended to the Arabs. That hand tragically never reached the Arab refugees.

With the experiences of the Holocaust in the Day of Atonement prayers, we did not just include the pious but also the perplexed and also those who didn't believe and some who committed suicide. All of them earned their right to be in it. So said Rabbi Dr Maybaum, the greatest theologian of Reform Judaism, and we agreed. I think the Additional and Memorial services in the Day of Atonement were probably the best work we did, and the work I am proudest of.

My own religious experience firmed up our commitment to a 'Beyond Life'. I didn't see how this life could be lived properly on its own terms alone. Also because of WW (Fred) there was a lot of God in the new book.

Reflecting on our work decades later, what were the shortcomings of the new liturgy?

It didn't use non-gender language. That hadn't emerged as an issue while it was being put together and written.

The services were far too long – sometimes wearyingly so. Like all insecure people, we were scared of missing anything out, though a lot was repetitious and not revealing. It is true the introduction gave permission to cut the prayers but much more precise bolstering-up was needed for a small congregation to get the courage to use this permission. As the Jewish community had lost belief in itself, its support was in the past.

It tried to believe what was sometimes unbelievable.

Prayer books are never perfect. Many other defects can be noted in ours but in the end it was more than a prayer book, it was a life book that spoke in straightforward English, which is what I had always wanted. It also didn't avoid the issues or the problems and it did not treat the Almighty like the headmaster of a minor public school (a private school in America). It also spoke to non-Jews and non-believers who kept it by their beds.

About thirty years later, I dropped out of the revision and rewriting which I had inaugurated. I was going one way and the prayer books were going another. They were becoming too fat and too scholarly – too professional, in fact. Scholarship can be a cover-up for fear of religious experience. You wouldn't dare 'throw the book' at somebody in synagogue. The person who received one of our prayer books full in the face would need medical treatment. But at least our prayer books spoke to God and about God directly without sentimentalism or moralism or too much use of the pathetic fallacy.

I am interested now in Simple Services in which the congregation are given the basic bits and tools to set up their own service. At present we go into a synagogue, pray the prayers written by other people, listen to the opinions of another person in the sermon, sing hymns chosen by a choir, or a cantor, stand up and sit down at someone else's command. We might as well be watching the entire production on TV, there is so little of ourselves in it.

In New York, where I was the guest lecturer of Rabbi Sammy Barth, a Leo Baeck scholar, I wandered into a crowded service in Manhattan. It looked as if it was being held in a disused warehouse, but it was crowded – scarcely standing room. I was curious and entered. The prayer book in use was a normal traditional one, and at one end of it there was an ark, a rabbi and a cantor, and at the other end of the synagogue warehouse there was a choir – all as normal, in fact.

But there was something about that service that was not normal. Tunes started up in the congregation not in the choir, and the cantor and the choir then joined in, taking the lead from the congregation. The rabbi started off the sermon and then voices from the congregation called, adding their truths to his, so the result seemed to me as if the congregation were preaching to each other. The prayer books themselves were used to give form to the service, but the content came from the people attending. Parents took children to the ark and they played hide and seek around it while the liturgy carried on. People in the pews also made arrangements to eat together in couples or families, to relieve the loneliness of bedsitter New York. Rich, poor, Jew, non-Jew – it made no difference.

Suddenly I realised the truth that was being taught me in that service. In a normal synagogue (or church) God lives in the ark (or on the altar). From there he dribbles a little of his truth down to the ministers, his servants, and these do the same to the wardens, the officers of the congregation, who in turn dribble a little to the congregation if they are good and behave. But this now is a misleading model. 'God dwells,' say the rabbis, 'wherever a human heart lets him in.' So he does not live in arks or altars, he lives in us! This made sense and has changed my view of what a synagogue is for and what books serve its needs. Once again, thank you, America!

A meditation from the Day of Atonement service in the new prayer book

Meeting God can be very simple. If it is not simple, and no voice speaks in our silence, and no hand reaches down to meet ours in trust, then we should ask ourselves these questions, for the mistake may be ours:

Perhaps God cannot be Himself to us, because we are not ourselves, our true selves, to Him. We have not prayed to Him as we are, but as we feel we ought to be, or as others want us to be, or as what we think He thinks we ought to be.

240

This last is the most difficult to unravel because it hides a confusion or a blasphemy.

Perhaps God meets us and we do not recognise Him. He may speak to us in a chance remark we overhear, through a stray thought in our mind, or by a word from the prayer book that resonates in us. Perhaps a side door is the only door we have left open to Him. Others we defended and barred, so he must steal into us as a thief in the night.

Perhaps we do not like what He says, but are frightened to say so, and so pretend we never met Him, and indeed could not meet Him for He is only an idea. The avoidance is natural because in the sight of God our success can seem failure, and our ambitions dust.

Perhaps we are satisfied with our lives and do not want to meet Him. So we chant our prayers and sing our hymns to prevent a few moments' silence, for He speaks in the silence.

Perhaps we have not allowed God to judge us because we have already judged Him, and anticipated His word. He may love us more than we know; He may know us better than we know ourselves; He may still surprise us.

Perhaps we are frightened where He may lead us. He may send us from our father's house; He may bring us to the wilderness; He may let us wander in it for forty years; He may ask for us to find our security in what we cannot touch. Will He give us courage equal to our need if we pray?

Meeting God can be simple, but nothing can happen if we do not will it. If we seek the Lord He can be found; He will allow us to find Him if we seek Him with all our might.

(Forms of Prayer)

A memorial prayer from the new service book liturgy
We remember our six million dead and all who died when evil ruled the world. We remember those we knew and those whose very name is lost.

We mourn for all that died with them; their goodness and their wisdom, which could have saved the world and healed so many wounds. We mourn for the genius and the wit that died, the learning and the laughter that were lost. The world has become a poorer place, and our hearts grow cold as we think of the splendour that might have been.

We stand in gratitude for their example of decency and goodness. They are like candles which shine out from the darkness of those years, and in their light we know what goodness is – and evil.

We salute those men and women who were not Jews, who had the courage to stand outside the mob and suffer with us. They, too, are Your witnesses, a source of hope when we despair.

In silence we remember those who sanctified His name on earth in dark times.

(Forms of Prayer)

57

Conversations, Divorces, Adoptions and Rows

Kim had gradually retired from yacht designing though he continued to sail, win prizes, and give lectures on design to yacht clubs and even to the Royal Society of Arts. The new breed of yachts designed and built in America were stripped-down racing machines meant above all to race and win. This was not Kim's style. The yachts he designed were gentlemen's yachts you could live in and holiday in with your family and friends, as well as looking lovely and race enjoyably. It was an English ideal.

This semi-retirement meant that London became our home and I could take a job in the Jewish establishment again. The only job going was as a backroom boy in Canon Law for Reformed Synagogues. I took it on in the late 1960s – apprehensively, remembering how I had loathed law as an adolescent. But for me it had one great advantage, I was free to join Kim on weekend sailing.

Now, I had walked out of the solicitor law exams when I was sixteen. I hadn't wanted to transfer tenements ripe for redevelopment from one member of the bourgeoisie to another. But ironically comforting the bourgeoisie and sorting out their routine sins and social problems became my principal task for over half of each week for the next twenty years. Together with my work on the liturgy and writing, it provided my bread and butter. Any jam such as expensive foreign holidays came from Kim.

As I walked back into the law, I told myself it was different now because it was God's law not human law I was administrating, though they seemed pretty similar to me. It was my friend Dow who had suggested the legal job. He wanted me back at my real work in the ministry, he said. Putting up sails and taking them down was no real work for a rabbi, he said disdainfully, and I admitted a bit sulkily that it was like putting up curtains and taking them down while standing on a rocking chair. (He did not understand the courage and the camaraderie involved.) The Clerk to our Rabbinic Court was retiring, and Dow said I should apply for the post but with a more elevated title. Not many people would apply for it because the pay was peanuts but I'd be back in the establishment, which is where I was needed. He was one of the selectors.

Now this was very nice of him because Dow and I had very different points of view on most of the issues raging around and through the Jewish community at the time. We came, it is true, from the same sort of background, poor Polish, but his was not so poor as mine and much more cultured. But he had suffered the war in a Russian labour camp, then repatriation to Poland, before going on to a new life in Sweden, while I had only experienced the Blitz in London. He was passionately attached to Israel, I was lukewarm about all nationalisms, our Jewish one included. I had become English, a bit Anglican even. But we respected each other and didn't fib much to each other or ourselves. He made it his business to understand gay people like me though he himself was anything but gay – he was as hetero as they come. I think we supplied a missing bit in each other. Despite his cool attitude to converts, he wanted to convert my friend Janny, and for me to marry her.

I decided to apply for the job with my usual muddle of motives. I would be a back-room rabbi and not too prominent at a time when gay relationships were still condemned socially and communally. Also because my life with Kim meant I could take only a half-time job. And yet another reason – and this was one that restored my self-respect. I asked a rabbi and colleague why he wanted me. His reply was unexpected. 'Because you like saying "yes" to people not "no", which is rare in a bureaucrat.' He was right. 'No' is easy – it's the end of problem. 'Yes' means another problem and another problem after that. I would face more problems than a no-sayer but I was coming to see God more and more in people with problems and less in arks, on platforms, and recorded in minutes.

I got the job in 1969 more easily than I expected, with an office and a secretary, and I started straightaway. I dealt with all the things that weren't supposed to happen in a well-ordered Jewish world, such as conversions, divorces, adoptions, and rows with rabbis, about rabbis and between rabbis, and arguments over tombstones. My colleagues married people chorally and florally on Sundays and I divorced and sundered them on Mondays, Tuesdays, Wednesdays and a half of Thursdays. Having been sort of married and sort of divorced from a non-Jewish partner, I sympathised with my clients and knew only too well how they felt. So I tried to make things nice for them by not telling them off, which is what most of them expected, but by comforting them in the waiting room as they sat there looking glum and angry, with good quality coffee and fresh moist cake, even the homemade sort when my secretary had the time to bake a batch, trying to help them sunder as pleasantly as possible, and without denying the original attraction or affection. I remembered what the writer Colette said about her first husband, the infamous Monsieur Willi. 'All the women adored him and I admit he had a certain something.' You can't get more charitable than that.

Through the seventies I was also Cookery Correspondent to the *Universe* – no, not the real one around you but the Catholic paper which bore that name, which was a popular, populist paper of religious journalism, cheery, chirpy and rather traditional. But that is another story.

This is what administrating our little court gave me because as in any good work, the satisfactions are on both sides.

Firstly it gave me an office, a secretary, a diary, appointments and stability. For the first time for years I was back in one of my own worlds. I wasn't a cuckoo in someone else's world. I got back my self-respect. I now appreciated the importance of all the things I had tried to break away from. I was not like my old romantic uncle Abie. I was as much bourgeois as bohemian.

The court brought both sides of me together because I recognised myself in my clients. With their divorces and conversions, their lives were in the same mess that mine had been and still was. My own experience helped me understand them and the mess they'd made of their lives. I did not look down on those problems from a high unnatural height. I kept my distance, of course – I had to – but I was on their side and they recognised it. We all wanted the same things: a home, realistic fidelity, another chance.

My first secretary was a good-natured Orthodox lady and so

was my second. Both liked listening to the people who passed through our little office, and we used to discuss them at length, confidentially and kindly. They educated us.

My second secretary, Phyllis, who remained with me for most of my time, was a beautiful bonus because to our astonishment we were part of each other's prehistory. I was dictating my CV to her one day when she looked up at me and I looked at her and we recognised each other. She used to live over the road from me in the little streets behind Whitechapel. Our fathers were both out of work and she used to take me to school with her little sister. Then years later, she reminded me, she had worked as a secretary under my mother. We went over the histories of those who had lived and those who had died and we became family to each other as Jewish people often do. I told her all about me and she survived the shock because people and family mean more than theology and abstractions in Jewish life.

Because of our shared background we knew that life was tough and, as I said, religion isn't there to make it unnecessarily tougher for people but to help them get out of jams even of their own making. Phyllis and I were touched when a sweet-natured but over-accommodating convert returned to visit us proudly showing us her new engagement ring and thanking us for her conversion, her two religious divorces and her forthcoming religious marriage, which both previous husbands would be attending. (All of them were neighbours, so the flavour was unexpectedly domestic.)

Beneath such curious cases were bigger issues, one very big indeed. We were at the cutting edge where medieval canon law could no longer cope sensibly with the needs of modern Jewish society. That law presupposed a closed society, but most Jews preferred to inhabit an open one and yet got upset when they got the bill for the consequences – when their beloved son, circumcised, bar-mitzvahed, confirmed, the lot, fell in love with the nice blonde girl next door whom his parents had always praised and was now going to receive his engagement ring. An open society meant an open door. Some would leave Judaism, some would enter. This should come as no surprise as the Jewish community is descended from converts – you only have to look at them to see. The question is whether $.0000 \ldots \ldots \ldots 1$ per cent of Abraham's blood flows in ours. Unfortunately there was so much propaganda in the Nazi time asserting that Jews were a race, a little of it even trickled over into Jewish minds as well.

And as well as being open, this new Jewish society was pluralist. Each section of the Jewish community had hopes of knocking out the others or of prophesying their demise. Just like the warring Christian denominations and sects in the religious wars of the sixteenth and seventeenth centuries. Time has marched on and in a secularised society religious groups no longer have the power to go to war, I told myself – wrongly as it turned out, because a lot of them are at it again. We still haven't reached a world council of synagogues like a World Council of Churches, but we may get there quicker than they did. At present, Orthodox don't recognise non-Orthodox and even fellow Orthodox, and the same situation applies to the non-Orthodox too (Conservative, Reform, Reconstructionist, Liberal and Progressive). As ever, two Jews – three opinions.

All this non-recognition is not as disabling as an outsider might think, because in times of emergency most Jewish groups have to work together, temporarily at least, and Jewish history is the story of one emergency after another. Also, the majority of Jews are a pragmatic lot and don't take ecclesiastical pretensions too seriously. In my experience, unity of the family is rated higher than articles of faith. Because of this lack of universal recognition and misuse of religious power in Israel, I kept a notice over my desk which read 'If you believe in me, I exist.'

Some of my problems came not from our clients but from my colleagues who staffed our courts conscientiously and voluntarily. Our little court, which dealt mainly with status, was the last stronghold of rabbinic power where a rabbinic 'No!' could still affect people's lives, e.g. remarriage in a synagogue after a civil divorce. The use of medieval power is seductive, and Phyllis and I had occasionally to point this out tactfully to young, over-zealous and freshly learned judges, suggesting the way back to common sense. Theoretically Jewish law covered everything – whether you could wear a self-winding watch on the Sabbath or whether Israel was a Messianic event, or whether a pot-bellied pig is kosher. But the greater part of Jewish law for the greater part of ordinary Jews had dwindled into custom. Even the devout made their own anthology of the Jewish legal past without benefit of clergy. A lot of my work was akin to heraldry, and its pretensions could unbalance ordinary rabbis, who were usually so practical. Rabbis were no longer in command of Jewish sociology. (And a good thing too! Religion cannot handle power – as the events in the newspapers show clearly.)

But my colleagues were an honest lot, and most realised that the learning had to work both ways. They had to learn from their clients as well as vice versa. The following cases remain in my mind as ones where the examined became the examiner. I have altered the details though all these cases happened long ago. A foreign girl came before us wanting to convert. It was the normal situation for such requests. She had come as an au pair to a Jewish family. The family had a son. No doubt she would marry him and be absorbed into the suburban Jewish life around her.

'When do you intend to marry him?' asked the Beth Din – our court.

'I am not going to marry him,' she answered, surprised. 'He already has a girl friend and they will soon become engaged.'

'Do you want to marry one of his friends?' asked the court.

'No,' she replied. 'After my conversion I want to return home to my own country.'

The Beth Din looked astonished. 'Are there any Jews in the town you will return to?'

'No,' she said, sadly but philosophically.

'Won't you feel alone?'

'Sure!' she answered, surprised.

'Won't the priest be opposed?'

'Oh, yes,' she said firmly.

'How do you know so certainly?' asked the Beth Din.

'Because he's my uncle!' she said.

End of conversation, and she was asked to leave the room as the court wished to confer.

When she came back, the questioning started up again but more obliquely this time. 'Have you ever felt depressed in England?' they asked.

'Homesick sometimes,' she admitted.

The court became more courageous. 'Have you ever had a breakdown?' it asked.

She looked at them levelly. She sighed. 'I am beginning to think you do not realise the value of your goods. You do not have confidence in the drawing power of your own religion. I am sorry for you and me!'

The court once again asked her to leave them. When she returned, the court stood up for her and an old rabbi humbly thanked her for her sermon to them. Like them, I wanted to cry.

Another case occurred when I really felt proud of my court. An old Gaelic woman from the provinces came before us wanting to convert. The court asked her the question it puts to all converts who once had a living non-Jewish faith. 'Could you please tell us the main differences between Judaism and Christianity?' it asked. Did she know what she was converting from and what she was converting to? Judaism has no monopoly of salvation and it was not our task to destroy someone else's religion so that that person could be a tabula rasa for ours. We were not conversionist.

The old woman knew a great deal about Jewish lore and kitchen law, more than me in many ways, but when she was asked the question above, her answer dumbfounded us. 'Are there any?' she said innocently. We gulped, ordered tea for her and for us and asked her to tell us about her life and her studies (she lived in a town a long way from any Jewish community).

Her story was simple. She had come from a Gaelic-speaking peasantry as a young girl half a century before and had worked for an old lady and her son who had fled the Holocaust. They kept to themselves, for the old fears still dominated their lives. The lady had instructed the young girl in all the dietary and ceremonial laws of Judaism and, after her death, the girl (now a woman) married her son in accordance with her wishes. The couple had passed the years of their enclosed household happily enough together until the husband died. There were no children. The woman, now old, in turn wanted to become Jewish because someone had told her she could not be buried beside him and her mother-in-law in the cemetery until she converted to us.

Again the court tried. 'Think back to your childhood,' they said. 'Aren't things different in your present life?'

'Yes,' she answered. 'In England we light the candles at a different time.'

The court persevered. 'What about Jesus and Mary in your life?'

Her answer had the same naivety. 'No,' she said wonderingly. 'I haven't heard them mentioned lately.'

The only differences she knew were not those between Christianity and Judaism but between the Ireland she had been born into and the England in which she had lived. It was useless trying to explain theological and practical difference. English was not even her native language. She spoke it laced with Gaelic and Yiddish.

Eventually the court accepted her. It was cruel to keep her from burial beside her husband and mother-in-law. She didn't know or want an interview with a sympathetic Catholic priest, which we could arrange for her. We wished her a good pious life and to go the way she felt right. If anything felt wrong, she could always ring me or Phyllis, my assistant. She never did. I would have put her on to the Sisters of Sion, who had a kind and understanding heart for people who had wandered unwittingly over the frontiers of faith.

Yet one more case. The legalities are too complex to explain in detail. It concerned a woman who wanted to remarry in one of our synagogues; her parents had only divorced in secular courts before their secular marriage to each other. Was the woman 'illegitimate'? The younger members of the court wanted to find a tortuous way of justifying our permission. Rabbi Dr Maybaum then said, 'We do not justify ourselves. The law is filtered through the living consciences of the members of this court. We need no legal fictions and we ourselves are not automatons. We no longer entertain objections based on the ancient laws of Chalitsah and Agunah' – which concern widows – 'because of decency and justice.' The court stopped arguing abruptly and agreed. To my knowledge, it has never entertained evidence about such matters since.

Now in traditional Jewish law, the position of women is not equal to that of men. For example, according to the Talmud they, along with gamblers, idiots and morons etc., cannot witness a document. My policy was first to remove all and any practical consequences of such inequality before Jewish law was changed drastically and substantively. I couldn't approach such change directly because no one was agreed on what changes to make, and it was not part of my policy to split our movement. In the sixties, women were studying to become progressive rabbis and soon they would have to decide themselves as to how they wanted the old formal sexist anomalies to be removed. This was beginning to happen just I was retiring, and the discussions had already begun. It was certainly time. But I don't think rabbis alone should decide the new rules for people any more. They need to decide together with women or with gays or with members of any group they're setting the rules for. The new pluralistic society will have to be a democratic one too.

Now law is by its very nature conservative, but the changes in Jewish life have been rapid and law has not been able to keep up with them. Much of the law was used to keep a hostile world out but in an open society the outside world has come into the Jewish world and is there to stay. This background in real life must be borne in mind constantly. Between a quarter and a third of all marriages in Britain where a Jew is involved are mixed-faith marriages and this is not counting cases where the non-Jewish partner has converted. When I started my work with the Beth Din these marriages were ignored. The non-Jewish partner was not excluded and some rabbis were helpful and sympathetic – but the law was clear. Only the child of a Jewish mother was Jewish unless he or she converted in his or her own right. It does not take many minutes to work out the tangled situations and absurdities that could arise from this. When the last Polish Jews had to flee from Soviet Poland under the anti-Semitic regime of General Moczar, it was impossible to work out who was Jewish and who not according to Jewish law. The community had known only two regimes – that of Stalin and that of Hitler. It was said after Moczar that only fourteen Jews now remained in Poland: Jesus Christ, the twelve apostles and Mrs Gomulka.

In the chaos of those years, law could not do justice to the price that non-Jews and half-Jews, who had thrown in their lot with Jews, had paid for their loyalty and adhesion. What really annoyed and shocked me were little rabbinical authorities pontificating over the ruined life histories left over from the Holocaust. Fortunately, such were few and far between. My colleagues were a kind lot who had the sense not to ask the wrong 'clever' questions. After all, if you were legally strict, you could probably invalidate most past marriages in Anglo-Jewry whether traditional or progressive.

At the end of the eighties, after nearly twenty years in this post, I resigned because a new way of doing things was being foisted on me (politics again) of which I disapproved. But back to me and my problems. I learnt a lot about them while administering the court, such as:

- Keep your promises but if your love turns into hate it's best to make a break. To really divorce someone, to be sundered from your partner, means letting go of your hate. You can be bound by it as strongly as love. Don't be bound together for the wrong reasons. I am talking about deep love and deep hate and bitterness.
- Let God and your friends into your break-up. You'll need both. A good decent divorce is much more difficult than a good marriage. It may take time before you can acknowledge the good times and the old affections.
- Particular remarks have stuck in my mind. You can't wave a wand in life over your mistakes so that they never happened. You can't obliterate your past. But you can learn from it, if you examine it with care. (This lesson turned up in my life in many situations.) The examination will be painful but it will make for better luck next time.

I sometimes asked myself: where was God in my peculiar job? Where was the spirituality I had became a rabbi for? Then I realised that He was in the cakes and coffee with which Phyllis and I comforted the troubled people in our waiting room. They were in the quality of the attention with which we listened to our clients tell their stories. Whatever the job description, the real work isn't poring over archaisms in committee. It was providing cakes and coffee to comfort people in their difficulties.

Remember that in a good marriage the couple divorce and remarry many times within the same marriage. People change. So do their needs.

My colleagues gave me a parting present and a dinner. They wanted to give me a ritual cup but I already had too many. I asked them for some office equipment instead and they gave me a photocopier (as well as a kidush cup). I had to get on with life and save for my old age. They invited my partner as well, which was decent of them. I had learnt from my years as Convenor of a court to listen, and also about the need for form and stability for troubled people in a troubled time – I needed such things myself.

At the dinner I thanked my colleagues for trusting me. I had used my personal problems as an aid to understanding not for scandal or politics. I had tried not to let them down.

58

My Radio Congregation!

Radio religion was something I certainly didn't plan for. It just happened. But it set me on a different course, answering new spiritual needs with a practical spirituality, and a career as a joker – which is the biggest joke of all, having been a Dostoevskian depressive and a po-faced pedant. But the 'wireless' did have a pre-history in my life during my evacuation years when I listened to it entranced by the horror and heroism of the world in which we lived, when our fate hung in the balance.

My next encounter with religious broadcasting took place many years later when I was in my mid-thirties – and it wasn't nice but awful! A friend had asked me to take over his chat line on a commercial radio while he was away on holiday. Bewildered, nervous, and terrified by the vast console deck of switches in front of me, I oozed false bonhomie. Unthinkingly I brought in a commercial about ladies' boned bras just before a news item about an alleged vision of the Virgin Mary. This finished me off and I wasn't asked again.

But after a decent time elapsed, and this episode was forgotten, radio religion entered my life once again in the sixties. I was guzzling rich chocolates during a short trip to Belgium to conduct a continental wedding when a telegram from a synagogue in England arrived asking me to return to Britain hotfoot. The BBC were recording a sort of 'down your way' programme, which included a synagogue I had once taken services for but which at the moment was in between rabbis. To hide this shame and save their pride I was recalled out of continental obscurity.

I promptly took the cheap night boat train back to London via Dunkirk. It was a stormy crossing and I regurgitated into the North Sea all the chocolates I had munched so eagerly only hours before. To cheer me up, because the boat was almost empty, the steward told me jokes over cups of wine, 'Red or white, sir? Sweet or sour?'

I arrived late in London looking white and wan and took a taxi to the synagogue. The nice BBC man asked me a question and, feeling disorganised, I confided in him and the listening public one of the steward's more unsuitable stories. He looked at me curiously, asked me another question and I told him another one worse than the first. I was on a losing wicket – one unsuitable remark followed another. I couldn't stop myself. Never mind – perhaps they'd edit it out in the cutting. I didn't ask them if it was live and I just wanted to disappear and weep!

I returned to the Continent crestfallen but, as my work (servicing new congregations, taking retreats and organising Jewish–Christian–Muslim meetings) was there not in Britain, this was no skin off my nose and I promptly forgot about it. I was more concerned with immediate issues such as how to compose a blessing for the Belgian royal family in pidgin Flemish.

So I was surprised and gratified when later on I received another invitation from the BBC to do one of their morning five-minute 'godslots'. I had apparently stumbled by sheer chance upon the secret of radio religion, which is really very simple. If you have the courage or naivety to say what is really in your mind and not what you think ought to be in your mind or what others think you should think ought to be in your mind, it works out very well. The new transistors were becoming our small friendly companions that worked best when broadcasters confided in them.

After several shifts I ended up on the *Today* programme doing the 'godslot' fairly regularly, mostly on Monday mornings when people felt at their lowest.

This suited me fine because I was still working my way out of my own depressions. I've never had a permanent contract with the BBC. I was sometimes dropped and sometimes resurrected. I escaped the cull of oldies by the skin of my teeth but, in the words of the Abbé de Sieyès after the French Revolution, 'I survived.' I'm not sure how long I've been on, off and on, but I think it must be about thirty years.

I soon learnt that giving a BBC 'godslot' is not like giving a sermon. To give a sermon I was taught to dress up in special robes. (I had to learn from my mother and aunt how to get up stairs in skirts.) Choirs sing or moan as I climb into my pulpit. There I am expected to say special things, holy things, restate the pearls of tradition. The congregation are looking special too in their creaky Sabbath best. In fact we are all rather special. Preachers get no thanks for being matey in such an exalted situation. It feels wrong.

But a godslot is not like that. This is how it goes with me. I get up at about five in the morning. There's time for cleanliness or godliness, i.e. a shower or prayers, but not both. So I get to the BBC too early, looking a mess. (I get twitchy arriving late for anything. I am always the embarrassed first at parties.) There I forage for my breakfast. When we were at the BBC building in Langham Place I used to examine the trays outside the offices of the great and good to see if I could find a piece of smoked salmon, undented by human teeth, left over from the night before. I get a plastic cup of BBC coffee strong enough to put hair on my chest though I am already endowed with enough.

I also go early because I like feeling part of a team. Many of the assorted technicians, journalists and presenters have been there for hours, half the night or the whole night, and I feel proud to be of their company. I admire their good nature and their pro-fessionalism. When a bomb falls anywhere, it not only blows up whatever it's supposed to blow up but it also blows up the order of their hot news programme, and I admire their calm as they put the pieces together.

I also get there in good time to catch the early news. Yes, I've read out my script the night before to check it for time and timely advice (some election might be in the offing) but a late-night tragedy may have happened and my cosy jokey script won't do and I've got to write another one fast. That's pretty rare, but very usual are last-minute adjustments so that a listener doesn't feel she or he is exiting the 'real' world and entering a religious ghetto when the godslot comes on.

I also arrive early because I've got to pray – out of need, not piety. Sometimes it's just a one-word affair like 'Help!' which often says it all. Sometimes it's making God present to me. Sometimes it's singing under my breath a verse of one of my friend Sidney Carter's popular, penetrating modern hymns: 'One more step along the world I go . . .' And always it's remembering the people I'm talking to, not my own vanity. What are they up to before 8 o'clock in the morning, in bed doing whatever they're doing, in the loo or in the bath, in the kitchen crashing into kippers or rashers, or swearing blue murder in a traffic jam? What are their real needs? What can I pass on to them? Can I give them one thought for the day that can help them through the rat-race, networking, consignment to home, or a Home, or a hospital, or a hospice or the less defined relationships of our time?

I also needed to pray for myself because I was frightened of speaking more than I knew, confidently, too confidently, stating knowledge I had never experienced and therefore had no title to. Was the media inflating my ego and making me false to myself? Whosoever Whatsoever solved that one. Sipping a plastic cup of BBC coffee, him sitting next to me 'as it were', I realised that I was speaking the truth but a truth I was only partly entitled to. A bit of me had gone ahead of me, that was all, and it would take time, perhaps a lifetime, for the rest of me to catch up. Quite often my own words lay in wait for me several days or weeks after saying them, like a trap. With a shock I realised a situation had arisen in which I could not broadcast one thing and do another. My own words told me what I must do and how I must change. I did change – but one step forwards, three-quarters of a step backwards, like the hesitant person I am. But I've been in love with Whomsoever Whatsoever for a long time and I'm not going to rat on him. It was a relief to know that my sermonettes were changing me as much as my listeners and perhaps even more. That felt right. I was my own proof. You don't reach much more proof than that in religion.

And when I got less nervous I always said Good Morning to the presenters just before I went on, because I became fond of them and respected their integrity. I admired their cool even when interviews became tougher as the world's become trickier. Gone are the days when interviewees admitted they didn't know or when Sir Alec Douglas Home worked out Britain's economics with matchsticks and actually confessed it! Some interviewees have ceased to bother about the questions. They just say what they want to say regardless.

Then some interviewees talk through their time relentlessly and can't be interrupted with uncomfortable questions. But I noticed another ruse some nights ago when I couldn't sleep and fiddled with the radio, listening to the same interviews from the world's hotspots over and over again on different stations. Not many of the interviewees seemed to admit their side had ever done anything wrong. Their side, whether revolutionary, religious or national, was of course as pure as the driven slush with no responsibility for child murders, bombings, lootings, land-grabbing, kneecappings, torturing, persecuting, bad mouthings, sexism, assassinations and bulldozing. They were only for peace, God and justice. And if they got caught out, poor things, it was all the fault of provocation from the other side.

Well, it takes two to tango, and too much self-righteousness makes me suspicious of anybody's including my own. The Hebrew scriptures warn, 'Don't be righteous overmuch' and the Gospels, 'Be as innocent as doves and subtle as serpents.' As my secretary Phyllis used to say, 'And the band played, "Believe it if you like", Lionel!'

The interviewers on the other hand struck me as a helpful lot not trying to take advantage – though occasionally exasperated – but some interviewees just wouldn't be helped. The presenters genuinely tried to be honest and fair but also not to let go, a combination which is rare in politics and religion. They are a good investment for the BBC: they give it distinction and integrity.

When I first started with the godslots, I asked an old rabbi what I should talk about. 'Tell them, Lionel, about the Jewish Problem,' he advised. But how could I? The listeners were suffering from so many problems. There was a recession on and a deep freeze and several strikes. I couldn't sprinkle the Jewish Problem over their cornflakes. It just didn't seem decent. But in prayer my inner voice, old Whosoever Whatsoever, intervened again and told me not to put on the style or ecclesiastically inflate myself, or get any big ideas. My mother incidentally told me the same. My job was to help people get out of bed on a difficult Monday morning and give them and me enough spiritual stiffening so that they didn't dive back under their duvets. It was that simple. And this I have tried to do.

Gradually I had to learn the realities of media religious life the hard way, that on the radio you don't preach at people, you talk to them. You have to, because they possess a power ordinary congregants don't possess. If what you say is irrelevant, they don't have to make a conspicuous and embarrassing walkout. They just flick a switch, turn to some soothing wall-to-wall Mozart and you're dead. So you have to think where your listeners are in life, not where you would like them to be. Also, don't try to sell your listeners religion, not even your own brand of it – especially not your own brand of it. They're used to the manipulation of adverts and can easily discount your puffed-up goodies. You're there to help them, not sell them pious soap. Your own religion can't help coming out but without you realising it. A radio voice is a giveaway of integrity. You can't fake it.

I learnt a lot too because my congregation came from all faiths and none, mainly none, so it was no use clinching advice with scripture texts, because they used different scriptures or none, as I've said. It was no use starting off with 'the rabbis said' or 'the prophets proclaimed'. For many of my listeners there were no scriptures, there were only old books.

What carried credence was my own experience if it was one they could relate to, or share, or trust. So gradually, to do my job, I had to assemble my own scripture, the religious story of my own life. This was usable if it sounded trustworthy, because it wasn't that different from the lives of my listeners.

I also had to speak out my hesitations, my doubts and wobbles, provided I didn't do this aggressively. If you can set out your doubts, your beliefs become more credible. Nobody expects you to believe the lot because a lot of it is unbelievable. Now many of these wobbles I'd never even spoken out to myself, but when I spoke out about them my religion didn't collapse as I'd feared, it just got stronger. Not allowing your Sunday School religion to grow up with you is the most dangerous.

This way of approaching religion lays much more weight on individual religious experience. I tried to tell people how to get their own. I could help them by telling them how I got mine, but I could not give them mine. I also tried to explain the difficulties of this path, that religion was not magic, for example. It didn't remove your problems but it did give you courage to face them, and without so much fear those problems could look very different. Your minuses become pluses and your failures your spiritual capital. You could see opportunities in them you had never expected.

It does mean, of course, that you have to have experienced the kingdom of heaven for yourself, to have touched it – even if it's been for a moment – and that that experience is within you. And unless you do know for yourself that that kingdom exists you'll end up in fanaticism, in banality. Thank God for my analysis and so, I suppose (I say this reluctantly), the problems that made it necessary.

The most important lesson the BBC taught me is, like all important lessons, very simple: that people come to religion out of need and they try out certain answers because they seem to work, not because of their labels or provenance. This is sometimes very difficult for clerics to take on board. They think in terms of 'The Jew' or 'The Christian' or whatever. They are committed to the brand, the particular establishment, the right designer label. But more basic than any religious labels is being human, and on this level we aren't much different. All you need is a little translation and the message of one gets through to the others without much difficulty. Also, our worlds are increasingly alike with globalisation. People dance to the same tunes in Tel Aviv and Jerusalem as they do in New York, Beijing and Paris. None of us is that special except in the eyes of God. Now some people like this but others find it very worrying. They want to feel very special, very 'chosen', but we weren't made that way. I am one of the people who like it like that!

That alikeness isn't only a plus. It's also a minus. People are also alike in their prejudice, and insecurity. Not a pretty thought!

I stumbled over another problem with radio religion and godslots, and other religious broadcasters found the same. One told me that his bishop really thought them vulgar – haha! – and not real religion like preaching in an empty church in full canonicals with a sermon bespattered with texts and quotes. Many older rabbis felt the same. I had to point out that more people listened to a godslot than all the worshippers in all the synagogues and churches put together on the weekend sabbaths. They provided the spiritual 'daily bread' of the nation. More people listened to a sermonette or Thought every day than ever before. People were coming to religion in a new way, though it took time for the establishment to notice. And it was good that such sermonettes and Thoughts were sandwiched into fast news programmes and chat shows. It stopped religion seeking comfy refuge in a semi-sealed ghetto from the facts of life.

It's a hard message and has to be swallowed with humour. But that's for another chapter.

The most precious gift the BBC gave me was membership of a congregation again. A congregation outside internal politics, points of order, money (you get paid peanuts on the radio, unlike TV), wrangling over constitutions, or heresy hunts.

It hasn't always been easy to survive. The difficulty hasn't come from listeners, but from ecclesiastical and political establishments who occasionally put pressure on the BBC for someone more conformist, more 'official', and less idiosyncratic (i.e. less personal, less spiritual experience) than the likes of me. But so far the BBC establishment has resisted it in the spirit of Lord Reith, whose Latin words are written in gold letters in the foyer of Langham Place, and I pray it continues to do so not just for me but for its own sake. I guess that the higher political establishment also presses on the higher echelons of the higher BBC establishment too – in the polite, subtle English manner, of course. It packs quite a punch and has a lot of pressies and honours to offer. (To my surprise I got an OBE, which astonished me and which I therefore treasure.) Once again I'm not into higher councils, but so far the BBC establishment has resisted pressies, pressure and siren voices. They should keep up their guard. This is not a moral time and I'm not talking about sex.

I meet my congregation in supermarkets and trains, at the bar in theatres and through letters. I try to follow what is important to them so our relationship is more two-way than it seems. Occasionally someone gets obsessive about me (the media produces unwittingly a kind of neurotic transference) or someone wishes I'd gone up in the smoke of the gas chambers, or that I was unfair to Ireland (which is untrue – I probably read and appreciate more Irish literature than my accusers. It's just that I like patriotism but am highly suspicious of nationalism, whatever colour it drapes itself in).

Without intending to, most listeners have impressed me with all they go through in life, and deserve a medal for survival. Every bit of my life has come in useful trying to be helpful – poverty, old-tyme Judaism, bars in Germany, saunas in Amsterdam, Anglo-Cat piety, dating agencies, the spectrum of my body and soul. I am not as stubborn as Ste Thérèse of Lisieux or as ruthless as St Teresa of Avila, but I've also tried to seek the truth – though with me it's been a jerky journey. But then I've had problems they couldn't have imagined (and of course vice versa).

'Good morning, Sue, good morning, John, good morning, Jim . . . and of course good morning, to ALL of you!' And I mean every word of it!

59

Bread of Heaven

There was a lot of spin-off from the BBC. I had never realised the power of the media even for a medium shooting star like me. Because of it I became an entertainer, which was logical, and because of it I came to write for the Catholic press, which was unexpected. At the time I thought it all happened by chance. But 'Chance is a fine thing' as the adage says and can be a cover for the Holy Spirit which bloweth where it listeth.

Many decades ago it listed towards me when I was preparing an ecumenical demonstration meal for TV. What would be your menu if you invited, for example, a Muslim, a Jain, a Jew, a Hindu, a Trappist, a New Ageist and a Far Eastern monk to drop in for dinner? The last was the biggest worry. When the meal took place, the monk had to sit three feet from the table to separate himself from womankind and eat whatever others were moved to put into his bowl. When they were deep in conversation about comparative ethics, they were not moved at all but forgot him and he starved. But during the pauses, they piled his bowl high. He just smiled, consumed and never commented on his erratic mixed menu.

But my friend Rowanne Pasco commented and felt for him – for she was in the studio with me and food turned her on too. It was Rowanne who enrolled me in the ranks of Catholic journalists, and this was the way of it. Not long after my drop-in dinner, she became editor of the *Universe*. Finding no copy for the cookery column, she rang me asking me to do an emergency job for two weeks on ecumenical eating while she settled into her new post. The two weeks lasted over ten years. I boasted to my mystified rabbinical colleagues that I had been appointed 'Cook to the Universe'. I remember starting off with *latkes*, the Jewish version of Irish potato cakes. Having learnt cookery from my pious granny, I naturally mixed religion with the recipes. Food is after all the centre of the Jewish Sabbath sanctification, and the Passover feast, and the prologue and epilogue to the Atonement Fast, and of course the centre of the Christian Eucharist and Mass too, though in these last its worldly nutritional value is now nearly nil. This wasn't always so. My friend Monica Furlong told me that her namesake, St Monica, Augustine's mother, took a picnic basket of goodies to the grand church in Milan and was told off for keeping to such old-fashioned country customs. Spirituality was more refined than digestion.

One of the nicest things about the *Universe* when I joined it were the convivial buffet lunches for staff and contributors. They melded us into a cheerful Catholic family. There were Fathers there, and secretaries, and Sisters, and Monsignors and eminent Catholic editors such as John Wilkins of the *Tablet*, and me. Rowanne dashed out through one door with a plate and then dashed back through another clutching copy. There was better class vino than at Jewish gatherings but the smoked salmon was scarcer. When I stumbled back to my office I had to take to my sofa for an hour before tackling the problems of my Reformed Jewish ecclesiastical court – conversions, divorces, tombstones, rows with rabbis and between rabbis. I felt at home in Catholic circles. It reminded me of my granny's kitchen. There was the same familiar combination of food and faith, high ethics and low gossip, creative chaos and contrition. (More contrition among Catholics than among Jews.)

I noticed something in those free-for-all lunches which I had previously remarked upon at ecumenical meetings where we were carefully divided up into our denominations and confessions. A real division in our discussion cut across the old formal categories. On the one hand were the rigid rigorists and on the other the loose liberals. They both had more in common with their counterparts than they felt comfortable with. I certainly felt cosier with the Sufis than with ayatollah-style rabbis. *In vino veritas!* (The Sufis drink only grape juice.)

I felt a strong bond with Monica Furlong and also with John Wilkins. My religious friends separated themselves generally into two camps. They either represented the deep meditations of medieval piety and guarded it against the competition of the enlightenment, or were the other way round, making sure the deep truths of the enlightenment were not muddied by an 'age of faith'. The bond I felt with both Monica and John was that they knew it was not a case of 'either or' but a case of 'both/and'. The question was how the two worlds would come together constructively in the world and in ourselves. They are of course deeply Christian and I am an idiosyncratic Jew, but the same discussion is in all faiths. Monica's early teacher was Archbishop Joost de Blank, the spiritual Anglican Archbishop of Cape Town, and her books, such as *Contemporary Now*, show the depth of his guidance. But this helped her, it did not stop her, from bringing women into the Anglican priesthood. Similarly, the *Tablet* under John's editorship encompassed liberalism and faith, showing often that they were two sides of the same coin. Listening to both of them, I learnt a lot of truth my own religion needed. Their friendship to me was another enlightenment for me and a pleasure. In different ways they spoke the truth.

After the Second World War we had all peered out of our ghettos, were faced with the same questions and had given not dissimilar answers. Some felt this was splendid and some as frightfully wrong. Having been both rigorist and loose at one time or another and sometimes both at the same time, I was used to seeing the world both ways. Members of ecclesiastical establishments develop necessary protective squints. They just get on with the job and the role-playing that goes with it.

I saw that both post-war Catholicism and Judaism were experiencing a crisis in tradition. The ecclesiastical machinery in both was still there and with little change. In my patch there were rabbis administering law in courts as they had done for nearly two millennia, and with my Catholic counterparts there were lines of authority stretching to the Vatican and beyond that to St Peter, they said. But neither machinery worked in the old way. Something had gone wrong with the transmission. For most Jews, even most of the Orthodox, a lot of the law had dwindled down to custom and congregants made their own selection from the past. It wasn't just pick and mix, it was an attempt to join together codes of conduct for a closed society with the customs and lifestyle of an open one, i.e. doing a job the clergy hadn't the courage, independence or self-assurance to tackle. For the Catholics, similar problems were clothed in extended use of 'conscience' and the areas of individual decision. All this was made necessary because we clerics were no longer the only learned faithful. There were psychoanalysts, social workers, lawyers, doctors, lay theologians, historians and anthropologists of all sexes and genders in the congregations whose knowledge dwarfed ours.

There were obvious demarcations between the two faiths, of course. I began to read the Catholic as well as the Jewish press. The former focused on divorce and birth control and the latter on intermarriage and food laws (pig and lobster). Both found the preoccupations of the other odd, but they were different aspects of the same problem. Rabbis were too concerned with communal survival in this life to take on Catholic worries about soul survival into the next.

I asked myself how I fitted into all this. I began to realise that being a Jew I could raise points and say things a card-carrying Catholic couldn't. I couldn't and didn't ever directly criticise the Catholic Church. It was not my place, not part of my remit. But in describing my own religious world and its problems personally and honestly, curious Christians felt free to note those which paralleled their own. I congratulate the Catholic press for choosing me – not out of personal pride or hubris but because no Jewish journal I normally read has ever dared employ a Catholic priest in that capacity. It is as yet too closed a world except on ritual occasions.

That is why when Rowanne left the *Universe*, and John Wilkins took me to lunch (Indian vegetarian), inviting me to come out of my kitchen and become a *Tablet* thinker instead of a 'Universe' eater and drinker, I accepted though I was hard pressed at the time. There was a sweetener, of course, and it wasn't my salary – which was similar to the BBC (radio not TV) – but a *Tablet* party at Christmas time where I get glasses of champagne and very superior wines with perseverance and nose and canapés so chic I can't work out how veggie they are. But they are exciting and I position myself strategically.

I had never had much contact with Roman Catholicism before, only with the Anglo-Cat kind at Oxford. But I felt very much at home in it except for the problem of obedience. I am temperamentally free-range not battery hen, and after Marxism I was wary of any confession or ideology which has too many answers. On the pro side, though, 'Roman' Catholicism was neither established nor just national and was reasonably realistic about its clergy, just like Judaism, so I felt at home in it. It was also very Irish, just as I was partly Russian and Polish, so it was able to laugh at itself, a necessity for all over-heavy organisations.

Catholic journalism has given me a fresh and sometimes startling look at my own faith. This is what ecumenical work done in good faith achieves – not conversion.

It has also acquainted me with Catholic religious orders and the startling variety of their religious gifts (they call them 'charisms'). It's like opening a box of spiritual chocolates with different and exciting centres. Being an only child, I appreciated the entry of Sisters and Brothers into my life. It was with regret I came to realise early on that you had to be a Christian and a Catholic one too before you became a monk.

I don't know whether it was the backwash of the Holocaust and the changes of Vatican II it brought about, but I was invited into the kitchen of Catholic life as I was once invited into the kitchens of my early Reformed Jewish congregation. I joined the family as a distant cousin on the distaff side. I am not using this just as a figurative turn of speech but as an actual happening. For one glorious week I cooked for vegetarian contemplatives. I got great joy in throwing out the lard (vegetarian huh!) and substituting olive oil as used in ancient Palestine. It doesn't take much for me to feel as a Catholic – though not to think as one. I was deeply touched to help a Catholic priest prepare a homely Mass on a boat as the day was dawning, and before the rest of the crew had got up to shave and drink their first mugs of tea.

Back chatting at lunch I realised that the Holy Spirit crosses all faith boundaries. (So does the rat-race!)

I also learnt to make Irish soda bread and how to pop in for prayers when the mood takes me. There's always some Catholic place to pop in to and you can't say that about other faiths who brood too much about insurance.

I brooded a lot about the Eucharist and Mass and realised how important spiritual table fellowship was. With my friend Eva, whose life resembled *The Perils of Pauline*, I started up in the seventies a free-range inclusive synagogue on the Portobello Road in London, whose service was the traditional eve of Sabbath meal. It was rather like the *Universe* lunch. Everyone brought along some food and we blessed the bread and wine we handed to each other.

Our meetings took place in a hired hall along the Portobello Market and sometimes at the Sisters of Sion and sometimes at a friendly Unitarian church. God directed who would drop in so no one was unwelcome. A Jewish lord dropped in, so did Aussies and New Zealanders, and many living on their own in bed-sitterland, and a Christian evangelical choir which tried not to convert us but to delight us. At its best you could feel the Holy Spirit supping with us. At worst it was a rather ramshackle religious happening – but honest and well meaning. Ma, who hadn't gone along to a service for years, loved it. So did Kim when he came along with the dog. Ma held out her fake fur mink, chatted with the boys on their way to the nearest pubs, straight and gay, and said her mother, my grandmother, would have been proud of me. Mmmmmmm? A Catholic group from a Spode retreat centre, the Dominicans of Spode, where I had given talks on Jewish spirituality, helped us start up and the Reform Synagogues of Great Britain lent us their duplicator, stationery and good will, which was very nice of a formal straitlaced organisation.

We asked our guests to give us an inspiring word before the parting blessing, and say something about their home. A New Zealander got up and told us that in his country the men were men 'and the sheep get nervous'. Ma cackled and some old ladies cheered. What they thought he meant I don't know. Don't ask!

We tried to give space to everybody, not excluding Jewish converts to other faiths, and asked them to tell us what had made them change over. The answer was always the same. Too many committees and not enough God. Too many services and not enough prayer. So many words to be recited, you had no time to wait for replies to form in your mind. Too exclusive to include people like them.

Looking round at their faces in the light of the Sabbath candles, I realised with pride that we had managed to turn ourselves into a fellowship and sometimes even a family. It lasted several years, but then I had to go away at the weekends. It was too much for my friend Eva on her own and I hope our floating congregants floated away to other congregations which didn't manipulate them or force-feed them.

These Friday meals also brought the unconnected parts of my past life together. I tried to cook for our congregation – many needed a solid meal. Token blessed bread and sips of wine were inadequate for them. Every part of my life had taught me something. I had picked up cookery not just from my granny but from all my partners.

The poverty of the East End had taught me potato cakes and chips, as I've said. My granny had taught me soups you could extend for ever. JB (who was a very good cook) had shown me how to make upside-down cakes and not be frightened of pastry. Kim had shown me how to make a white sauce and flavour it. In Amsterdam I had made 'cemetery soup' under supervision (it was Ezekiel's 'valley of dead bones' but tasty nevertheless and nutritious). I didn't of course make Amsterdam 'Electric Coffee' – I was too scared, the ingredients being illegal. Jim taught me scouse and blind scouse. A 'Jewish' nun also divulged her mother's secret dried-fruit salad, the last remnant of her Berlin existence. And my friend Father Gordian taught me the art of 'Tablet' – the sweet, not the journal. But for that you need too much muscle, which he has and I haven't.

What did I get out of it (because few of us are capable of truly disinterested service)? I made myself a family of friends with a real religious centre and under the guidance of the Spirit became less sniffy about oddities, less exclusive and more inclusive. No one was ever turned away, and a member of the born-again Christian choir told me Jesus would have been proud of me. What a nice thing to say! I have never forgotten it.

60

My Brother, Father Gordian OP

While I was living a quiet life with Kim, both of us supervised by my mother and Re'ach, a door to a spiritual world opened up for me just when I needed it badly. I was conscientiously trying to be a tidy ecclesiastical bureaucrat in an office but this was not enough. I also needed to find a new spiritual balance to make myself a good bureaucrat and not a mere bureaucrat, i.e. a bureaucrat who tried to solve people's problems rather than creating some for them. Now, heaven had happened once before when I prayed for help and then met Colin, so I prayed again and got a new guide in 1970. His name was Gordian. Ma liked him. Kim respected him though he wasn't that keen on RCs and Re'ach accepted him though he didn't bribe her with dog chocs. But he did take her to the park and let her get on with her insane barks, her bursts of speed, and forlorn yelps when she thought she was lost or a pair of lovers in the long grass swiped her. For me he became a brother in a human as well as an ecclesiastical sense. He was a Scottish Dominican and a Roman not an Anglo-Catholic. After I became Convener of our Ecclesiastical Court, he helped me with my spiritual life.

I met him because of my lifelong inability to say no. If I did, I felt guilty because being religious surely meant saying yes to everything self-sacrificial (Gordian disabused me of this pious sentimentalism). On another level, I didn't like being left out of anything that was going on. On another level, monasteries and priories attracted me. With all their oddities I felt they pointed heavenwards and might give me a hitch in that direction.

Now the Dominicans of Spode in the Midlands had organised a retreat on prayer for Catholics, postulants and novices of various orders – male and female. It was decided to provide a new view on the subject by inviting a Jew. They had consulted the Sisters of Sion who were trying to be a living link between the Church and the Jewish people, and the Sisters, who lived round the corner from Kim and me in London and had become my sisters in a very deeply human way, asked me. And as the retreat would not take place till the following year, and for the aforementioned mixed reasons, I doubtfully said yes, because like many neurotic people I never quite believed the future would happen.

But of course it did happen, so while others headed for the Costas I headed for the heart of the industrial Midlands to the Dominican centre in Spode. The place was impressive but odd. A mock chateau had been married to a priory and both stood on top of coal mines. So the floors in corridors could open up before you in surprising ways – like the hole through which Don Giovanni exits into hell in Mozart's opera. A big crack once opened up in the priory pond, draining away the water but leaving the smelly floundering fish. The brethren tucked up their white robes (a most unserviceable colour) and stomped about in the mud, catching the slithery beasts in buckets.

It was a vast rambling place. If you took one corridor, you bumped into brethren ironing their smalls, domestic rather than divine. Another way and you stumbled past the public telephone (blocked by Irish coins) into a dusty, princely library worthy of an Oxford college. Yet another way led to a memorable chapel decorated by Eric Gill and his pupils. There was a genial bar and innumerable bedrooms – some so narrow as to be fit only for emaciated contemplatives, and others vast with cavernous wardrobes, and wonderful for games of Murder. That's certainly what the Jewish rabbis and retreatants I introduced to the place used to play in them.

But these are its outward description. More importantly it was a grand shabby spiritual home to all sorts and conditions of people, many of whom felt confused and abandoned after it closed. I certainly did. There are not many places where you were welcomed to be yourself. So skiffle groups met sodalities (whatever they are) and earnest meditators screwing up their eyes for yet another assault on the inner life. Some youngsters were looking for a nightcap and some for a night-time novena (I wasn't sure what that was either).

I was constantly surprised by the openness of the brethren.

One Friday evening just as I was preparing the Jewish hallowing of the Sabbath in the refectory, I found I had left my silver (plated) goblet behind. 'No worry,' said the brethren and I was given their silver (solid) chalice instead. Jesus must have celebrated the Sabbath many times, they said – an obvious truth but easily forgotten.

I now had brothers as well as sisters. There was Father Joe, posed picturesquely in a nook, willingly stroking his silver beard whenever visitors wanted to snap him. There was Father Geoffrey, a former Methodist minister of enormous girth, who wouldn't diet, accepting the risk of an earlier death because he liked his food. He wrote two remarkable books on the liturgy which showed that he had prayed through his subject and absorbed it into him. And then of course there was Father Isidore, my friend who accompanied me occasionally on holiday, for whom I helped prepare the table for Mass on canal boats before I brought out the bacon for the rest of the crew. I, being a sort of veggie, consumed rissoles with relish. Isidore still suffered from the after-effects of fevers after his stint in the West Indies. It was because of his kindness that I no longer bore grudges against the Dominicans, who in the Middle Ages had burnt the Talmud and strengthened the Inquisition. Such old hostilities had passed their sell-by date. Isidore is also an artist and has a remarkable way with down-and-outs, being compassionate, kind and realistic.

The director and administrator and centre of the priory was Father Conrad, who holed up in a paper-stuffed office, researched medieval English mysticism, hunted for lost central heating bills (enormous) and directed souls. I was too much in awe of him to carouse with him so Father Gordian had to service my soul as best he could.

Now this is how I met my friend Father Gordian. I turned up at the retreat, arriving late for the afternoon service. I stole in and sat at the back, only half listening to the priest who seemed to be in charge. I picked up some of his words while looking round to see if there was anyone I knew. Occasionally I listened and the words I expected popped out like carved birds from a cuckoo clock.

Traditional questions, traditional answers, hoary with age, I thought cynically, and decided I would have ten minutes of private shut-eye. But the words did not pop out in the way or order I had expected, and I sat up and listened.

The gist of it went like this and it was rare spiritual plain speaking. Now these are not his words verbatim, they are what I thought were his words, and of course I couldn't take notes. To the younger novices and retreatants and to me he seemed to say, 'You have come here to deepen your prayers so that you can become better Sisters and Brothers. But prayer is open-ended and you do not know what will be the answer. Perhaps you will become better Sisters and Brothers. Perhaps God will lead you away from the religious life. Perhaps he will lead you out of your religious security.'

I noticed one girl looking at him as curiously as me. The penny had dropped for her as it had dropped for me: 'religion' had triumphed over 'Religion'. The firm, pleasant, Scots-accented voice had asserted the sacred and subversive over the bureaucratic and pre-programmed.

I was so taken by this deep level of discussion that I hastily revised my own talks. Tradition says you should know what answer to give to heretics, and of course from the traditional Jewish point of view Christians are if not heretics certainly sectarians. But I did not give the standard answer. I was not playing theological bridge and taking and counting tricks, I was talking to fellow souls, and I had to match his honesty with my own honesty. I was also touched by what these young novices would be taking on in the jungles of Africa or drugged western slums in the work of their Orders.

So instead of listing all the cosy comfortable bits of Judaism (family life, mother worship, collective farms in Israel, Jewish jokes and Jewish intelligence), I tried instead to tear myself away from *Fiddler on the Roof* country and give a straightforward honest account of a post-war Jewish suburb in a big city after the Holocaust, at a time when rabbinic authority was coming to an end and the future had not yet revealed its hand. In other words, to the places where I numbered their confusions, inconsistencies, their loyalty and popular theology, their trust and distrust in God at the same time, their generosity, their golden age of intellect so recently murdered, their folk exclusivity.

A nun, I think, recorded some of those talks. Somehow those recordings found their way to an enterprising young Catholic publisher, Robin Baird Smith. He was taken by them and wanted a book on Jewish spirituality from me. What he got wasn't, I suspect, what he wanted because there is a profound respect for materialism among Jews – which doesn't mean the worship of success or the rat-race but respect for the world as it is, liking it even, despite the disasters of Jewish history and the Holocaust. I called it *To Heaven with Scribes and Pharisees* and it won the *Jewish Chronicle* Prize for the year. I understand Robin's reservations because an awful lot of Christian spirituality is finding a way out of the world, not immersing oneself in it and having fun with it. But my modest success swayed him, and we have become close friends over the years – though my views sometimes exasperate him. They are not what a saintly Catholic cleric should hold. But being fair, he would I am sure admit that this is his problem, not mine. I am not a saintly sacerdotal but a mixed-up Jewish believer in bits, influenced by Marx, Freud, Emma Goldman and a lot of other disreputable unrespectables. And influenced by some respectables too, like Anne Frank, Ste Thérèse of Lisieux and Nicholas Berdyaev.

But back to Gordian, who is a Catholic sacerdotal. Perhaps he is my closest friend – I'm not sure, he keeps his own counsel. We've romped round Europe together persuading German bishops to fund get-togethers for Jews and Muslims. Through him I half stared into a Dominican world which wasn't easy for me, still thinking of past persecutions and acrimonious disputations. Partly through me he has become a member of the Jewish family, and has had to draw the line of separation carefully. We've conducted retreats together for a mix-up of Jews and Christians, some Jews who have become Christians, and some Christians who have become Jews, and a sprinkle of straights and gays in relationships.

He has the great gift I have noted in real religious people – he sees the obvious, the reality that is there in front of him. And I constantly check up with him what is really happening. The honesty remains and is a rock I rely on. He is of course not infallible. And now he is back in Scotland he has begun (in my view) to use mythological history to justify present history. Jews do that a lot, so I find it easy to spot. He also throws in the occasional English critical quip. But they all do it, whether I'm in a Glasgow pub or at an Edinburgh Tattoo. Me – I'm suspicious of all nationalism, my own favourites included. All nationalist revivals start off creatively with a burst of energy and a literary revival, and they usually end up by trying to love their own more by loving others less, which is a kind of blasphemy, and the reason why I am no longer a Jewish nationalist and I'm cautious about communalism.

On a personal level, Gordian has turned up trumps. He was the only friend who thought Jim and I could make it together, and he offered during one of our early partings to go up to the Wirral where Jim was living and explain us to each other. He has his own scale of priorities. I don't quite know what they are, but I think I come fairly high on the list. When we phone there's a competition as to who can get in first with 'And how are YOU?'

He thinks he would have made a good rabbi – he has a feel for Talmud, and I have more Christian-type religious experiences than him. It's a matter of temperament, not belief.

I told him once he had my permission to convert me. I was serious. 'Whither thou goest I will go.' But we didn't go very far. He started off with gambit one: 'Now you believe in the Messiah, don't you?' But I couldn't play the game, I was playing a different game altogether. 'No, I don't,' I said. 'It's post-Torah mythology. The dream of every child that a good adult from the sky would come down from above to put your life and the world to rights. If there was any messiah going, then we were all bits of him or her, redeeming each other. Perhaps I was the messiah to my dog Re'ach.'

We do have things in common. I like the way he translates what at first seems like theological gobbledegook into something that makes practical sense.

What does original sin mean when it's at home? He had a quick clever answer which I've taken over. 'It means that the world isn't perfect, nor me, nor you. Just do the best you can. Don't use perfectionism destructively.'

He did the same with the Immaculate Conception, the Incarnation and the Resurrection. If I'd been disposed towards joining his Church, they might have eased my entry. But I wasn't. On an even more practical level, I was gay. Condoms as a barrier against HIV seemed a semi-effective remedy against Aids, and, though I was awed by the work and self-sacrifice of Catholic individuals and groups in the Nazi time, I had little time for Pius

XII, Opus Dei, the Vatican and *Osservatore Romano.* It was quite a feat while witnessing the rise of the Nazis and their Holocaust, to make a concordat with them, and never make one clear reference to Jews or concentration camps. (Homos of course were beyond the pale and unmentionable. Homos needed a lot of self-discipline and fidelity in their relationships in the new situation caused by Aids. Religion didn't help them. And all sex can easily become irresponsible and obsessive.)

I must add that the Jewish establishment too might/would have walked on the other side if the Fascists and Nazis had only tortured gays, shot gypsies, and hanged socialists. But we were never given the choice. Perhaps this was a grace of God. As the Jewish proverb goes: 'With such friends, who needs enemies?'

As in all friendships, we have to find each other again. He has leukaemia and is working double time instead of half time. I'm now eroding too and quaking much more. Like my granny in heaven, I don't suffer pain, only 'Egony, egony'. I can enjoy it more that way.

61

Sisters

The first Catholic Sister I got to know was Sister Louis Gabriel NDS (Notre Dame of Sion), who I met at the house of Hephzibah Menuhin. She lived with her community just around the corner from Kim and me in Bayswater. I didn't take to her at first because she was a convert from Judaism (which was a quite irrational prejudice on my part in view of my own religious peregrinations). I also thought she looked furtive. Later on I found out she was just keeping 'custody of the eyes'. She was accompanied by her quiet shadow, another nun who was as retiring as Sister Louis was dominant. Kim and I had just come to settle in London, but I wasn't sure if Sister Louis and I would become friends.

We did, however, and I got to know her very well, and also her silent chaperone, Sister Theodore aka Mary Kelly NDS, who was no mere chaperone in fact but a considerable scholar in her own right. (Nuns at that time still went around in pairs.) Sister Louis's life story mesmerised me and I sat for hours in their living room drinking it in with the excellent sherry the Sisters provided.

Sister Louis had been born Charlotte Klein and lived with her very Orthodox Jewish parents in Nazi Berlin. In 1938 or 1939 she got married and went on her honeymoon to Italy. Shortly after she arrived she ditched her husband (I don't know why) but continued her honeymoon alone. Why waste tickets?

She also fell in love with an Italian doctor (just like heroines do in Hollywood films). Then a princess warned her not to go back to Berlin but to get away from Europe fast. Charlotte took the advice and got to the Holy Land just in time. There she worked for British Intelligence (she was very intelligent), read the Gospels, unlike me got converted, joined the Catholic Church and became a nun, where she was known for her strict observance. Sister Louis aka Charlotte Klein never did anything by halves, which is what I like about her. Her preferred text from the Gospels was 'Enter by the narrow gate, for the gate is wide and the way is easy that leads to destruction and those who enter by it are many. But the gate is narrow and the way is hard that leads to life and those who find it are few.' These are strong words from the Gospel of St Matthew, another Jewish Christian.

After the war she came over to England, wrote a book on anti-Semitism in the Church which didn't make her popular, and got a doctorate examining the demonisation of Jews in English theatre. The honesty of her writings was not universally welcome, and Cardinal Heenan called her 'that dreadful Prussian nun'.

Her chance really came with Vatican II. The religious orders had to re-examine their purposes and it was with the energy and learning of Charlotte that the Sion Sisters ceased to missionise Jews (they were founded by two Jewish Catholic priests) but become instead a living link between the Church and the Jewish people. Charlotte suffered but she gave others a rough time too, and it was because of Sister Theodora aka Sister Mary that she didn't get battered by her own 'charisms'. She wasn't an easy person to live with. But then neither am I. Jews can be difficult and excessive. Anyway, thank God Sister Mary was there, so she survived and did work no one else had the courage to touch. Charlotte gave Mary a lot too. When they met, Mary was just a typist but, with the belief and encouragement of Sister Louis, she became a scholar, a writer, a lecturer and the first Sister to study rabbinics at the Leo Baeck College. I understood why Mary was so attached to her and fond of her.

The big change came after Louis left for America. There she responded to the call of the new social radicals among the clergy. I went to visit Louis on her return. The door opened and my jaw dropped. Sister was dressed in pants. She also smoked from a long cigarette holder, Marlene Dietrich style, and told me nonchalantly to call her in future Sister Charlotte or even Charlotte. But she still wore her nun's ring. 'That's to tell men I'm not available,' she said. Well, she had a good figure but her face didn't match it, mutton dressed as lamb, so I don't think she was in mortal danger. In fact she remained underneath a very strict nun – in her own way of course.

She had done very important work for her order at a critical time and, however irritating she could be, her sisters remembered that and tried unobtrusively to make her life easier. It was through her that I met Sister Mary and I shall always thank her for that. Very quickly Sister Mary became the sister I never had and completed my family.

The Sisters who were becoming my sisters did so much for Kim and me during the very difficult time when we both trying out new lives. They made a non-Christmas party for their Jewish and non-Catholic friends in which we were given non-Christmas presents from a non-Christmas tree and we ate non-Christmas pudding and non-Christmas pies. How they contrived it I don't know, but my mother and aunt even won prizes for Biblical Knowledge – though what they knew wouldn't have covered a postage stamp and even that would have been excessive. The old ladies marvelled. I was touched.

There were occasional spats, of course. Charlotte told Kim, who had helped prepare a Passover meal for Jews and bedsitter folk, that being Christian he shouldn't go along to it (nonsense!). She of course was different being Jewish (which she wasn't). Kim got his own back at a cocktail party. 'How shall I get home?' said Charlotte. It was raining hard. 'On a broomstick!' said Kim sotto voce. But Charlotte heard. Mary and I were their principals and it took us some weeks to negotiate a resumption of relations.

When Charlotte died, her requiem Mass was unusual and outstanding. It's not often you see some of the most eminent rabbis in the country attending such a service for a convert out of Judaism. In her last years Charlotte (Dr Charlotte Klein NDS) devoted her life to alcoholics. She died in harness.

The Sisters did many things for me. When I went to Rome to take the progressive Jewish service for a new Jewish community, I found everybody had thought everybody else was making the preparations. It was Sister Edward, another Sion sister, and her nuns who got me candles from a church (from Nostra Signora del Soccorso, which seems appropriate). They lent me one of their amethyst rings so that some old Jewish ladies could kiss it in the Roman manner and they provided the scroll and eternal light from their own museum of Jewish antiquities. They also provided me with English cucumber sandwiches and Earl Grey tea after the service, which went swimmingly because of them. After it was all over, I needed an English reviver.

I think their kindness that I shall remember most is when Kim and I split some years later. The home we had built together was going to be disassembled. The result was that I was moving to an unfurnished suburban house all alone – though Ma and Lil soon joined me there once they could no longer cope with living by themselves. What a mess I had made of my life, I thought. And then the wonders happened. One Sister got up at an unearthly hour to take me in her car behind the furniture van. And when I arrived at the empty house, I was surprised by the curtains in the windows and then by a tea party with cakes and cucumber sandwiches and all the Sisters waiting to greet me. Charlotte made a little speech of welcome. I now knew I had acquired a real family, a Catholic family, and I shall never find better. Thank you dear, dear sisters!

After getting to know the Sisters of Sion, there were other nuns too who were important in my life: Sister Sunny of the Benedictines, who didn't just theologically love Jews but truly liked them, which is harder on the nerves; Sister Nilda, who put new life into me and some businessmen (all businessmen need cheering up) at the Foxtrot Oscar restaurant; Little Sister Esther, who let me into a way of life that purified me; Sister Mary Bozena, who joined me in retreats for people with Aids and their carers, and many, many others.

'Get thee to a nunnery!' I would have if I could, but I couldn't.

Note: After Vatican II many Sisters returned to their original baptismal name. So Sister Louis Gabriel became Sister Charlotte Klein again and Sister Theodora became Sister Mary Kelly. They not only changed their surnames but many also changed their attire. It was very confusing until it all settled down.

62

A Death in Venice

But I have gone ahead of myself as regards my personal life and Kim's too. I think this is because I already saw in advance what was happening – I had experienced a break, a gay divorce, before, though for Kim such a split was new to him. This is how it happened.

As I've mentioned before, when our life moved to London from the yachting village, Kim transferred to a new doctor who changed his treatment and it worked – he zoomed from a low to a high. Understandably, he now resented the presence of a carer like me though he was still fond of me – we were both still fond of each other. I understood his situation. He wanted to taste and test life as I had once done in Amsterdam before I met him. I was in the way.

It was in Venice, about 1978, that I began to think the unthinkable. I began to realise a gay divorce was inevitable. Kim and I had gone on holiday there to repair the damage left by our second honeymoon which never happened. When I brought up our summer holiday plans for later in the year, Kim was silent and I knew he had found someone who was not anyone and that that summer there would be no holiday together. The fabric of our life together was fading and getting thinner. I also noticed that he was not wearing the ring, one of those which we had given each other for our ceremony. Now we had not made love together for some years, and our relationship had become an open one. Both of us tried other partners – he more successfully than me. Below the surface I sensed a lot of hurt and anger in him and in me. It was beginning to explode above the surface. You have to be very generous for an 'open' relationship and I wasn't generous enough. I also had the feeling that if we stayed together Kim would hate me and I . . . I don't know what I would have felt. Probably we would have hated each other. Old love can easily go into reverse when it has passed its sell-by date and turn sour. Nearly twenty years of my life had led me to another dead end.

Through the years of Kim's illness and convalescence I had got used to taking refuge in a chapel or church when the going got rough, and I left him without comment, not trusting myself to say anything. So I dropped into a chapel, where I remembered the affectionate times Kim and I had passed together. How he waited for me at an airport in winter to welcome me home. How I held him when he had bad dreams. How he held me when a wave of anxiety broke over me. How we shut the world out and the two of us and a dog were for a few hours sufficient to each other.

In the little church my old familiar Friend, the only one whom I'd never broken up with, showed up and spoke inside me. 'Lionel,' it said, 'in this life you only enjoy reflections and glints of love but one day you will meet me, love itself – the real thing that you've been talking to all these years. Be patient, I won't let you down! I'm at hand here and I'll be waiting for you there.' I understood that he was referring to my dying and the day of my death.

Not long after, Kim and I decided on divorce in Amsterdam, the city of our coming together. We had a drink. I raised the subject. He said I was probably right, he already knew it was coming. We left the cafe and went our different ways – he more joyous than me because he had somebody to go to. I felt empty, overwhelmed by memories of past affection. It was best to get it over before everything in our life together turned sour.

I remember thinking how little there is in prayer books that helps you in such situations – even the prayer book I had half edited and composed myself. Lots of prayers for marriage were in it when you don't need God much – society and your body do most of the work for you. But for divorce you need a lot of God and the support of friends but there is no ritual for it. You're on your own. Friends also don't like a divorced acquaintance around. He or she might be a dangerous loose cannon or an uncomfortable reminder that even twenty years together is no permanent glue, no divine fixative.

'Here is no abiding city,' as Augustine said.

Back in London we tried to sort out the debris of our life. We quarrelled over silly pots, and mementoes of past holidays. All valueless except as markers of our inner anger and bitterness. But when we were quarrelling over a silly holiday jug, Old Smokey intervened. I suddenly saw his face outside Kim and then he was speaking inside him, out and in, out and in. He made faces at me and I burst into laughter.

'Let's go to the pub,' I said, 'and toss a coin for it.'

'That's the most sensible thing you've said for years, Lionel,' said Kim.

It was the way we brusquely tied up the loose ends in our life. We dealt with the finance in less than fifteen minutes and arranged to sign a document renouncing all claims on each other. Old Smokey had done the trick. Once again I experienced how real was my see-through friend. And I had a bonus. I was no longer frightened of death, only dislike of pain. Death was a door to a meeting. Parting was also a kind of death, now it was not unknown but familiar. With help I could get to the other side.

If you invoke God into situations, unexpected things happen. Kim had already found his Jim who became his partner, and who has since looked after and cared for him through every illness. I was about to find my own Jim. I had learnt to finish a relationship decently, not denying the good times, nor trying to find someone to blame, some convenient villain. I could wrap it up politely. And so could Kim because he was a gentleman. At fifty, I had begun to grow up. Just in time too!

We have remained together in a sort of way ever since, Kim, me and the two Jims (his and mine). We meet for lunch every few weeks or months. I still want to live my life on the water. No longer at sea, that is no longer possible, but in a barge, a canal boat that can move. Kim showed me my element. I am Aquarius, a sojourner in this world, a gypsy like my mother.

Kim says I gave him an education and I certainly discovered in him a most sensitive taste in art and music. He taught me spiritually as well as materially. At the beginning of my sailing career, I couldn't see buoys. Everybody else could but not me. Patiently Kim showed me again and again the tell-tale signs, what to look for. After I saw one, I saw them all. It was the same with God and angels. After I learnt to see one door to heaven, I spotted such doors in every situation. Whether I was prepared to go through them is another matter.

Kim also advanced my Oxford education. In a wobbly way I was becoming a gentleman. I had also begun to be the kind of chap my father would have wanted. What Kim never managed to teach me was tying bowlines, telling the difference between right and left, and how to hold a sextant straight. He did teach me never to go into a pub unless I had enough money in my pockets to be able to take my turn to buy a round . . . and many, many other things. In return I taught Kim art, museums, opera, chamber music and bohemia.

63

Another Inner Journey

As my relationship with Kim got rough, I started to break up. Couples often act as if on a seesaw. When one goes up the other goes down. Kim and I had experienced these seesaw movements many times before. It was now his turn to go up again.

At a Jewish–Christian–Muslim conference in Germany, I was managing well on the surface and putting on a good show but I was going to bits underneath. Only Irene saw and understood what was going on. (You must not confuse her with Irena, though both are refugees from Germany.) I hardly knew her though we both taught at the Leo Baeck College. She told me to come and see her at University College Hospital where she was a senior psychotherapist. I could see her on the NHS, she said.

Having gone through a Reichian depth analysis I didn't think there was much she could add, but any port in a storm. I came to see her when she was the only one at work in a darkened empty building. She was seeing me in her free time. 'Aren't you frightened of me alone in this empty block?' I said. 'Not at all,' she replied, 'and certainly not of you. Now tell me what's happening.'

I took to her courage straightaway. I knew little about her, but gradually I began to assemble the bits of her life. It wasn't easy because this was outside the syllabus of psychotherapy and Irene was German and kept the rules. She was a Jewish schoolchild in the Nazi Berlin of the thirties. She had two friends, girls like her devoted to athletics. They all belonged to the same sports club. Their friendship was so close they were called the three-leaf shamrocks. But it could not continue and after Hitler came to power in 1933, her two friends walked away from her, they could no longer know her or be seen with her. Irene's name was removed from the sports club list.

It got worse but Irene stood her ground. The Jewish shops in her neighbourhood became forbidden to Aryans, and SS guards stood outside to enforce it. Irene was fair and tall so they tried to stop her, thinking she was Aryan. 'But I'm Jewish,' she answered firmly, 'and therefore I can go in.'

One day her father, a professor of psychology, told Irene and her sister to come to his library. There he showed them their two phials of poison in case they should need them if the Gestapo came.

Irene was in Palestine during the Second World War. She saw what many in the heady days of Zionist achievement did not see. If they had, the situation of the new Jewish state might now be less dark, tragic even. Here is an incident she told me about. During the war she belonged to a Jewish platoon working in a British military hospital in Palestine. Masud, an Arab servant boy, was suspected of pilfering. A corporal contemptuously said he was 'one of those wogs who would even steal your pants'. Irene said she laughed. It was a joke. But then she thought of all the demonisation and false accusations that she and the others had suffered, and how unkind stereotyping was. She never laughed again at such prejudice. The consequences were too serious.

Now psychotherapists are a mixed lot and they regulate themselves as do psychoanalysts. Most in my experience are concerned and caring. But some use it to make a fast buck and some to inflate their own egos, and some for a lazy way of earning a living. I stuck to Irene for twenty-five years because though I have disagreed with her, in a time made dishonest by advertisement and self-advertisement, she possessed a transparent integrity and a loyalty to her clients which continued long after they ceased to be her clients. She didn't enjoy power over her clients. From the very beginning of her career as a psychotherapist, she learnt from them just as they learnt from her.

I worried her because we met too often, being involved in the same Jewish world. 'We mustn't keep meeting like this,' I croaked at her during an academic sherry party and she shot to the other end of the room, which amused me. I also stayed on with her years longer than a client should. I told her that attempting to know God without knowing oneself led to fanaticism, banality or disaster, because God is not just out there but deep inside. Also I needed help to make sure the imaginative mythical part of my mind never became more real than the hard realities and facts of life. She considered this, understood it and carried on.

From me she began to consider the importance of humour in self-knowledge, and she tried to understand religious religion. She listened carefully to her closest colleague, the Catholic priest and professor at a London hospital, Father Louis Marteau. She also listened to me. She nevertheless died an agnostic or atheist. Religious people played too many tricks (her tried friends excepting). They could be wonderful but they played games she didn't understand. I understand how she felt because she was right, we do. Unfortunately our language, which is so exact with the outer shell of reality, is inadequate for the spiritual and aesthetic heights and depths of our experience.

Part of her continues to live inside me, and in dodgy situations it speaks to me though I don't have the strength to practise it. I did learn a lot about myself from her but her greatest lessons to me were integrity, honesty and courage to face the truth. In religion such virtues are often in short supply because there is too much role-playing, pretending and insecurity. Irene's agnosticism meant nothing to WW. In my prayers he told me she was his messenger and I should listen to her carefully. I did. She reminded me, for example, of an obvious truth I had forgotten – that jokes and humour are not just joyous and helpful, but when made against somebody can be among the painful experiences that person endures in life. Many of us in adult life still remember the jokes made against us at school when we were at our most vulnerable.

She deserved a verse in Jonathan's Cavalcade but I am not good at writing such things. She was a great teacher at the Leo Baeck College, though undervalued because she did not inflate or put on the style.

After Irene died, I sat back on a bench at the crematorium and considered what it meant to me not having her support during my difficult days. A lot, though I did not feel bereft as I would have felt years before. That is her achievement.

It is now the time in my story to recap the difficulties I have had to cope with through my life. My problems were not abnormal, just the neuroses many people share. As a child I was compulsive and obsessive. These behaviour patterns were common signs of insecurity which lingered with me later than most and into adult life. I can give various reasons for them. Like many children who had not experienced the Holocaust directly, I was nevertheless close enough to it to be deeply disturbed by it. Another reason. My mother's family, whose only child I was, looked to me as a messiah who would lead them out of their poverty and insecurity to the good life and good living. But of course the sensible part of me knew I was no god or messiah, and this left me feeling puzzled, inadequate and letting down people I loved. Perhaps another reason was that I found happiness harder to handle than its opposite. It was less familiar, so I used to punch myself to avoid even worse from the cosmos.

During these times a depression descended like Churchill's Black Dog. I couldn't get out of bed. I tried to masturbate myself into oblivion. I just let the telephone ring and ring and I couldn't draw the curtains. But after my analysis with Leslie, I never tried suicide and in the end, about 2 p.m., I did get up and shakily face life. My animals helped me and also involuntarily even JB, because it was better for me to have someone in the house.

Fortunately, I had a good mobile mind and could cope more or less with my obligations even though I had made no notes and could not keep a diary. I wasn't up to such organisation. Also fortunately, problems could turn from a minus into a plus as I had found out at the Quaker meeting. I could recognise and understand my own problems in others. Feeling compassion for them was like feeling compassion for myself. And problems were like coiled springs – they thrust me into painting, writing and religion. With regard to the last, my saving grace was self-honesty. I could stand aside from myself and watch myself – this was not schizophrenia but common sense. I could also talk straight to WW. In that relationship I trusted, and there was no need for nonsense.

I was quite aware I came to religion out of need. And I stayed with it because it worked. Some people thought it was my escape into never-never land where I could consume pie in the sky, but this was not so. The B-movies running round in my mind were never-never land. WW and religion carried me back to the real world of obligation, the enjoyment of small things and common sense.

In my work, I met many people inhabiting their Cloud-cuckoo-land. Like many neurotics and occasional psychotics they could be shrewd and manipulative but without the courage to face self-awareness, which thank God I had. Some of them wanted me to go up in the smoke of a gas chamber, some 'loved' me (a strange self-regarding love), some wanted me to play their neurotic games.

The combination of analysis and religious self-examination got me through the dark wood of middle age, like the one mentioned by Dante at the beginning of *Il Purgatorio*.

I thought a lot about religion and truth and honesty. Religion was good with higher truth but it wasn't good at lowly honesty. It wasn't open or honest or exact when it dealt with sex, power, ambition and preferment. It had to cloak them in fibs, half truths, little white lies, and accommodations. As a religious bureaucrat I had to do so myself. I excused myself by telling myself that I at least knew what I was doing. A little bit of me had touched real holiness, but it might take a lifetime for the rest of me to catch up, or even more, if it ever did.

Beyond God and the gods who are the shadows of our desires there was another dimension which existed for itself. Profound atheists and agnostics like Irene know it as well as self-labelled religious folk.

Irene taught me some inside-outs too. That I shouldn't torment myself with perfectionism. That I had a duty to enjoy myself. That I wasn't the saviour of the world and should be careful of religion that led me in that direction. That I shouldn't get obsessive about prayer. That I didn't have an obligation to pray in each chapel or synagogue I passed or to follow every funeral procession for at least three steps. That I shouldn't use religion compulsively and neurotically. That God had sent her to tell me this because I was getting it all wrong. That my main success now was if I plucked up enough courage to enjoy myself.

She succeeded. Since Irene's death I have enjoyed myself quietly and pleasantly. And the self-understanding which started with Leslie and herself has continued with the aid of other counsellors and psychotherapists. It did not only continue professionally and continuously but through self-examination and contemplation in my Priory or while sitting in the great hall of a London station and considering the human comedy and human tragedy of which I am part and which are being played out before my eyes. I have a good brain and little difficulty in being clever-clever, which is why I feel most indebted to those like her who planted in me seeds of self-awareness.

64

'Dear Merseyside . . .'

As Kim and I divided up our house and our lives and separated, I sank into a bewildered depression. I decided I had developed a talent for friendship over the years, but I had no talent for love except for the religious kind. Life still puzzled me and I needed advice.

One friend told me that a relationship could only work if you had the same interests, the same intelligence and the same amount of money. It sounded wise but I didn't want my clone, I wanted my complement. Another said perhaps what I needed was just an uncomplicated answer to my love needs and some straightforward enjoyment and all this idealistic sentimental talk about Jewish marriage and my granny's home was just confusing the issue. I should keep it simple and not make a meal of it. Yet another said that I should think about a straight marriage again and risk Disaster à Deux. Another knew of a sympathetic masseur.

But in the end I didn't go with a woman, a matching clerical clone, an escort or toy boy, or wise masseurs. I wanted a mature chap, who was sexually compatible and wanted to set up a home. This didn't seem too much. Wearily, I thought I'd have another try.

Phyllis, my assistant at my office, then took a hand and added her advice. She is and was a good friend and didn't like seeing me suffer. 'You can't carry on like this, Lionel,' she said.

'But what do I do?' I answered desperately, crying out like Bunyan's Pilgrim. 'I'm not built right for cruising in bars and I don't want to end up as the oldest swinger in town.'

'What about that gay paper you read?' she suggested.

I turned to the personal column. 'They're probably all fifty-one who look forty-nine and a half in the dark and into leather underwear,' I replied crossly.

'There must be some more normal ones,' she said – and she was right. One advert said simply, 'Merseyside. Ordinary working class guy seeks friend. Age and looks unimportant.' He may have added a few vital statistics, I've forgotten.

I whipped out a pen and wrote a short note. 'Dear Merseyside,' I replied, 'I am fifty (with the following measurements) and fed up because I am just finishing a long relationship. Over to you. Sincerely.'

A fortnight later I got a cautious phone call from Merseyside. He hadn't expected a reply from as far away as London, he said, but he had got in touch because all the local replies were zilch and he was finishing a relationship probably longer than mine. He had a weekend free from work so I invited him down. He was older than me, about the same age as Kim, which was familiar.

He was slim, wiry and must once have had golden curls. We sat in pubs and talked. What he made of my collapsing household I couldn't know because he never said much, just glanced around, but we were company to each other. After he left I wrote him a polite letter saying thank you for his visit but I didn't want another affair. He wrote the same to me and our letters crossed in the post. But we went on holiday together, Kim lending us his flat in Amsterdam, which was nice of him. It was a disaster. We were going for a fortnight and returned after three days speaking not at all or in chill voices. Our backgrounds were too different. Everybody said so. Without thinking I'd dumped on my scouser Jewish ecclesiastical Golders Green, Amsterdam Bohemia, my Sisters and assorted weirdoes accompanied by their counsellors, therapists and analysts. Later he told me he thought he was in a madhouse.

For just over a year it was on off, on off, on . . . We stuck it because after all who else would have us at our age? Also, we were both agreed about wanting a home (despite the geography) and having a desire for an exclusive faithful relationship. We were getting on in life and getting old on your own is a mug's game. So we made up, parted and made up again.

Gradually we resumed contact. Physically we fitted. We also both came from poor backgrounds and I instinctively knew my way around Scouseland – it was the old East End of my childhood with its fish and chippers, decaying houses of worship, charity shops and black humour which stopped you getting poisoned by your own bad vibes. I got the hang of it and stepped easily from Kim's squirearchy-on-sea to Jim's trade unionism and works club.

He had to get accustomed to me and I had to get accustomed to him. There was me making witty conversation over high tea emphasising points with my spoon and then discovering in one of my dramatic pauses that Jim had taken away my plate, washed it up and dried it. He was a tidy chap like all my partners.

A few friends of mine thought the situation might not be completely hopeless. Sister Charlotte (Sister Louis Gabriel that was) liked him, partly because she was having one of her recurrent spats with Kim and partly because she romanticised The Worker as only an upper-class radical nun can. Gordian offered to explain us to each other, as I've said before. Rabbi Dr Albert Friedlander, my colleague, told me not to give up but try again, because there was obviously some bond between us which kept us trying. Jim's ex also told him he was a fool and wouldn't get anyone better. Kim wasn't sure but, being in love himself, didn't have time for my muddled affairs. Sister Mary, my sister, invited us over and cooked comforting meals for us both. Jaap, my confessor in Holland, gave us less than a 50 per cent chance and advised caution because we couldn't laugh at the same things. Could he laugh? he asked. I didn't know.

I think we both got to learn that the secret of any relationship is in the will and, unlikely though it was, we never gave up. It took us three years before we could come back from a holiday still speaking to each other. We usually kept our polite self-restraint and only blew up at the last minute in the returning departure lounge.

We also got to learn what we could give each other. I discovered that Jim had a natural feel and appreciation of modern art – much more than me – and of strong tough plays put on by passionate local dramatic groups. Sometimes his sense of order and tidiness got us into trouble. At an exhibition Jim saw a random heap of rubble in a corner and, being conscientious, was about to tidy it up into a wall. He was just about to start when the curator came in and had a *crise de nerfs*. The randomness of the rubble was 'the art' and Jim was about to tidy 'the art' out of existence. Feeling put-upon, Jim ceased to be creative and the curator was grateful and pacified.

I liked sitting in pubs with him, and visiting works clubs, and learning bingo calls – 'legs 11, 88, two fat women dancing, 69, everyone's favourite'. I also settled happily and cosily among his friends, who were far more friendly to two old gay guys than I'd expected. I discovered how much of my whisky grandpa there was in me and I uncovered a layer of English life previously unknown.

Getting away from that bloody Jewish Problem was also a relief. On the TV came a picture of Israeli troops marching into Lebanon. I nearly shot out of my seat. 'What you getting so excited for?' said one of Jim's friends. 'Because I'm Jewish,' I babbled. 'Well, Ken here's a Baptist, so what?' came the puzzled answer. They had their problems like benefit, finding a job, the wife, working the system. The Jewish Problem wasn't way down their list, it was nowhere. This helped me in my BBC talks. The world was more than one big Jewish Problem.

Because we came from the same poor respectable background, I relaxed with him. I recovered my delight in small things, and free treats, like listening to the bandstand, walking the promenade, gazing at the towers and spires of Liverpool from across the Mersey. Once again it reminded me of Bunyan's Celestial City beyond the River of Death. We hunted in charity shops through the debris of other people's lives, and studied shoppers while enjoying a sausage roll tea in the local precinct. The streets and malls were theatres like London's East End. My jaw dropped as I saw a little man slip half a lamb from the butcher's tray into his loose grey raincoat and then scuttle off. Pinching a pie is common enough, but a whole half sheep!

In religion it was a case of give and take with no pressures. I'm still intrigued by Jim's religion, whatever it is, but I've also learnt not to make windows into people's souls. Jim was many things before he met me. He'd been a Bevin boy, a sergeant in the army, a steward at sea, a cabin boy, an engineer, a sailor and a funeral director. Because of the last he was dubious about life after death and all religion, but on the other hand sang out plangent hymns in church and synagogue, crossed himself at communion and lit our Sabbath candles. Ritually he was quite a stickler, so we welcomed in the Jewish Sabbath and fasted on the Day of

Atonement and he prepared our Passover table. (I cut down the liturgy and don't stretch it out like the bubblegum of my childhood because I don't think quantity is a substitute for quality, nor scholarship for spirituality.) He never became Jewish, because he got too muddled by the Hebrew vowel signs. But if the powers-that-be ever get our bodies, any ashy bits will be buried side by side or mixed up in whichever cemetery, preferably Jewish, will have us. But I don't think WW (Fred) will carry Jewish exclusivity into the afterlife. Some colleagues are now beginning to discuss mixed-faith burials, provided there is a path between the couple. I imagine our bony hands stretching towards each other underneath it. Did you ever!

In America a former pupil of mine was very nice to him but obviously thought, 'Why couldn't Lionel have met a nice old Jew instead?' He changed his mind, though, when after the Atonement Fast (twenty-five hours) ended, Jim stayed on in Synagogue through the additional service of Separation (Havdalah), the next day's evening service, an extra sermon for the devout, a lesson in law and a clutch of miserable, wailing, mystical hymns. (Miserable, I suppose, because we were all starving.) After that my old pupil regarded Jim with new respect as a self-made Jew and a peculiar model of God's grace. Sergeant Jim would have regarded anything less as falling out without permission on the barrack square! Many years later one of my colleagues offered to perform a ceremony for us, but we declined with thanks. Having been blessed by the Holy Spirit for over twenty years, further warrants of respectability seemed superfluous. Jim had a feel for the real thing, whether it was art, Greek drama, or religion. But what he believed or believes I still don't know.

In our early years together I used to go up to Liverpool every weekend. Later on, when Jim was made redundant, he came to London and for over ten years he, me, Ma and Lil lived together in suburban Finchley. The old ladies loved him and he loved them.

Even when they went to the nearby Home for the last year of their lives, he visited them every day, bringing them presents and taking them out on excursions and treats. He knew exactly how to treat them. It was Jim not me who showed Ma how to wear incontinence pants, and use the bedside chemical loo. He cleaned the house, did their washing as well as mine and turned into a rather ruthless gardener. The plants knew who was boss! But through him the whole ensemble worked. We'd all changed roles, that's all. He and I were the parents and the old ladies were our mischievous children.

He looked after me as well. Once when I had an epileptic fit in Belgium by a canal, I came to in the ambulance and the nurses were worried about the brown fluid oozing from my lips. They thought my guts were coming up. Knowing some Dutch, I tried to reassure them saying, '*Nee, nee m'n heeren t'is alleen een Marsbar*' – to which I'm addicted. I'd been chewing one before I fitted. It was Jim who looked after me in that and many other hospitals. He saved my friend Robin's life too, when Robin fell off our boat into a canal lock and could have got crushed. He also took to my dear friend Amsterdam Bertie and helped him stagger around on a crutch after another of Bertie's lovers' tiff. Bertie was one of the wisest and most discreet hairdressers I have ever met. He looked like a blond Tarzan, a great golden labrador, so he had many lovers and many tiffs.

Jim and I now look after each other in the way two committed old codgers can. After twenty-three years together we've got to know each other's fears and needs, bodily, sexual and emotional. For example, I have to use an erection injection. Jim fixes it for me. All our lives we've been saving up for our old age and we've suddenly realised that the old age we've been saving for has now come, so three weeks after writing this we're going off on a romantic cruise (two weeks en suite £700 full board). We'll watch the young marrieds for tips. Jim is jolly good at line dancing. He straddles round like a real cowboy. I'm not even good enough to be the horse. We not only feel for each other, we amuse each other – but then we've been lucky. We've been the first generation of gays who've enjoyed a legal middle age together. 'You earn love as you earn your living,' says the prayer book. Our love hasn't dropped from heaven, though heaven helped us. We've worked jolly hard for it and it's happened.

I was well received in Merseyside by Jim's friends, family and neighbours. Nothing was said but nothing was condemned either. Jim had a more difficult time down south. He may have been (in my eyes) 'a thing of beauty' but he was also clearly 'a goy forever' (goy means Gentile). Jewish people were polite to him but didn't stay with him at parties. At prestige functions, we were both seated at Table 13, the one by the swinging kitchen door, along with the wisecracking au pairs and the self-doubting divorcees. Twenty years later we've made it to the top table now and have got to behave.

Old age is a stiff test for all of us – especially if you've got no children.

Jim said that if I went first, he'd never want anybody else. I told him I probably would because I've never really lived on my own and it was too late to change in my seventies and eighties. Jim on his own sets out a knife and fork and dinner mat. I would take out a tin of tomato pilchards and another of rice pudding, a tin opener and a spoon. We trust each other now. I tell him about my paranoia and depressions. He unlocks his worries (if he has any). We sit together in synagogue and church and say our own thing to Whoever. You can't get closer than that.

65

Don't Put Your Son on the Stage, Mrs Blue!

My mother was not the only one who changed with age. I did too because of the arrival of Jim and the new security in my life. And with me it was the same kind of changing and ageing. I became lighter like her and easier to live with. It also became easier to live with myself. It was my friend Gordian who said: 'Do your best and leave the rest to God. That's what he's there for.'

Now these words came as a great relief because for my little family I had always been a little God. Other people wrote books, I wrote scriptures. It was wonderful in a kind of way. I enjoyed the perverted power it gave (though I never really believed in it). Megalomania could also serve as a sex substitute. In difficult times it seemed to make me safe, cocooned in solipsism. But I was never really happy and the perfectionism it brought with it wrecked my childhood. As I got older I became freer of the load I had carried through life. Instead of changing my partner, I now enjoyed him. I learnt to say I don't know and even 'No!' if I was very courageous. I no longer resorted to fibs to protect my sanctity. I did what my mother advised – I no longer put on the style. I was no longer God or God's Gestapo. I was just a mildly gay gay making the best of it. To my surprise I became rather nice – or at least nicer than I'd ever been before.

I also became more honest without hours of kneework and mental flagellation. I decided I didn't want to take ordinary services any more because I didn't know what I was doing in them or whom I was doing them for. I felt silly reminding the Almighty how mighty he was and how everything he did was wonderful when it manifestly wasn't. He seemed as bound by necessity as we were. Simone Weil says that, and I agree with her. So after completing three good volumes of liturgy with Jonathan Magonet, I decided not to carry on my work on the prayer books. The old 'Stand up! Sit down!' no longer meant much to me. Perhaps I'd find my way back to liturgy again but first I had to go on a journey. I knew God or WW was waiting for me round the corner but he hadn't yet revealed his hand. I didn't mind taking services to help out overburdened colleagues, of course, and it felt nice being helpful to small rabbi-less congregations.

But something did happen in my life which was totally unexpected – just like the BBC, in fact. First a rabbi and then a businessman came to my office asking whether I'd consider going on the stage, treading the boards, turning myself into a jokester and entertainer. I had entertained old age homes unintentionally as well as intentionally but this was in another league and I blinked. But feeling younger and gayer (in its conventional sense) than I had ever been, I said yes straightaway. For two reasons. I might find God again (an overdose of religious bureaucracy had taken away his freshness) and I'd certainly be able to top up my pension again. My CV had been too erratic for the normal, safe-as-houses provision for old age that most of my colleagues enjoyed.

'Beware of the grey days when I shall say I have no pleasure in them . . .' (Ecclesiastes). I had no children to fight my corner and money would certainly be a help for Jim and me during the cheap winter months in Benidorm, if prostate and Alzheimer's didn't get us first.

But my real motive wasn't so materialist. I wanted to meet at last the people I'd been talking to through a mike or a TV camera. I was attracted to the flesh and blood of them. Somehow over the years we had become members of a congregation and, as in all good congregations, the giving wasn't just one way. I wanted to listen to them speaking, to hear what they were thinking and plug into their spirituality. They had more than they realised. We were a congregation of all faiths and none, mainly none, and it was the best congregation I ever had.

WW had had enough liturgical compliments, complaints, chants and moans from me. Perhaps he wanted me to entertain him so we had a rendezvous in a theatre.

66

I Tread the Boards –
the Only Honest Profession

Graciously saying yes to the rabbi, the businessman and God was one thing, treading real boards on a real stage was quite different. I was let loose on the provincial circuit which I thoroughly enjoy. Actually talking to and touching people (steady, Blue!) whom I'd only been making contact with before through a mike was wonderful and I warmed to them all. I wanted to throw my arms around them – though of course I didn't dare.

Unfortunately, I had always been an accident-prone person, especially in later years. Being epileptic, I couldn't for example take a strong front stage light in my eyes. If I did there was always a chance that the audience would get a show it didn't bargain for. I was also so keen to be near my audience I nearly tripped over the edge of the stage and fell among them. (From a pulpit I had once actually fallen among my wardens, knocking off their bowlers.)

What helped me with all these problems was prayer. I used to pray to God or WW before I went on, telling him that if I made a fool of myself, let me make myself a fool for him. I also asked him for help so that I didn't fall into the numbers game – because he was as present with an audience of only five as he was with fifty or five hundred or a thousand. Yes, the money helped but there were other reasons just as important. The warmth of people warmed up the embers of my own religion. We warmed up each other.

I also kept the house lights full on because although my entertainment may have seemed a monologue, it was really a dialogue. I needed to see people's faces and find out what engaged them. Did they want to be cheered up with lots of jokes, especially raunchy ones, or did they want me to help them face their problems of mortgages and mortality and the horrors in the media? They got both, of course, but I altered the proportion according to what I read in their faces. So they partly fixed the programme.

In the interval I sign books and chat with the people, and after the show I stay in the theatre until the last one who wants to talk to me has left. As in a hospital ward or waiting room, I get overwhelmed by the Original Goodness of people. God is among them and shines out of their faces and also in their worries, as he does in paintings of old people by Rembrandt. It renewed my own professional religion which had got tired.

Theatre people are a friendly lot. The theatre staff are interested and helpful and there's real camaraderie, much more than in official religious buildings, where officials think they know all about God and what he ate for breakfast and can waste their time on the specks and measly little details of custom, forgetting the charity and generosity that are the point of the whole exercise.

For about fifteen minutes before the end, it's over to the congregation. They can make any points they like and ask any questions. They get my truth neat because I've got too old to play games and I've never been organised enough to fib successfully. (You have to say exactly the same fib to everybody, but even as an alert youngster I never remembered it!) So they get my gay bit, my anxieties and depressions and my doubts and also my amusement when religion goes over the top. I've got to like these points and questions more and more. Because of them we get to an honesty which formal religion rarely reaches.

I've also learnt some humility while touring as a spiritual entertainer. In Edinburgh at the Festival I wandered among the buskers and marvelled at their dedication. Unlike me, they did not have a warm pre-booked theatre and a name made known by the media. They had to gather an audience surrounded by the competition of other buskers and collect their fee even while performing. (Crowds can melt away fast when the hat's passed round.) I watched a lady sword swallower with respect and amazement. She demonstrated the sharp edge of her sword and it convinced me. Her glass of water had got knocked over so she had to swallow her sword without whetting her whistle which she did successfully and alarmingly. What she received was about enough for a supper. I asked her why she did it. She'd tried various ways to make a living, she told me, but this was the most honest and that's why she carried on.

There was a man with a whitened face in Jacobean costume who slowly struck fascinating hypnotic attitudes. It was too slow for most of the adults, but some children appreciated it and even contributed some of their pocket money into his hat. Working without the response of a crowd was a tribute to his integrity and I admired him too.

The audiences were my new congregation, and I was a minister again and of course they ministered to me more than they realised. It had its limitations, of course, because we probably would not see each other again, but our one show contact was the real thing. It was the best one-night stand I had ever experienced.

Quite often without any fuss at the end of the programme we sang an unprogrammed hymn together. It wasn't kitsch, it felt right!

Returning to a more conventional pulpit, I realised how much the theatre had affected me. I am much less snooty and ask the congregation to put up their hands if they can't hear me and then redirect my voice accordingly. If they can't hear, what's the point? Me talking to me? Or a classy ego trip?

I am much more conscious now that my congregation own the service. It's theirs. In the old Hebrew term, I am only their 'representative', their 'agent'. The service is not a private conversation between me and the Almighty which I graciously permit them to overhear. I make sure they've got time for questions and points some time after the service. If I don't know the answer, I say so. We begin to give a sermon to each other. We're all the people of God and the best parables come out of everyday life, not libraries.

I also make sure my sermon has an ending as well as a beginning, so that I don't flounder on and on. I learnt this from the radio where the greatest sin is not in the ten commandments – it's delaying the eight o'clock news or the tired staff clearing up.

And I'm supported by tradition. Rabbi Baruka, says the Talmud, met the prophet Elijah in Lapet fair. 'Who is worthy of eternal life here?' asked the rabbi. Elijah was just about to say, 'Nobody!' when he caught sight of two men. 'They have a portion in eternal life,' he said. Rabbi Baruka ran to them. 'What is your profession?' he asked them. 'We are just comics,' they said. 'We cheer up sad people and tell jokes to stop them quarrelling.'

And many modern scholars say 'The Song of Songs' is a play with choruses, characters and even stage directions!

I am proud that Jonathan and I got some words of Bud Flanagan into our liturgy. He tells how good show business has been to him. He has made people laugh and helped them forget the troubles of the world. During the war his kind homely voice did just that. I am proud to be a member of his profession.

I'm proud of Jim as well. We've become a team. It's bed and boards with us. He sees to my books, tells me when to wrap up my 'spiel' because there's only five minutes to go and whether the deaf old lady can hear in the gallery. He makes sure I get my sandwiches because they take away my tension like the cigarettes I've long ago given up. And he also knows when to leave me because old WW is around. He drives me around England because he enjoys it and because they took away my licence on account of my epilepsy. He also tells jokes better than me but won't. He makes sure I don't go on stage with my mobile. Afterwards we relax with red wine in our room.

67

Pilgrimage to Amsterdam

I did return to Amsterdam at different times with all my partners, except JB – which is significant. I returned at different times with Janny, Kim and Jim so that they could understand what this place had meant to me. It was the unofficial college where I had learnt to grow up. True, it was no longer the raw poor city I had first known just after the war, when youngsters dodged the draft to Indonesia and the hopeless war to retain the old colonies. 'War for whom?' they asked. 'For the old bourgeoisie and the genera-tion which had helped bring on the tragedy of Europe?' The seeds of revolt were in the air as they had so often been in Amsterdam's turbulent republican past. I remembered the riots that greeted a repentant Prince Claus, in his youth a conscript in Nazi Germany.

I remembered the hippies with a new message of peace, but it got taken over by the business world it so much despised and ended up annexed to the drug trade or, less dangerous but more demeaning, to the fashion industry. I met many on the way to Nepal to seek enlightenment from some grisly guru. (They also became high fashion.) It was a spiritual revolution that failed.

I remember the time of bicycles painted white. When you saw one you just took it and rode off with it. When you got off, someone else could take it. Anything white was for anyone and everyone. Some women wore only white! And a few men too, but not many. And then there was the rise of the Provocation Party, some of whose activists shouted, 'Vote Provo for better weather!' and won seats on the Amsterdam town council.

It was the time of the squatters, some of whom adopted me as a curiosity. I tried to cook for them. They ate mushrooms which they collected for free. 'How do you sort them out?' I asked uneasily. 'We don't,' they said, 'but some we only eat once.' I ate my own baked beans. It was my religious requirement, I said firmly. But I did go along to a big hippy house where I attended a cookery course. We contemplated rice for forty minutes and then burnt it!

Now many think of Amsterdam as a sex city or a drug depot, and in my time it's been both. What saved me was my naivety. I brought a pot of geraniums to a friend's birthday party. 'Much more colourful,' I said, 'than those straggly green pot plants you see everywhere.' The guests hooted with laughter, but how was I to know the economical Dutch were growing their own hash?

But above all, for me, Amsterdam was and is a holy city which makes me wonder and worship, a modern holy city. There's the statue of a stolid dockworker, one of those who went on strike when the Nazi deportations began. Not many risk their lives against the evil that happens to others. By the red light district is Bet van Beeren's cafe which sheltered the resistance. Near the Westerkerk is the attic where Anne Frank still hoped when I would have hated. And by the church there are three pink marble triangles, recalling the badges worn by gays in the concentration camps before they were tortured. The memorial is user-friendly and you can sit on those triangles as you wait for your clanging tram. Amsterdam is the only city I know with such a memorial.

Other holy cities like Rome and Canterbury don't want to know the struggle and fate of small minorities like gays and lesbians, though God knows they've benefited from the great gay contribution at all levels like all denominations – but have never acknowledged their debt. I don't think such safe silence is decent.

Near the memorial there is the plaque in the Westerkerk which says that Rembrandt was buried nearby in an unknown pauper's grave. He represents self-honesty, not flinching from the dereliction and failure of old age. He was one of those people not conventionally pious, but one of my unofficial saints.

When in Amsterdam with Kim, I took him to a hippy house for dinner. We sat on the floor and Kim complained politely but firmly that the soup was badly burnt and he objected to paying for it. The waiter looked at him compassionately and said dreamily without irony that as it was all free, it didn't really matter. Kim and I tried to make polite conversation, first to the diner on our right and then to the diner on our left as good manners dictate. They were silent but looked at us dreamily and contentedly. Kim touched one to make a point and a whole row of our fellow diners keeled over. They were stoned!

Kim grew to love Amsterdam too. He was also educated there in social honesty as I had been, and learnt the basic lessons much faster than me.

It was in Amsterdam Kim discovered the excellence of his artistic taste. He would saunter through one of the great exhibition rooms of the Rijksmuseum, glance round and then make a beeline for the unobtrusive jewel of the gallery, a small Corot, an Isaac Israels, a Gerard Dou, one of Rembrandt's pupils.

He was struck by how nice to him my Amsterdam friends were – this was not because of me but because of his own qualities. He was not only a real English gentleman, his troubles had made him a rare open-minded one. He was also a courageous man who could sail across the Atlantic and could calmly take charge during North Sea storms. He could also sing rude naval songs after a *kopstoot* (beer and genever together or mixed) or two.

Kim and I spent our honeymoon in Amsterdam. But there was a hint of future troubles. He wanted me but he also wanted to be free. The poor chap had been bottled up so long. I had wanted the same thing a decade before but now I wanted an exclusive Jewish home. So we were out of sync. Pity!

Now that so many of my old mates have disappeared with scarcely a clue to their memory, I want to continue Bertie's story, though this was some years after Kim and I broke up, when I returned to Amsterdam with Jim.

Not many even in Amsterdam will remember my Bertie now after his death. His liver couldn't cope with his life. An old, old friend asked me to say memorial prayers for him. Which I did willingly. After all, the last time I was in Amsterdam, some friends of his told me with a giggle that some chap in his squat (next to the Rembrandthuis) was worshipping him as God. Jim and I dropped into Bertie's squat out of curiosity and so it was. 'It is not right,' said Bertie virtuously to the trembling worshipper at his knees, shaking with pious ecstasy (or was it sexual excitement?). 'Lionel can tell you, darling, because he has studied such things and knows all about God.'

Bertie had tripped over this junkie lying among rusty needles in the gutter. He'd carried him home and was trying to wean him off the hard stuff on to hash. The poor chap had delirium tremens and the shakes and was skeleton thin. He'd spent his childhood in institutions and his adult years in jail. But as he got stronger under Bertie's nursing, he sallied forth with a bolt-cutter lifting fridges and freezers and TVs as offerings to his great God Bertie. Bertie became frantic trying to repatriate them and, exhausted after three weeks of rows with angry shopkeepers, had said, 'You will just have to go back to prison, dearie, because I need a holiday, but when you come out, I will nurse you again.' The chap quietly broke some windows, was taken back into prison and it came about as Bertie said. This carried on till the junkie died. Bertie's was the only home he had ever known and he was too weak to survive.

Now Bertie was no god but he was the poor chap's Good Samaritan. Most people would have passed him by on the other side. Some like me might leave a few coins beside him. But Bertie was the only true redeemer in the junkie's life.

I think people look for the Messiah, the redeemer, the Good Samaritan in the wrong direction. They are not in the skies or in books but at work inside us. I feel pleased about including this story about Bertie because a story is a better memorial. In the end the heritage of the Holocaust, after all stone monuments have crumbled, will be a handful of stories about Jews who shared their last crusts in concentration camps and about a nun who went with Jewish children into a gas chamber to comfort them. And about Ettie Hillesum, who tried to keep sane and decent in the insane time of the Nazi occupation and whose story is a modern spiritual classic.

In a bar I did meet two of my old drinking mates, big jolly sensible chaps who embraced each other and everybody they could clutch. They had once looked askance at me because of my profession. I belonged to 'the crows', they said and I should be ashamed of myself. But this time the difference in them was obvious both outside and inside.

Outside they wore purple and mauve pants, and a framed portrait of their seraphically smiling jaunty guru nestled in their abundant curly chest hair which extended from their neck to their navel. They clanked holy medals and objects of piety as do many pious Hindus and Catholics. To quench their inner needs they mauled me with great bear hugs, sat me down and, breathing heavily, asked me to reveal the Cabbala there and then to them in the bar.

I treated them to a long lecture and they gazed at me pop-eyed with awe which embarrassed me. They fed me with Dutch gin but they drank only juice. Now some people, including me, can get snotty-nosed about fancy faiths but once again Amsterdam took away any remnants of spiritual snobbery. I was told that it was the Jehovah's Witnesses and Plymouth Brethren who had suffered most under Hitler because they were not among the big establishment religions and not compromisers. It was about the jaunty guru who had woken a spiritual longing in the hearts of my two 'bear' friends, though the spiritual cognoscenti made fun of him and thought he was a laugh.

I took both Kim and Jim in their turn to Tina's sauna. The new owners were polite and courteous and pleased to see me. Kim and Jim were uncomfortable. Perhaps because Tina had died and I could see her ghost, her holy ghost, but they had never known her and couldn't. It was her holy ghost that made me come out of the closet.

Tina had had cancer and I visited her in hospital in the seventies. Then when I returned and asked about her, they told me she had just died and her funeral would be taking place in a day or two's time. How fortunate that I had arrived just in time! But was it fortunate for me? She had helped so many people, many of them important. The press would be there and I was booked to give a public religious lecture at the weekend. Perhaps it was better for me not to put in an appearance. There would be no lack of mourners. So I stayed away.

I later learnt that very few had turned up for her funeral. Many, whom she had helped like me, must have thought like me and been made cowards like me. I tried to apologise to my inner voice, old WW. But he was not in an accepting mood. I knew then I could not live a lie any more. It would murder my soul. I could choose how and when I came out of the closet, but the crunch had come. 'The truth shall make you free' resounded in me again.

Back in England I told my own story to a journalist and it was duly printed in a newspaper. It created less of a stir than I thought. It was no big deal because nearly everybody knew and it would soon become public in any case, a helpful unknown woman's voice told me over the phone. But it was a big deal for me. That was the last great lesson Tina taught me. 'May her honesty shine out as one of the stars in the firmament of heaven.'

I also remember not a person but an apartment overlooking the old Amsterdam Flea Market. In it lived Theo (who is still alive though that apartment has gone). I discovered that apartment in about 1969. It sheltered a steady stream of people for days, weeks or months – me too among them. The apartment was my home, Theo was pa, and the inhabitants were my rival siblings and family. I remember the sweet tap dancer from German light TV programmes who only wanted to clean and clear up, the complex intense intelligent Dutch Indonesian pondering his double heritage (I'd been through that one myself). He was in love with Theo but he kissed me affectionately too. There was the Spaniard who was also in love with Theo but grrrrrr'd at me to tell me to keep off.

About ten years later when Monica Furlong and I were on our way to Berlin to lecture on 'Sexuality and Spirituality' we holed up at the apartment, while Monica sobbed her heart out over her divorce and rejection by the chap she had always been in love with. 'Lionel,' she said, 'let's cry off Berlin. They'll never miss us. They know more about sex and spirituality there than we'll ever begin to know in London. Let's just stay here and talk and drink in brown cafes instead and exit from the world in this wonderful apartment. Will they let us stay?'

'If you can find floor space you can stay,' I told her.

For four days over gin we wept out our sorrows to each other.

Monica was a wise woman and told me my destiny was with my friend Jaap who, she said, looked at me with love. Well, she was right about the destiny and the look of love, but there wasn't any bed in our friendship. Timidly I asked him and to my relief he told me I was wiser than the wise woman.

We had been like that since our first meeting. It was at a farewell party for friends who were off to the Arctic with children, caravan, the lot. I had just arrived from Germany and had dropped into the party unexpectedly and was having too good a time to think straight. I had been thinking too straight and spiritually crooked at ecclesiastical committees in Germany. It was a relief to relax among straightforward atheists. We waved off the wanderers goodbye and I was just about to recover my cases when I found that they'd gone off in the caravan and were heading with the kids sitting on them towards the Arctic. The guests were all leaving and where would I go at past two in the morning? A chap at the party took a compassionate look at me sitting on the pavement, rescued me from the gutter and took me back to his flat. It was my future friend Jaap.

At his home he gave me a bowl of bone broth – the speciality of the house. I looked through his books to find a nice romance to send me to sleep but all I could find were Marxist, though not Stalinist, tomes and I didn't need them because I passed out on his floor.

We lived together after that many times, Darby and Darby without It, just chaste kisses and mutual respect. In desperation one night Jaap rang up the love of his youth, whom he had worshipped from afar all his life, a sensitive, beautiful, famous actor. Jaap invited Joop over to dinner. To his surprise Joop said he had been waiting for such an invitation for many years and had never forgotten him. After dinner Jaap pushed his luck and asked his friend if he would stay. They have stayed together ever since. Dreams did come true in Amsterdam but for me mainly spiritual ones.

The chaps and girls and in-betweens I used to hang out with in the streets at night-time had long ago disappeared. No one had heard about them. Some were truly affectionate. But those narrow alleys and canals were as hauntingly beautiful as ever. I still saw old WW, JC, my Inner Voice, my Guardian Angel among the bottles and cigarette smoke of their small bars. I didn't need other arks or altars. I had known three holy cities: London's East End of my childhood, my Oxford Anglican one, and De Mokum – the Yiddish–Hebrew name for Amsterdam. The last was where I found a ladder to heaven, sturdy enough to take the weight of my body and soul.

68

At Sixty-Five I Get a Jolt! –
a Miserable Business

But I must retrace my steps in life for I am always going round in circles, being so disorganised. When Kim and I were breaking up and our house was dying, the way houses (and churches and synagogues) do when love has left them, I had to think about new arrangements for myself, my mother and Aunt Lil. I didn't want to return to the suburban nest it took me so many years to leave. So I rang up a really nice Home to make enquiries for my elderly mother and aunt and get the miserable business started.

'How old are they?' enquired the pleasant voice at the other end.

'In their seventies,' I answered.

'Oh, you've really left it too late.'

'When should I have enquired?' I asked. 'When they were in their seventies or sixties?'

The voice at the other end was hesitant.

'Do you mean I should have enquired when they were in their fifties?'

'Oh yes,' said the voice enthusiastically, 'that would have been just right.'

'You mean,' I said, 'I should have been enquiring for myself.'

'Yes, sir,' said the voice quickly, 'leave your address, Rabbi, and I'll send you particulars.'

The voice rang off.

I had a shock. Ever since, I no longer visited Homes just to see people I knew in them but also to work out how I myself would fit into them. I wouldn't, I decided. I'd do it my way together with

Ma and Auntie, and Jim if he left Liverpool and came down to London. That's what happened and so far my late sixties and early seventies have been one of the best periods of my life. Ageing has its advantages. I am free of the rat-race and its sticky corruption – big meals with 'big' people and handouts for compromises with your integrity. I am no longer in thrall to the Bitch Goddess Success. I am open about sex but not media sleaze. I don't have to prove myself to myself any more. I don't have to save for my old age any more. This is it. This is the old age that I've been saving for.

I am a lucky guy, I told myself. I have a partner, Jim. We would never leave each other or be unfaithful. (We wouldn't dare!) Love has grown between us faster than our puzzled understanding, and the needs of companionship have become more and more important. I resign myself to setting up that suburban home for all four of us. Being alone as you get older is a mug's game. As in package holidays, you need someone to complain to and someone to complain about. You also need someone to fight your corner for you or with you . . .

Having had to fight the corner for many old people, I know only too well how communal care which can be very good can also deteriorate into a communal con. Most of the workers and carers do a good job, with affection and even cuddles and kisses. But some bully old people into certifying that they've worked an hour when it's barely ten minutes. Because of my name and title I could sit by the phone on behalf of my congregation, mother and aunt and force my way to the official responsible for oldies' welfare. Most old people would not have the strength to do it by themselves. All they would get is an inane and hurried recorded answer dodging all responsibility. This is admittedly the worst scenario and many officials are very decent but understaffed. There isn't enough money in the system, but that's not the only shortage.

Worst of all, of course, I've been told about 'helpers' who try to make money out of old people, stealing a little bit here or there (they claim it as a gift), or even an inheritance (though that is being stopped now).

I do not want to paint too rosy a picture of ageing. The weak part is the body, and it is almost impossible to say what will happen to it. One old lady I know has taken up belly dancing at the age of ninety-six. On the other hand, my friend Sidney Carter, the hymn singer, ended up with Alzheimer's and I could not follow him into whatever world he inhabited. There are all stages in between, many to do with the indignity of crumbling water-works, and many with life-threatening illnesses, like cancer, paralysis or strokes . . .

Sooner or later we will all come to the river of death like Bunyan's pilgrims. It may help if we glimpse the celestial city from afar on the other side. After initial shyness, people (including my therapist) wanted to know what I thought about life after death. In that matter I have reverted to ancestral attitudes and don't think about it much. It's in God's hands or WW's hands and I leave it to them or him. Like Ma, I'm more concerned with this life than the next. I've got so much more to do here, I don't have the time or energy to dissipate it in speculation.

I have to learn, am learning, a new form of giving, which is not 'giving to' but 'giving up' and I should like to do it with grace. If I can learn the art of that I might be more comfortable with age. At least that will help the younger people waiting in the mortality queue behind me – those who will die after me. Also I have a lot to repent, and repentance for me is not going soggy on my knees but breaking out of old patterns of behaviour and not repeating my mistakes and sins. I have just begun to be aware of them and need to turn that awareness into practice and action.

Many therapists I know are not helpful. This is not their fault. They usually specialise in sex and success and the distance that has to be covered through puberty to adulthood and adultery. Few are trained to cover the distance between late middle age and old age. Perhaps they think there is no nice success story at the end. Many old people feel that no one is really interested in listening to them. They are just recipients of thoughtless bromides and placebos.

But I could do with some counselling and these are the situations I need help with:

I have a shorter fuse and get irritable.

I'm too judgemental about changes. I need to remind myself that the old order wasn't that wonderful, and I won't have to live under these changes, a younger generation will – poor sods!

Their own mistakes, if they are mistakes, might be more useful than my unwanted advice.

I'm frightened of being dependent. This can translate into money and I can get mean, because I don't like to see power leaking away from me.

After seventy, the goal posts shift continually and fast, the seasons succeed each other with unwelcome rapidity. I have to recalculate my capacities regularly.

The horizon is approaching, and so is my Judgement, whatever form it will take (I don't believe WW is a sadist and if he was I wouldn't follow him). I've got to think more of this Judgement than the social Judgement of friends or foes.

Also I can't put things off, like the pictures I may want to paint or the books I'd like to write. Unless I start them now, they'll never be done.

Life hasn't worked out as badly as I thought. To my surprise my hair fell out far more slowly than I feared long ago in Amsterdam, and life did not turn out as I had feared. But this still does not stop me being apprehensive. I shall live with my anxieties till the day I die. But becoming familiar with them has helped and I have also learnt to use them and even make friends of them. They're very good fodder for sermons and spiritual talks.

While looking around for a Home for Ma and Lil, I noticed things were not always as they seemed in these days when the concentration is on accountants, brochures, money-raising, TV chairs and equipment. All these are worthy activities and objects but I would prefer myself to go into a small Home I encountered which was not as well provided with state-of-the-art lifts, foam baths etc., but the inmates were given a large ration of cuddles, kisses, hand pattings and encouraging kind talk, where the entire staff, not just the nurses, had a team spirit and were clear about the purposes of their Home. Agency staff are very necessary and can do a very good fill-in job, but they do not have the time or experience to get motivated about the Home they have been sent to. Old people, even if their personality is eroding, are not just children to be played with. They are also on their long journey to their eternal home and should be treated with this in mind. Cuddles and kisses cannot be quantified in any annual report. That is where an accountant's or visitor's outer view and a client's inner view can differ.

Our suburban house also turned out much better than I expected. Ma was quite right. I was worrying much too much. I did the bills, Ma typed, Lil sewed, and Jim saw to the plumbing, the electrics and everything else. In case I was worried about money the two old ladies left their building society books on my pillow, telling me to take it all. That was all they had and I was welcome to it. When Jim came to live with us, he looked after them and organised jokes for them.

This saintliness didn't stop Ma playing her tricks. After we'd moved, Jim came back from work. 'You must feel tired,' exclaimed Ma, shaking her head. 'I expect you'd like a cup of tea.'

'Yes, I would, Hetty,' said Jim gratefully.

'Good, then make me one too!' said Ma briskly.

Jim and I roared with laughter. This cut through any false sentiment nicely. The old ladies hadn't changed. They were more themselves than ever.

'There's hope for us yet,' Jim said to me.

69

A Balding Orphan

Before she died my mother said to me, 'You and Jim should enjoy yourselves more, Lionel, while you still can. When you get to my age, it's not so easy. So travel, have a ball. All the money for you is in my building society book.' And she said, 'You worry too much, Lionel. I know you. Don't waste time on feeling guilty about us. You've been wonderful to Lil and me, you've looked after us just as our mother would have done.' What a nice thing for a sick woman to say! It was jolly nice of her and everything she said was helpful.

These are the big pluses of old age. You can (with care) say what you like when you are an OAP, and you can be what you are. You can eat cold baked beans from a tin. You can fall in love and make love. I know youngsters don't like that – they think it's obscene if anyone does it except themselves. They don't see the young person that inhabits an old body and they don't want to, because many of them are frightened of age. But science has stepped in. For a price experts can suck out your surplus fat, and remove hair from where it wasn't intended and find replacements for where it was intended. If you're a man you can keep your pecker up by injections (painless and on the NHS), vacuum machines, inserted plastic rods (which keep it up all the time so you have to bend it down) and Viagra, which I don't know anything about. The foreplay is of course more important now than climax, and you manage the whole thing much better because you're relaxed. It's far less fraught. Religious spokespeople often seem to think sex is so easy. To do it well requires a lot of thought, imagination and consideration. To take pleasure and lead your partner into pleasure is an art. Practice also makes perfect, as it does in so many activities.

I met an old couple in an Amsterdam cafe. They had been childhood sweethearts, got separated, married other people, and then found each other again in their eighties. On their anniversary he provided a bottle of champagne, pinned a rose on her, and we drank to 'Love on the Blink'– the nicest love of all.

It's not only that, of course, there are more complex changes. When you're older, you live life backwards and, before you experience second childhood, you have some years of painful second adolescence. A lively old chap I knew fell into a decline when his even livelier mature lady friend tried to let him down gently from his illusions.

About seventy, I watched myself rushing here, there and everywhere speaking, lecturing, broadcasting and bounding across a stage like a rejuvenated pop star with ants in his pants. I tried to simmer down. In my alone time, my quiet time, I re-experienced an old familiar feeling. WW said, 'You'll be doing the can-can next,' and chuckled.

I began to understand what was happening. I was being born again into old age. I was passing a frontier to the second most puzzling period of my life (the first was puberty) and I was nervy and out of my depth, that's all. My mother had died, followed shortly afterwards by Lil, and suddenly I realised why I was so nervy. I was an orphan – a big overweight geriatric orphan baby.

Now you have to be flexible because you (I mean me) don't know how old age is going to hit you. Many friends are of course dead and I'll never see their like again – at least not in this world. No, I'm not being sentimental, the youngsters I meet are just as nice, but there just isn't time for the long investment of time and attention, rows and reconciliations that an old matured friendship requires.

I comfort myself because so far I'm a survivor. At seventy there are still lots of men like me around. At eighty, it's a woman's world, and men like me a scarce lot, an endangered species.

But when you get old, you can't rely on sex for a lift. It's after all only a part-time activity that goes up and down in importance and is often of no importance at all.

At Ma's funeral I asked for a short service. She loathed liturgy which went on and on and sermons that couldn't end and prayers extended like chewing gum. Kim and Jim both asked me for a Thought at Ma's celebration send-off in the crematorium cafe near the cemetery. I reminded them that the only tombstone Ma ever said she liked was a life-sized marble one with a marble motor-bike driver astride a marble bike. I couldn't put up anything like that! She was a true Yiddishe Momma, despite her blue films and askew hairpiece. I was about to cry, I felt so lonely.

I suddenly remembered a burly oldie who at Christmas time used to go around a pub patronised by Ma, Kim, Jim and me, collecting for The Orphans. I gave reasonably, Ma gave enthusiastically. I later found out why the clientele guffawed. It was a regular pub comedy. The Orphans were a group of tough grizzly gay guys who drowned their 'sorrows' with the proceeds. Self-righteously, I complained to Ma. It was bringing charity into disrepute, I said preachily. 'Don't be like that,' said Ma, 'it's when you're getting past it that you really feel lonely. I always thought all that religion couldn't be good for you. Give those orphans a fiver, Lionel.' I did so. Now I knew what she meant because for the first time I felt an orphan too and wondered if I could join them.

70

I Learn to Listen

Old age wasn't for me a time of standing still. I learnt to listen, laugh and to make others laugh as an entertainer. It was the listening that affected me most. (I remember that in her old age my mother had begun to listen too.) I had to learn to listen with my whole heart, the kind of listening that requires empathy not just sympathy, when you enter into the feelings of another person and not just feel for them but with them. I needed to learn how to listen not just for my social life and professional life but also for my prayer life and my eternal life. I had to listen to God as well as people.

My best teacher was my friend Father Bill Kirkpatrick, an Anglican priest. He knocked two coal bunkers together in a swinging part of London and set up a listening post. Word got around that he would be in residence as the bars, dance halls, backrooms and clubs were closing to whoever dropped in and to whatever they wanted to talk about and they didn't even have to talk – they could just stay silent with him. He would just try to listen with all his attention whether to their spoken language, their body language or their silence and wouldn't counsel or advise unless asked to do so, and even then he preferred to help his caller advise her or himself.

And all sorts of people did drop into his converted coal bunkers because London is very big and very lonely and feels even lonelier when you have not found a partner for the night to keep you warm or keep you company.

Some who came to his listening post wanted to seduce him or rape him, some couldn't utter but their body language said it all and they just held hands, which also says it all. Some wanted to mug him, kiss him or strip in front of him. But after the vaudeville was over, many stayed talking, crying, or in silence while he gave them his attention as he promised with all his heart and mind.

Giving even ten minutes of one's attention to someone else is one of the most difficult things I know. At the Leo Baeck College I was taught to talk fluently and wisely. Like any healthy youngster, I enjoyed hearing the sound of my own voice, so if you needed an impromptu sermon, or an engaging after-dinner speech, or a funeral oration, or a stand-in for a lecturer who hadn't shown up, I was your man.

But nobody taught me to listen. I was expected to pick that up en route. And I found that it required not just techniques but a deep change in me – a spiritual one. It means that the other person had to matter to me as much as I mattered to myself – and that is religious bull's-eye!

Here are examples of what I mean.

At the beginning of my ministry, I used to cheat when doing my hospital visiting. Well, I entered a ward cheerily and said upbeat things to the patients in a firm confident voice. The patients looked interested in what this visitor from outer space who had erupted into their ward was up to. 'Why, you look well, Mr So-and-so!' I exclaimed. 'Why, you're beginning to look better already, Mrs X.' And so Mr So-and-so and Mrs X stared back at me blankly and wearily, knowing they weren't looking any better than yesterday. They also knew I wasn't saying all this garbage to help them. I couldn't solve their problems or even cope with their having them. I could only say my party piece. I couldn't listen and enter into their situation. So I took the easy way out.

It was the same with dying people. I tried to encourage them by telling them that the body has all sorts of powers of recuperation. I didn't mention the word 'death', though that was the subject in their minds and mine. I wanted to brighten them up and me too, even if the good cheer I was peddling was based on avoidance. For this sort of bromide it was better if I did the talking and they just listened and didn't interrupt.

It was only later that I learnt I didn't have to talk at all, and I didn't have to have all the answers. Listening was just letting their hand lie loosely in mine, so that they knew I was with them and they could drift away when they wanted. Once again I learnt from my friend Father Bill that my hand should not clutch them nor seem to restrain them. Once again body language was truer than talking.

One last example (which I've made up). Say a man came to see me and says, 'Rabbi, I've just knifed my dad.' He is naturally in a state of shock. While he continues talking, some of the following thoughts and questions race through my mind:

- Oedipus?
- Did I ever want to do that with my dad?
- Should I make him a cup of tea? Where's the sugar?
- Is it a fantasy?
- Does he need therapy?
- What an interesting morning!

All these thoughts meant that I was not listening to him but to my own solutions, my own thoughts, my own bromides, my own theology. I was certainly not giving him my attention. My own self-absorption was too strong. There may come a time for theology and solutions but much, much later when he has finished what he has to say and I've listened, really listened with my heart as well as my mind and chewed it over.

This lack of attentive listening, or indeed any type of listening, is a great problem and preoccupation of people now. It is a paradox that just as the means of communication such as mobiles, counsellors, therapists, internet, social workers and analysts has increased, the amount and quality of true deep listening has contracted. Talking is a way we use to cover up the truth – not to communicate it or reveal it. It is the Tower of Babel problem.

Here's an example of how the lack of such listening affected my own life. In my late teens I realised beyond doubt that I was homosexual, the expression of which was a criminal offence in Britain before 1968. I needed advice urgently, being an only child with normal needs and having no brothers who could enlighten me. I went to see some ministers of religion, who ordered me out, or who discovered a late appointment and disappeared fast over the horizon as soon as I put my problem to them bluntly. And it was the same with clergymen, youth leaders, teachers, Marxists and rabbis. My mother burst into tears and said it was all her fault, which didn't help her or me, and a doctor took the easy way out and told us all not to worry about it because I was bound to grow out of it – which I didn't. In the end by chance I met my analyst Leslie at a party who asked me what I thought about it and how the world appeared to me and actually listened to my reply. This was true listening and it released the floodgates of my pent-up feelings. It was a new point of departure. I wasn't going round in circles any more.

Why is listening so difficult for us? Probably because our parents, like most parents, never listened to us very much as children. They always knew better about how we felt than we knew ourselves. Since childhood experience goes very deep, most of us still do not understand what real listening is. This is a great handicap. So how do we set about learning it now that we ourselves are adults?

My best teachers have been my problems and failures in life. They are not exactly listening but my stepping stones towards it. They are my spiritual capital. They are the only way I learn compassion, mercy and what it's like being at the wrong end of the stick. They point the way by which I can go beyond feeling to that deeper listening which is feeling with.

A lady stands outside a London supermarket. She is wearing cast-off clothes and two plastic bags beside her contain all her possessions. A big city is full of such down-and-outs. At Oxford I had a bad breakdown and nearly became a drop-out too, and I empathise with them.

A young man asked me if I would help him with his CV. He was applying for jobs after university. Sure, I said, and then he told me the help he wanted. I was a smooth writer, he said, which I took as a compliment, and he wanted me to help him remove all his mistakes, failures and problems from the record and we should do it so smoothly that it would appear as if they had never happened. I told him to think again because anyone who presented me with such a smooth life would get no job from me. I repeated to him those words of my teachers that 'Only your failures will make you wise.' My young man then told me I was not of this world and would find someone else. I agreed with him that success and failure are dependent on the world you wish to enter. Failures and problems may do you no good in the rat-race world focused on success, but they may be very relevant for you in the spiritual life, the Beyond Life which encloses it and which we experience even in this one.

What is the difference between feeling for and feeling with? Well, the former is hierarchical, which is why most religious or ideological establishments prefer it. It implies someone on high who helps someone below. It is also quite self-conscious. The latter is the fellow feeling which is so much part of us that we are scarcely conscious of it. It implies that we are both in the same boat and we listen and speak to each other out of fellow feeling. 'Hath not one father created us and are we not brethren to one another?'

Now religious institutions, churches and synagogues do not like hearing their members out. For a variety of reasons – which include a desire to be helpful, avoidance and megalomania – they prefer to answer problems rather than listen to them. Like the parents in our childhood, they know more about how we fancy than we do ourselves. I found that Marxism was exactly like religion in this. The leader might even be sympathetic but they were above you and knew what was better for you than you knew yourself, so why waste time listening?

Perhaps this is why so many religious congregations are in a state of crisis now. Perhaps the crisis arises from the fact that at their best they are sympathetic institutions but not empathetic ones. They can give answers, but find it hard to listen and feel what they are listening to. They still have to learn another way of listening – not to give 'correct' answers which don't answer. Perhaps their answers do not fit our situation because they have never really felt what our situation is. Religious wisdom flows down but does not flow up. Perhaps the task of the Church is not to be so ready with answers at the present, but instead to help us grow up and find our answers ourselves. Perhaps the sympathetic religious congregation has to become the understanding silent fellow feeling congregation before we can all move on.

It was time this change took place, I thought. The alternative was standard answers to set questions. The official religious answers in our time have not been that good or even applicable, and their involvement in our world's problems has not always been for the best. It is no secret that religion does not have the answer to all our problems because it is a part of the problem itself. We only have to look at the political hotspots today to see this, whether in the Middle East, Far East, Ireland or Yugoslavia. Unfortunately the faith of big sections of 'faith' is expressed by shouting, fulminating and condemning rather than listening, especially deep listening. But the sheer amount of noise does not hide the insecurity and fear they try to cover.

I was told this story about the death of Gertrude Stein. It is anecdotal and I cannot vouch for it but it fits. While dying, she drifted back into consciousness. 'What's the answer?' she said, puzzled, and then drifted away again. Then she suddenly opened her eyes and remarked, 'But what's the question?' We could all learn from her, especially clerics and ecclesiastical bureaucrats like me.

So now, I try to tease the feeling behind the words when someone comes to see me. I am not so ready with my own solutions. I help them to try to find their own. The trouble is that this takes time and I haven't got much. I pray for patience. If someone rings me long distance to find out how I am, I ask them how they are first. It's only recently that I understood what listening with my whole heart meant and involves. That is why I never wanted to become a therapist or analyst. I could possibly start training now but it is too late.

71

Go North, Old Man, Go North!

As you get older you have to learn how to make yourself at home in hospitals, because you are going to spend an increasing amount of time in them. It's the same with airport departure lounges when you're young. You will have to accustom yourself to waiting, so a long novel with a happy ending, papers to correct, a bar of chocolate and a thermos of strong tea are all helpful.

Like my parents I was never frightened of hospitals after I learnt to cope with the nausea of blood. I have found them a kind of relief from living, which I still find difficult though I get more cheerful as I get older. One of the loveliest weekends of my life was spent in hospital after a full epileptic fit. Nobody knew where I was, it was a bank blank holiday weekend so I was the last admittance and I watched the rain peacefully run down the windows. An Indian chap in the next bed fed me with samosas that his wife had made, and another patient found me spare toiletries and lemon barley water. I released myself from worries and gave myself permission to enjoy my bank blank holiday from life. I am not usually so nice to myself – but when I'm ill it's different. I forgive myself and give myself a break.

At night, though, I let my thoughts wander and as usual they settled on the might-have-beens of my life. Miserable stuff, because we don't get second chances. But against all expectation I did get a second chance some years later just after another spell in hospital – back to university at least. A polite letter asked me if I would accept a one-term Holgate fellowship at Grey College in the University of Durham (renewable). And Jim was welcome, which made it possible. I had wondered what it would be like reliving my university years but with the wisdom I had learnt later. A silly idea, I had thought, because it would be like saying

I would be very happy if I wasn't me. But the gift had come. It was presented to me on a platter.

I could scarcely wait to answer yes. I began to pack my splendid gold and blue doctor's gown, honorary not academic but a stunner all the same, from the Open University. I looked very splendid. I'd treat myself to Calvin Klein underwear lookalikes in Durham market and some snob silk ties from the charity shops. I was rarin' to go and make up for lost time.

I learnt so much in that term and the two that succeeded it. I made my peace with so many inner conflicts. I remembered Eric and the telephone number I had never given him. Now I was going north to his country. But he had been much older than me, I didn't know his surname, nor the name of his mining village. I never traced him. He was probably dead. But I remembered the tune from Sweelinck and hoped I'd have another chance with him too in the Beyond Life to which we are all travelling, because some seeds of recognition had been planted and began to grow between us. It was a strange episode and I prayed for him and contributed to charity to seal my prayer in Durham Cathedral.

Trying to locate his world, I walked the north country he came from. I ended up sitting on a hill on the Durham/Northumberland border and spied all the cultures and peoples that had washed across the landscape. All had left their signature. Small unpretentious Saxon churches, Celtic crosses, stones from Roman temples and altars, some embedded in those churches and crosses, the straight Roman roads, the ponderous Norman cathedrals and castles, the frail traces of Saints like Cuthbert and Aidan. The settlements of Danes and Vikings – all next to modern Indian restaurants and rural Chinese takeaways and over-the-top Jews like me. Bede, my original religious inspiration at Oxford, came alive for me again. I decided to visit my priory again soon and experiment with a bit of monkery once more. I had never lost my taste for it.

And sitting on that hilltop I saw this country not as a visitor on sufferance but as an integral part of it. I was part of the last wave of immigration but two, a Jewish wave, fleeing like all the others from poverty and prejudice to Britain. I wanted to give something to my new found country because I wasn't an East European refugee nor an Israeli exile nor a refugee to America who hadn't made it. This country I spied below me on the hillock was my provisional earthly home. What made the identification easier was the history of suffering and poverty in the North, like the Jewish suffering and poverty I knew in my childhood.

At Grey College I didn't have to give many formal lectures, just write and be available when any group wanted me. The lesbians and gays wanted me and I tried to describe life before the Wolfenden Report. They were shattered by learning about the dread of provocation, prison and blackmail that darkened my Oxford years just fifty years before. The young students could scarcely believe it. Thinking back, I could scarcely believe it myself. And being a Jewish gay too, a Jew of the Jews! – a minority of a minority!

But I told them that this had helped me spiritually. Being a member of two ghettos released me from the constrictions of each. They cancelled each other out. So I was free to burrow back through the layers to what was underneath both and was more fundamental and try and be a decent human being. Neither ghetto had a monopoly of love or caring, though both often thought so. Under the Nazis, gays had suffered under their pink triangle as Jews had suffered under their yellow star, and Stalin had sent both to the gulags. Both had suffered from religious power too.

Being gay, I also needed more personal direct spirituality than ordinary Jews, because my problems lay outside the legal religious framework. Neither society nor tradition could give me the inner strength for a faithful relationship. It had to come from me. I got it by connecting up to WW and Inner Voice. I had to go beyond the pieties to spiritual realities.

The give and take worked the other way too. Old people can easily get crushed and abandoned in the scrum of a gay bar. The reason is that many gays fear old age as I once feared my loss of hair in Amsterdam. But looking after their old is something that Jews are good at, and it gave me pleasure when I could link the strengths of both to the lacks of both. They might not realise it but they needed each other. The contact is coming hesitantly as old attitudes are melting, but each still feels deprived and both of course are right.

Judaism can show gays how to turn a house into a home and the gays I know can show Jews that this means more than repetitive ritual but real support. Both ghettos fortunately are good at jokes and can laugh at themselves.

I also think you need the experience of the Beyond Life to deal with 'real' life without illusion. Sex is not the purpose of our life on earth but it can be fun and enjoyable. Religions are not good at fun and enjoyment so they should learn it from gays.

At Durham I brought together intellectually the Jewish and the gay parts of myself. This was another healing from my fellowship.

The younger generation of students delighted me. Compared to my generation, they were neither ageist, sexist, racist, Stalinist or snob and I spent a lot time in the Junior Common Room propping up the bar just listening to them. They were not hierarchical, and oldies like Jim and me were welcome. This would not have been so fifty years before at Oxford when we were all pigeonholed and had our place.

I respected them and felt for them because life was in many ways tougher for them than it was for me in my time. They had loans not grants. Of course a few had wealthy parents but most searched for any vacation work that paid. One girl I met sold everything she had, invested in a gun and shot rabbits, which she skinned, jointed, froze and sold. Defurring and eviscerating rabbits is a bloody business as I remembered from war time. I admired her guts and wished her good luck.

I nearly split my own guts listening to the freedom of student backchat. One was throwing clothes and books out of a window to someone I couldn't see. 'If you treat me that way again,' he shouted, 'so help me God I'll masturbate inside your best trainers.' It was the 'best' that sent me into hysterics. Fifty years ago, if the 'm' word had been said aloud some students would have removed themselves to the next room away from any risk of contamination.

Hardly any of them attended the college chapel, though its priest was a sweetie. With the Jews it was the same. They were paranoid about me, thinking I might criticise their laxity, and I was paranoid about them, thinking they would criticise my theological liberalism. But they courteously fed me a lunch of smoked salmon bagels 'because that's what rabbis eat'.

I tried hard to work out what religion could give the graduating students in their situation, if anything. I told them it could help them resist the rat-race and prefer job satisfaction to money. Also religion could help them find out what they were really worth. It isn't easy when one moment you're a highly paid young executive, and then on the dole when the stock market sneezes, then a consultant, and then founding your own company which can boom or bust. In a changing world, religion may be important because it concentrates on what doesn't change. This is important when you have to be as versatile as a chameleon to survive.

Also an Inner Voice could help you with the loneliness of your computer, when your office is not a place of gossip and chattering typewriters but like a fortune teller you gaze into a crystal ball. People need someone, solid or see-through, to congratulate them on their successes and comfort them in their failures.

The students gave me so much. I am still dazed, absorbing their gnomic sayings on astrophysics and the diamond-sharp brilliance of their pure mathematics.

But the greatest thing they gave me was a rebirth of fun. They restored my youth, which had never been very successful. The exam results had been posted up and life became a party. The vodka breakfast was bliss and I watched the women's rugger team on the dance floor in smart slinky black sparkling with faux diamonds and pearls. To my surprise Jim was prancing beside them though he's more ancient than me. He should be tucked up in bed, I thought enviously, restricting myself to timid static karaoke and bellowing out our college song instead.

> You make me happy
> When skies are Grey, skies are Grey, skies are Grey . . .

Nobody minds. The ageism of my generation has gone. These youngsters are maturer today. Fuelled by champagne, I finally join the dancing, the first time in twenty-five years. My might-have-been return to university took me further than I ever expected. What a lovely thing to happen when you're ageing!

Now the elemental force that started the process that got me to Durham was firstly my friend Henry because the party is where Henry is. Henry is half Jewish, half Quaker, and a communing Anglican. He is *toujours gai* in whichever way, and the spirit of Grey, and he is on a spiritual search which is how I first came to bump into him on a retreat. Alan his partner looks on powerfully, silently, supportively, smiling enigmatically. He also is gay and Grey and good. Needless to say, neither has any prejudices about class or caste. Whatever the gender and however geriatric, you're welcome with them. They're very clever, very to the point and very Yorkshire.

It was Victor Watts, the scholar and Master of Grey, who befriended them and then me. He was the translator of Boethius and the authority on medieval English and French literature. But his greatest achievement was the trust of nearly two thousand students who knew 'he was on their side' and who went along with him even on the rare occasions he said no.

I wish I'd met someone like him long ago. He and his wife welcomed me and Jim into their hearts and their home as they did with so many others. I shall not look upon Victor's like again! He died unexpectedly just before his retirement from a heart attack.

Victor encouraged Henry to arrange art exhibitions at Grey, because education wasn't just exams and jobs but a feeling for the beauty and profundity of our inner and outer worlds. Some of the exhibitions were fun, some charming, some beautiful and personally revealing. But one day, strolling into a preview, I got a shock. I began to tingle, a sure sign with me. The exhibited artist was someone I had never heard of before, a Theo Major from Wigan. Like Blake he had had a vision too, his in the grimness of industrial Lancashire. He was saying what I had always wanted to say about the Beyond Life in the East End of London but didn't know how. This was the art teacher I had always wanted. But he had died quite recently in his nineties and out of sorts with men though less with women.

He explored many styles, but for me it is his workers in silent streets that make me hold my breath. They are North England as the early Van Gogh and Vermeer were Holland. I seriously wonder if I should paint again, though I have no easy talent. Perhaps I have written too many words and need to see, not think. Perhaps Grey would give me space and encouragement.

Victor and Henry would not have laughed at me. Both could intuit when something is serious. Perhaps I can explain it to the new Master, Professor Martyn Chamberlain – a nice man with a nice wife whom I only met once just as they were facing 'the JCR test' with the appointments committee and succeeding beautifully. Not schmaltz but true!

Some people are called to Provence or Tuscan Chiantishire. For me it is 'Go North, young old man, go North!' I need a teacher now even more than fifty years ago. Like the medieval scholars, I must start searching to find my own. Victor could have been it and so could Theo Major and so could Sid Holgate but I arrived too late.

Up at Durham I thought again of my father and the love of geography and maps that he taught me. Map-making had accompanied me throughout my life. It was the way I thought. It hadn't stopped with East End maps that got me home or London Underground maps that my mother meditated over so wistfully. It had developed into metaphysical maps that charted my jerky hitchhiking journey to Heaven.

72

Beyond, Not After

As I write this book I ought to be conscious that death is coming ever nearer, for the seasons are succeeding each other with surprising rapidity and I don't like being hustled. I am conscious of it in a matter-of-fact way certainly because I have had to make wills, the ordinary and the living ones, and get Jim to make them as well. Gays don't get married privileges when our partners die, however long we have been together or looked after each other. It is one of the injustices of those 'Victorian family values' so beloved of a comfy satisfied majority.

But death is not high on my agenda. Christianity is often death-obsessed; Judaism is obsessed by life and rabbinic rituals and in this instance I remain Jewish. Religion is to do with my life in this world. When this world ends, religion doesn't end with it but it becomes God's religion and he can worry about it not me. It will be a relief to get the world off my shoulders. Over to you, mate!

There are lots of reasons for my attitude, one of them being my ma, who had no strong feelings about death either, apart from enjoying wakes and family get-togethers. Both of us do our best to satisfy relatives and friends but the person we loved, liked or disliked is no longer here, and the grave just holds their memory, not them.

I remember listening to Ma on the phone. She sounded mournful and moved and so she was. 'Oh,' she said, 'how dreadful. He died on Monday and the funeral's on Thursday.' She was talking to the son of a former boyfriend who had just passed away. She paused and then added in her chirpy voice, 'Now what's news?' How that poor chap's jaw must have dropped! I felt sorry for him. Few people had enough GSOH to cope with Ma when she was upbeat.

It was the same when our good friend Tom rang to tell us his mother had just died. 'Come over straight away!' she said. 'Get a taxi, I'll pay for it.' (She was a generous soul.) When poor Tom arrived Ma gave him whisky, sympathy and cake and then said, 'Now, Tom, you've got to face facts. What have you decided on, a burial or a cremation?'

'A cremation, Hetty,' said Tom sadly.

'That's right,' said Ma meditatively, 'I'd make a curry out of the lot of them.'

Tom's jaw did drop and I hurriedly added, 'She said there's enough curry for the lot of us.'

Tom seemed to accept my version but continued to look at her covertly for the rest of the evening.

The problem for most people is that death is so difficult to conceive. By definition we can never know death, only dying. I can only know this life and whatever other life there may be within, after or beyond it. When we die, space and time will die with us. But what can life be like without space and time? I don't go in for saccharine heavens and sadistic hells. They're too pagan! I much prefer an old rabbi who said, 'I don't care about your heaven and am not frightened of your hell. All I want is You!' That makes sense. I want WW, that Voice that brought me back to life in Oxford a half century or so ago.

But even if 'after life' makes little sense to me, 'Beyond Life' does. And of that I do have experience. Experience but not proof. There is no material proof when we go beyond the boundaries of this sensed material world. Being mainly material creatures, worldly proof is of course what we would like. Which explains our unending appetite for material miracles, dancing madonnas, weeping statues, liquefying blood of doubtful saints, wars won by God's grace or partiality, and divine replacement eyes, ears and limbs. The Sunday papers are stuffed with them. We do not find the spiritual by itself satisfying. It cannot stand on its own – it needs material support, which by definition it cannot get.

Well, here is my support for the Beyond Life. I trust it but you are welcome to consider this as my imagination. But then so are my experiences of Bach and Rembrandt and love and reason and God. The Beyond Life of course also makes living in this life more interesting. It adds a little frisson. But ardour for it usually cools down when we find we have to pay a price for it. The Beyond Life makes demands and if we ignore these demands it dies on us. (It is this which makes it real.) The experience of it is there if you want it but even wanting it is not enough, you eventually have to become it or part of it or at least try to. You have to become your own proof of its existence.

Do not underestimate the punch it packs. Few alcoholics or addicts can prove stronger than their addiction. The few alcoholics I have met who have done so, tell how 'they have relied upon a power greater than themselves' not because they are formal believers but to attest what works in them. The recognition of it has certainly changed me.

On an easier level, like many or most people, I have occasional out-of-body experiences. A me steps out of me and from somewhere near the ceiling regards the whole scene below me with deep compassion. It lasts a few moments and than I snap back into my normal consciousness again. I feel as if I have crossed into another dimension.

I also cross into the dimension of the Beyond Life when I have done something good for the sake of that Beyond Life which I call heaven. Then in my experience heaven happens. I have invested some of myself in heaven, as it were. The feeling of exaltation lasts only a short time but I make sure it remains in my memory and I return to it in thought many times. (I use Arab worry beads, or an old rosary, the gift of an optimistic Catholic friend, or my Jewish prayer straps as remembrancers.) Some people say they touch that other dimension, that Beyond Life, through music or literature or art or making love. I understand them. I can get to that Beyond Life by meditating in front of a Vermeer or Rembrandt (a good reproduction will do). Let the quietness of the one and the compassion of the other steal into you.

To get to that other dimension you will need imagination. It must be disciplined imagination. Mysticism is not tricks arousing cosy communal feelings, it is a way to the hard stuff of integrity, liberation from lies, sacrifice and giving. Of course this prescience or presence of heaven can happen without doing anything. Then you have to be humble enough to receive it as a pure gift, as a grace. It can come to you in a supermarket, while washing up, or sorting out your laundry.

In life one can come to a black hole many times. In past experience if I really ask God to be present to me in it, the hole seems to turn inside out and in the darkness there is a hidden shining and as John of the Cross and many Jewish mystical rabbis have pointed out, a door appears in a blank wall, and a hand steadies me in the nothingness. This happened to many in the Holocaust and on their experience we rely when troubles hit us.

This happened to me personally in my breakdown and in the use I put it to afterwards. And when my second partnership broke up, what made it possible to part decently without rancour on my part was the message of my inner voice. My inner voice told me that I would one day meet the Whomsoever Whatsoever I've been talking to all these years. I assumed this must be when I am dying or dead and I look forward to it. Our meeting is overdue. I don't necessarily want to argue or settle points, just to put my arms around him/her/it and kiss. It hasn't been an easy hand to play but I've tried and he, Whoever he is, has made that possible.

I think all we can ever do in this life is to give the Beyond Life our attention and a kiss. This life is not the place where we can expect happiness as of right and, even if we get it, it won't stay around that long, because everything in this life is moving and permanence is not part of it, only obsolescence. It is a corridor as the medieval rabbis said, it is a departure lounge – but it is not our everlasting home and cannot be. Our mortality stops that. It is best to think of it as a school where we learn the three great lessons of acquiring, giving to and giving up. This seems to fit our experience best. In the old days traditional Jews used to leave a corner of their smart drawing rooms unplastered, to show visibly what Augustine knew intellectually, that here is no abiding city. Many, I am told, still do in the middle of materialist suburbs.

If we accept the transitory nature of our present 'reality' we shall not feel so hurt or let down when it disappears on us. It always will. It is not that eternal world or reality but we can already experience another dimension in it.

I accept the Beyond Life for the same reason that I accept religion. I go to it because I am in need and I stay with it because it works. By this I mean that it works spiritually. It works because I became more content, more helpful. Not because I can manoeuvre better in the rat-race. In other words, I become my own evidence for the Beyond Life. I have to become part of that dimension to 'prove' it. The material evidence insofar as it can have any is that it genuinely leads me towards common as well as uncommon sense.

If you want to make the Beyond Life yours in this life, then get familiar with it. There's nothing occult about it. Occultism is usually a hindrance not a help. Pray towards it, give it your attention in your meditation and reading. You will gradually become used to it. You will not yet be the citizen of the Beyond Life but a tourist, a day tripper into the life you came from in the first place. (Which is why you don't seem to learn about it but remember it.) The spiritual life, the Beyond Life, works like that invisible force we call gravity, as I learnt from Simone Weil. It pulls us towards it but to hold it we have to let it work on us, and be prepared to change in the way it suggests to us.

I am already experiencing death as a foretaste of coming home. I realised this in a departure lounge in an airport. This world was so much like that lounge. We make ourselves as comfortable as we can, we learn, we get acquainted but it remains a corridor, a place of passage. It is not our eternal home. But that is the home I want to get to, as the writers of Negro spirituals recognised so well. Like them I want 'to pass over into camp ground'.

Home is the source of goodness, of my soul, of my values, of the Divine within me. In the Holocaust literature it is evident that many who based their human life on that Beyond Life did not feel let down. The coming centuries will live (not just exist) on their example. I think they will be the true victors of this terrible time.

It is pain, of course, which distorts the matter of death so much. I used to wonder why such awful drugs as heroin and morphine had such lovely names, recalling heroines and Morpheus the blessed God of Sleep. But a medical student said they deserved such names because they took away the dreaded death agony. So I'm grateful to live and die in a time when the intelligence that God created in us has brought us sedatives and drugs that bring a relaxation of spirit in place of fear.

Some still die in pain, of course. But as experts tell me pain is not necessary, I don't understand why. From this you will gather than I do not dread death but I do not endure pain gladly or stoically. Like my granny, I scream and complain and demand a scientific happiness fix.

Death without pain is no great worry, no big deal. I've no grudges against whoever set up my deal. I used to have, but these last years of content have evened up the score. Also I've learnt how to turn my own minuses into pluses for other people, so they have their place. If problems have purpose, you grit your teeth but you accept them. It's the mindless suffering of this life which is so hard to bear.

In the latter part of my life, I've begun to enjoy it, but I also know I'll never be free of the anxiety states and depression that I can trace back into my childhood. So when I reach the horizon, I'll feel I've done this world just as I feel I've done a certain job or finished the liturgy of a certain festival. I'll want to move on because like my mother I've always been curious.

There is also the matter of my judgement – but it's not that of a divine headmaster or sadistic sergeant. These are the remarks that help me.

'Rabbi Zusya said in the final world, they won't ask me why I wasn't Moses, but why I wasn't Zusya' (i.e. why I wasn't myself).

I also remember two remarks about my last judgement from my teacher of mysticism.

'All that will happen is that God will take you on his knee, and tell you what your life was really about and you will see clearly what you did and that will be your heaven and your hell.' (I am already beginning to see and it is indeed like that.)

'What else will he say?' I asked my teacher.

'He will just look at you and say you did just as he expected – no better, no worse.'

One word recurs in the titles of the books I have written and that is 'heaven'. It is something I experience more and more. It is not a place, nor yet another place. It is another dimension in which I see the same places but transformed. Part of me is already in it. And heaven is home. I have tried to recreate it in many houses but it is not a building, it is in me or beyond this world.

Death is going home! Flowers fade and die but something grows out of them.

When I die, my remains shall be cremated (after medical research has made its claims) and I hope they will end up by those of Jim in any cemetery that will have us.

This is how it seems to me. But if you think this wishful musing, then I have no material proof to contradict you. I can only say the words I learnt so long ago from the agnostic emperor Marcus Aurelius. If there is a God, follow him. If there is no God, become godlike yourself. Give the Beyond Life as much time as you would give to learning the guitar or holiday French and you will probably experience it for yourself. You will of course have to become the living evidence of your own belief. This isn't easy but it is the only evidence that convinces. Go for it! Try!

73

Very Late

Just as I try to tidy up the manuscript of this book, and send it to the publishers, I celebrate my seventy-fourth birthday. I never expected to get beyond my three score years and ten, so another illusion hits the dust. Like my ma, I'm tougher than I thought. My seventy-fourth birthday has come and gone. Jim gave me a pen on a string which I can't lose – though I will. I give myself a large forbidden bar of wholenut milk chocolate, my comfort cholesterol for a few weeks, and from my Creator I receive a lump on my leg which isn't just another cyst but a Rare Cancer of an Aggressive Type, so rare that nobody knows much about it – just the type I would get.

I'm not surprised. When you're living on borrowed or extended time, something like that is bound to happen. It's the same with old cars going to their MOT tests. Men are the frailer sex and not geared to caring for themselves.

For a few days I'm on an emotional switchback. What's happened to so many of my friends may now be happening to me – it's my turn. Up to now I've been lucky, helped on by clever doctors and a witch's brew of tablets and capsules. Heart problems, prostate cancer, epilepsy and a huge hernia – I've seen them all come and go or get civilised. But a rare and rabid cancer may be one round I do not win. This is of course speculation.

What surprises me is how relaxed I am about it, and Jim compliments me. This I didn't expect. I concentrate on the present, look forward to small treats, and become kinder to myself. I'm no longer worried by rat-racing, success-searching, or networking. Instead I try my hand at bouillabaisse with varying results. Because I'm kinder to myself I become kinder to others. I don't invite many people round – I am enjoying myself too much with Jim alone. It's like the honeymoon we never had the time or money for. I tell him he had better check my will and power of attorney. It's now more his business than mine. I tell him to find a replacement rabbi if I go first, and then feel virtuous. He sensibly says I am putting on airs because I haven't gone yet and he may shuffle off before me, being older. I like hamming it up. (You should pardon the expression!)

I do wake up rather alarmed but lots of things help me. There was the voice in the chapel by the Rialto when I parted from Kim. There was a message from one of the last conversations of Ste Thérèse of Lisieux which made death feel purposive. 'It is not Death that calls us out of this life,' she tells us, 'but God.' I feel the same as when I exited from the work on the liturgy – I'd done it and was now interested in what comes next – and it is the same with this world. Perhaps I've done that too and it's time to move on. I want to meet the being, the Voice I'd been speaking to for over fifty years, since the Quaker meeting in Oxford.

I noticed I was getting nicer. Now a real saint wouldn't even be conscious of such thoughts but I'm not a real one, though like the curate's egg, nice in bits. If Margery Kempe is only a third-rate contemplative then I'm many notches below her   and this is not humility but reality.

I am conscious also of changes. An old me is dying and a new me is sprouting. I can tell that by the different way I treat people. When people used to ask me how I was, I used to tell them in extenso and at length. Now I look at them, stop and say, 'How's it with you, dear?' I actually want to know and they tell me in extenso and at length. I'm interested but don't propose solutions which do more good to me than to them.

At the National Gallery I was never that interested in Titus, Rembrandt's handsome son. I was more interested in his portraits of oldies and his late self-portraits. Behind the thinning flesh and emerging skull I could see a light, a luminosity. He was painting not just the surface but the soul. It's the same with me. One Lionel is withering but another is on the edge of being born. I don't think this is fanciful. Look at those Rembrandts, study them and decide for yourself. Late middle age brought me listening and laughter. I'm curious as to what or whom old age will bring, however short or extended. It might of course bring me

Alzheimer's as it did to my friend Sidney Carter the hymn writer, but then I am out of my depth.

To my surprise, I thank God for all the new happiness he has given me since the diagnosis of my cancer. I never found this world an easy place and am pleased it has a frame and boundaries.

I go to see the specialist. The news is hopeful, he tells me. I now have to adjust back again to living. But I learnt a lot during those days of detachment, and the experience will be useful when they come round again. I am enjoying the world hugely because I know it isn't home and don't expect things from it which it can't give. It can certainly give me a night zimmer beach party in Benidorm when I'm seventy-five which will be fun on the modest chap's Riviera. It can give me holy Sabbath nights at home when Jim and I bless the candles and offer each other bread and wine. It can give me opportunities to strengthen my hold on heaven and times to fall about the floor in laughter.

If there's time I also want to write a novel. The theme? What if I had given Eric my address and telephone number, what would have happened then? I should also like to write about ageing and dying because I don't think things properly unless I write them. I should also like to paint again and live on a canal boat – at least in summer.

Now of course is the time when you wish me Jewish style, 'May you live till a hundred and twenty years, Rabbi Blue!' And I reply, 'And the same to you!' It's a nice thought but I don't think we'll make it. Sorry!